W9-DEQ-848

JAMES L. ORR
AND THE
SECTIONAL CONFLICT

Roger P. Leemhuis

University Press
of America™

0772023   102932

Copyright © 1979 by

University Press of America, Inc.™

4710 Auth Place, S.E., Washington D.C. 20023

All rights reserved

Printed in the United States of America

ISBN: 0-8191-0679-8

Library of Congress Catalog Card Number: 78-65850

PREFACE

On September 27, 1865, the Columbia Daily Phoenix remarked that James L. Orr "has a strong will, with leading ideas which consort admirably with what is called the progressive spirit of the age." State legislator and Congressman before the Civil War, he was one of the most progressive South Carolinians of his time. Democratizing the archaic political system of his state, which a low-country oligarchy controlled, and making South Carolina economically more diversified --these were his main goals in the ante-bellum years. A spokesman for the hilly Piedmont area, he criticized the political economy of the great planters, and he wanted an expanded white immigration. He also defended slavery and would not accept the Negro as the white man's social or political equal.

In the pre-war era this up-country politician hoped that Southern rights, as he understood them, would be protected in the Union. Only when he became convinced that the North was hostile to his section did he favor disunion. In the late 1840's and early 1850's, during the controversy over the Mexican Cession, he advocated secession, but he opposed South Carolina's departure from the Union without the support of other Southern states. By 1852 he was satisfied that Southern rights were secure in the Union, and he became known for his moderation on sectional questions. Influential in Washington, he served as speaker of the House of Representatives from 1857 to 1859.

During the Civil War he sat in the Confederate Senate, where he was a bitter critic of Jefferson Davis' government. By 1864 he doubted the wisdom of continuing the war, and he participated in the movement for peace negotiations.

Governor of his state in the immediate postwar years, Orr actively supported the policies of President Andrew Johnson. Initially he opposed Negro suffrage, but he came to recognize that the South had to conciliate the North and make concessions to the blacks. He advised his state to comply with the Reconstruction Acts, which brought black electoral majorities and Republican rule to South Carolina. When Orr urged his fellow whites to enter and control the new ruling party, most of them spurned his advice. In 1872 he was prominent in an unsuccessful reform movement against a corruptionist element in the Republican party. Also, during the period 1868 to 1873, he served as a state judge and as the United States minister to Russia.

This study seeks to make a balanced assessment. At times his racism and conservatism blinded him to the need for change in the white society's posture towards the blacks. He was, however, more flexible than most Southern whites on the race issue. He was a pragmatic and calculating politician who worked to safeguard the interests of the white South Carolinians.

***** ***** ***** ***** *****

I have accumulated many debts while preparing this study, which began as a doctoral thesis at the University of Wisconsin. Avery O. Craven suggested this topic, and the late Robert S. Starobin guided me through the final stages of dissertation writing. John B. Edmunds, Jr., Arthur Makechime, Robert B. McNulty, Jr., R. Nicholas Olsberg, and Michael Perman offered ideas and brought materials to my attention. Before his death in 1968, I became acquainted with William A. Foran, who was interested in Orr, and our exchange of ideas was stimulating.

Acknowledgement for many favors is due the staff members at the South Carolina Department of Archives and History, the South Caroliniana Library, the University of North Carolina Library, Duke University Library, the University of Virginia Library, the Alabama Department of Archives and History, and the Library of Congress. Mrs. Lulu Orr Farmer of Anderson, great-granddaughter of James L. Orr, kindly made available to me some newspaper clippings preserved by her family. In addition, I benefitted from a publication subsidy from Clemson University.

Daniel W. Hollis, Otto H. Olsen, and Allen W. Trelease read early drafts of the manuscript, and their suggestions have contributed to its improvement. I must, of course, bear the responsibility for any errors and defects that remain.

CONTENTS

v

107932

I. THE EARLY YEARS

The United States was growing in the 1840's, looking westward, exuding the spirit of manifest destiny.
As the country expanded tensions increased between the
free and slave states. The issue of allowing or for-
bidding slavery in new territories was divisive, forcing
the nation to confront the larger and ultimately disruptive question of Negro slavery in American society.
This question involved not only political power and
economic advantage; it embraced symbols and cultural
values. The late historian Roy F. Nichols wrote that
the United States comprised a cultural federalism as
well as a political federalism. Before the fateful
1860 election there existed a Northern culture and a
Southern culture. After 1860 there would also be
separate nations.[1]

James Lawrence Orr lived in the slave section.
His public career, which began in the 1840's, spanned
a period of conflict between different labor systems
and ways of life. A slaveholder who became one of the
South's spokesmen in Washington, he adamantly rejected
any thought of abolishing slavery. At the same time,
criticizing the political economy of the great planters,
he urged his section to industrialize and partially
imitate the North. He believed in economic progress,
and he wanted the South and the nation to prosper. So
long as the North appeared friendly to the slave states,
he wished to preserve the Union. Hoping that dissolution would never occur, he deeply regretted the sequence
of events that led to civil war. Yet in his own way,
paradoxically, he helped to bring about the tragedy
that finally came.

***** ***** ***** ***** *****

In 1730 Robert Orr migrated to the New World from
Ireland, first settling in Pennsylvania and later moving
to Wake County in North Carolina. Jehu, the youngest
of his six sons, fought in the Revolution, and during
the 1790's he moved to Pendleton District in South
Carolina. His son Christopher married Martha McCann,
the daughter of Robert McCann, who had migrated from
Ireland around 1786. These were the parents of James
Lawrence Orr, who was born in Craytonville in Pendleton
District on May 12, 1822. He had two brothers and
two sisters. In 1830 the family moved to Anderson,
where Christopher operated a hotel and general merchan-
dise store.[2]

1

Anderson is situated on the Piedmont plateau in western South Carolina. Sparsely settled during the Revolution, this region drew a steady flow of immigrants in the late eighteenth and early nineteenth centuries. From the North, the British Isles, and the European continent settlers came. Cattle raising and grain farming became the chief livelihoods. Lacking easy access to the markets of the more heavily populated coastal area, the Piedmont was not fully integrated in the state's economic life until the western spread of cotton production and the railroad made their impact.[3]

Spurred by the cotton gin, the plantation economy penetrated the middle and western parts of South Carolina after 1795. Cotton production continued its growth along the Atlantic coast and accelerated in the interior. The state as a whole enjoyed a buoyant prosperity which lasted through the first two decades of the nineteenth century. During the 1820's the economy declined. Cotton prices fell, and the opening of fresh western lands lured many South Carolinians. Between 1820 and 1860 the state lost 200,000 whites and 170,000 blacks to other parts of the country. Soil erosion contributed to the migration; knowledge that fertile western lands were easily accessible discouraged many people from remaining in their native state to seek better farming methods.[4]

Emigration and internal migration occurred simultaneously, as the plantation system reached into the interior districts and endangered the livelihood of small farmers. Population patterns changed. In the middle and upper parts of the state the number of whites decreased slightly between 1820 and 1840, but the black population increased appreciably. Although several neighboring districts attained black majorities, Anderson, Greenville, Pickens and Spartanburg did not. In this section the landholdings remained generally small, below the state average (which in 1850 was 541 acres, the largest average size in the nation). Here the aristocratic values of the great planters never took hold as strongly as in the coastal and middle areas. Home manufacturing developed, and the hilly Piedmont districts took the lead in demanding industrial growth and economic diversification.[5]

Listed below are the population statistics for the area that Orr would represent in Congress in the 1850's. (When the legislature reapportioned the Congressional seats in the early 1850's, Laurens was separated from

2

his constituency while Spartanburg and Union were
added.)[6]

| | 1840 | | 1860 | |
	Black	White	Black	White
Anderson	5,746	12,747	8,587	14,286
Greenville	5,348	12,491	7,261	14,631
Laurens	9,012	12,572	13,329	10,529
Pickens	2,808	11,543	4,304	15,335
Spartanburg	5,745	12,924	8,382	18,537
Union	8,451	10,485	10,965	8,670

Anderson was located in Pendleton District until
1826, when the movement of people into the western
region induced the legislature to redraw the political
map. From the old unit two new districts were created,
Anderson and Pickens. (Together they still comprised
the Pendleton election district.) In the town of
Anderson, the judicial seat of Anderson District, the
Orr family resided. According to the 1840 United
States Census, Christopher owned twenty-five slaves;
the value of property was not recorded.[7]

"Larry," as he was known, attended a country school
and then an academy in Anderson. There he joined a
debating society and studied Greek and Latin under the
Reverend J. L. Kennedy, whose reputation as a teacher
was considerable. Under another highly esteemed teacher
and classicist, Wesley Everett, the young man continued
his education. [8]In his spare time he worked in his
father's store.

To prepare for a legal career Larry chose the University of Virginia, which was known as one of the best
Southern institutions of higher learning. Matriculating
in 1839, he spent two years in Charlottesville. His
courses included, in addition to law, such traditional
subjects as natural and moral philosophy, and political
economy. Upon completion of his first year he was cited
in the faculty minutes for achieving "proficiency" in
political economy and medical jurisprudence. The
second year he devoted mainly to the law. With particular zest he applied himself to the commentaries of Lord
Coke upon Littleton. He frequently remarked that his
understanding of English common law principles, specifically in real estate, were derived from that jurist.[9]

At this time the University of Virginia student body numbered between 165 and 225 annually, and there were usually about a dozen South Carolinians. Sons of John C. Calhoun, James H. Hammond, and Langdon Cheves, prominent public men in the Palmetto state, were among those enrolled in the 1830's and 1840's. The political atmosphere was congenial to Larry. States' rights and proslavery opinions, which he would embrace in his public career, dominated the campus.[10]

One of his student friends was John Reuben Thompson of Virginia, who later became editor of The Southern Literary Messenger. Another schoolmate was Henry Winter Davis, future Maryland Congressman and co-author of the Wade-Davis Bill of 1864. The faculty member upon whom Orr depended for his legal training was Professor J. A. G. Davis. After Davis was slain by a student, the university replaced him with an inexperienced Richmond lawyer. The young South Carolinian decided to continue his studies in his native state. Returning to Anderson in 1841, he immersed himself in history as well as the law. Among his favorite authors were Hume and Linyard.[11]

In January 1842 Orr entered the law office of Joseph N. Whitner, solicitor of the state's western circuit. He prepared for his bar examinations and, during the solicitor's frequent absences, gave counsel to clients. Whitner's assistant met many people and began his political career as a delegate to the Democratic state convention in May 1843. Meeting in Columbia, that body endorsed John C. Calhoun for the Presidential nomination in the 1844 campaign.[12]

His personality was well suited for politics. Bland and cheerful, talented as an anecdote-teller, Orr was pictured by one acquaintance as "a most insinuating person in his manners." Another contemporary noted that he was "careless in his dress, and did not cultivate the graces. There was nothing artificial about him." His voice was clear and ringing, his bearing dignified. A large frame gave him a commanding appearance. Tall and stout, he had black hair, hazel eyes, and rosy cheeks in his oval face.[13]

1843 was a milestone year in the young man's life. In the fall he launched his brief career as editor of the Anderson Gazette, and he opened a law practice in the courts of Anderson, Greenville, Pickens, Abbeville, and Laurens. At about the same time he married Mary Jane Marshall of Abbeville; two years later the first of their seven children was born. Agriculture engaged him in addition to law, journalism, and politics. The Orrs resided on a farm and were slaveowners.[14]

The family was among the small number of Episcopalians in their vicinity. In 1849 the rector of St. Paul's Church in nearby Pendleton began to conduct services in the Anderson court house. When Grace Church in Anderson was established in 1851, Orr became actively involved in the effort to construct its building.[15]

He mixed well in his community's business and cultural life, holding memberships in the Anderson District Farmers Society, a library association, and a forensic group. When the debaters offered the topic, "Was Washington a greater general than Bonaparte?" he was on the team which upheld the Frenchman. He spoke negatively on the subject, "Should the interest on money be regulated by law?" Orr was also a prominent member of the Masonic order throughout his adult life.[16]

All white males in the eighteen to forty-five age bracket were required to serve in the militia. The young Andersonian, who was a colonel, ran unsuccessfully in the fall of 1843 for the position of major-general of the first militia division. He drew 222 votes against 324 for Milledge Bonham of Edgefield, a future Congressman and governor. Major-generals were elected by division officers.[17]

The new lawyer prospered. In 1845, two years after admission to the bar, he formed a partnership with Jacob P. Reed, a well-known Whig politician. Lifelong friends, they thrived in their professional affiliation. Their firm enjoyed a large share of the business in the courts of law and equity in the area. Orr had a special fondness for practice in the court of chancery. In one case the presiding chancellor remarked that the young attorney's bill was the most skillfully drawn that he had seen outside of Charleston.[18]

*****   *****   *****   *****   *****

The Anderson Gazette, which he edited, proclaimed
what it viewed as the Democratic party's traditional
principles, "Free trade, low duties; no debt; separation from banks; economy; retrenchment and a strict
adherence to the Constitution." This was the dominant
political outlook in South Carolina. The Whig party,
the party of Henry Clay, Daniel Webster, national banks,
economic nationalism, and broad construction of the
Constitution, had only scattered support. However,
there were many Whigs in the Pendleton election
district.[19]

The Gazette's "separation from banks" plank applied
to national policy. In late 1843 this newspaper declared that the people had never been shown that the
Bank of the State of South Carolina was "either a
nuisance or an 'evil.'" The state-sponsored fiscal
institution was a major issue during the 1840's, one
in which the Gazette editor showed no active interest.[20]

In 1844, when Orr made his first bid for public
office, the slavery question was becoming more explosive, intertwined with the issue of the country's
westward growth. The Democratic party's compromise
nominee for the Presidency was James K. Polk of
Tennessee, whose support of expansion in both Northwest and Southwest enabled him to avoid a strictly
sectional image. Outwardly the party was united behind Polk, but there was internal friction between
its Southern and Northern wings. Calhoun had been
the leading Southern contender for the party's nomination, and Martin Van Buren of New York the main
northern aspirant. Southern Democrats favored Texas
annexation and low tariffs. In their constituencies
Northern Democrats were exposed to antislavery sentiment and pressure for tariff protection. Their reluctance to go along with a downward revision of the
Tariff of 1842, as well as their reservations about
Texas, annoyed many Southerners.[21]

In South Carolina a group that desired Southern
militancy against the North gathered around Congressman Robert Barnwell Rhett.[22] Speaking in Bluffton in
July 1844, Rhett proposed nullification or separate
state secession if tariff reform did not materialize
soon. Disturbed by Polk's vagueness on the tariff
question, he suggested that a state convention meet

in the spring of 1845 to consider action. Calhoun,
fearing that the "Bluffton movement" would harm
Democratic chances of victory in 1844, gave assurances that Polk would work for tariff revision.
Almost a political dictator in South Carolina, he
succeeded in turning back the Bluffton drive.[23]

In September 1844 another prominent Democrat,
the elderly Langdon Cheves, aided Rhett by helping to
keep alive the idea of resistance. Cheves advocated
a Southern confederacy as the appropriate response to
his section's grievances. This plan made no headway.
Most South Carolina Democrats, concerned that resistance
talk would hurt Polk, rallied behind Calhoun. The
tiny Whig following in the state miscalculated terribly
when it tried to exploit the Rhett-Cheves proposals
and pin the disunionist label on the Democrats. In
the 1844 election the Palmetto state Whigs were badly
beaten, left without any Congressional or state
legislative seats. With Polk elected, the Rhett and
Cheves schemes rejected, and the South Carolina Whigs
impotent, Calhoun's supremacy in the state was indis-
putable.[24]

While the Presidential campaign between Polk and
his Whig opponent Henry Clay was in progress, Orr ran
for one of the seven seats from Pendleton election
district in the state house of representatives. The
Texas question was of paramount interest, pro-annexa-
tion meetings were held, and legislative candidates
were asked to discuss this subject. Orr described
the immediate annexation of Texas as vital to "the
security and existence of the South." While he did
not support Rhett's Bluffton movement or Cheves' plan,
he assailed the Whig-sponsored Tariff of 1842 as a
"shameful fraud upon the people."[25]

Winning the first of two legislative terms, he
resigned from his editorship shortly after the election.
The young man, who had many friends and acquaintances,
made an impressive showing. His 2,429 votes comprised
the highest total for any candidate in the district;
he outpolled three Democratic incumbents. In an area
that had backed the Whigs in the recent past, the
Democrats swept the legislative contests.[26]

7

The new Anderson representative, a Calhoun follower on national issues, wrote to the elder statesman for advice after the state balloting. He asked if "any movement should be made" in the event of Polk's victory, and he wished to know if Calhoun counseled South Carolina's "moving at all without the cooperation of other Southern States." The freshman politician was cautious, watching for signals from the state's revered patriarch. He was reluctant to offend or oppose Calhoun on national questions.[27]

Retiring Governor James H. Hammond expounded separate state action in his message, thereby provoking a confrontation in Columbia between the Calhoun people and the Blufftonites. One of Calhoun's lieutenants, Senator Francis W. Pickens of Edgefield, presented resolutions pledging South Carolina's confidence in the new Democratic President and Congress. Should the incoming federal administration fail to remedy the tariff grievance, the state reserved the right to "protect her citizens in any future emergency that may arise." In both chambers Pickens' move succeeded. Orr backed the resolutions, exclaiming in debate that Polk had always been an anti-tariff man. He saw no reason for distrusting the new President before he took office.[28]

In late November the state encountered a challenge from Judge Samuel Hoar, a Massachusetts agent who came to contest South Carolina's Negro seamen law. Confinement in jail was mandatory for blacks who disembarked at any port. The legislature passed resolutions asking the governor to expel Hoar from the state. Orr voted for the resolutions, which included a declaration that "free Negroes and persons of color are not citizens of the United States within the meaning of the Constitution which confers upon the citizens of our State the privileges and immunities of citizens of the several States." Also proclaimed was the right of a state to exclude "seditious persons." Aware of the indignation which his presence aroused, Hoar left quietly.[29]

War with Mexico erupted in 1846, with consequences that eventually put the country on the road to civil war. Calhoun, who had desired Texas annexation, voted against the war declaration and broke with Polk. Arguing for a defensive line strategy, he warned that additional expansion at Mexico's expense would create

dangerous tensions in the United States. South Carolina opinion divided, yet Calhoun remained dominant
in the state. His forceful stand against the Wilmot
Proviso in 1847, and the conviction of many politicians that Mexico was not suited for slavery, discouraged the growth of any groundswell against the
senator.[30] The belief existed that the "all-Mexico
movement," which had appeal elsewhere in the South,
would damage Southern interests in Congress. Also,
Mexico's intransigence in 1847 about negotiations
raised the prospect of a long and costly war.[31]

     Although many South Carolinians had misgivings
about the conflict, they felt obliged to sustain the
military effort. One newspaper asserted, "The step
has been taken, be it for weal or for woe, and it is
our duty now to stand by our common country in her
hour of peril and danger." Orr, who was a Calhoun
follower, believed that the military commitment
required support. In November 1846 he offered a
legislative resolution pledging South Carolina's
assistance to the state's volunteer regiment.[32]

     The Palmetto Regiment was organized in June 1846
and called into active duty in November. Initially
the call for volunteers drew a disappointing response,
and this apathy was reinforced by the War Department's
announcement in July that the regiment was currently
not needed. In the remaining months of 1846 the
length of service was changed from twelve months to
the duration of the war. This altered requirement,
war weariness, and the controversy over the Wilmot
Proviso dampened public enthusiasm. In several western
districts, among them Pickens, Anderson, and Greenville,
no companies were recruited for regimental service.[33]

     Not until late 1846 did Calhoun articulate his be-
lief that territorial aggrandizement in Mexico would
menace slavery in the United States. Early in 1847
he publicized his stand, and throughout the remaining
months of that year public opinion in South Carolina
moved decisively to his side. The state accepted his
contention that the United States should not absorb
into its society alien people who were antagonistic to
slavery.[34]

9

The young Andersonian backed Calhoun and was
solicitous of his views. In August 1847, after returning from a trip to Mississippi, he wrote to the
senator. He derided the Mississippi Democrats'
"ultra" support of Polk. In his words, they knew "no
higher duty than absolute and unwavering allegiance to
party." The letter writer continued to be a discreet
Calhoun man.[35]

***** ***** ***** ***** *****

On internal questions the young representative
usually did not follow Calhoun, who reasoned that any
reform movement might weaken the state's unity. Orr's
position closely paralleled that of Benjamin F. Perry,
the well known Greenville editor, lawyer, and legislator. Both wanted to weaken the low-country planter
gentry and expand the scope of popular democracy.
The "Compromise of 1808," attached to the 1790 constitution, gave the coastal parishes a disproportionate
weight. Its formula for legislative apportionment
included property as well as white population. The
tidewater area, which was heavily black, possessed a
veto power in the legislature.[36]

Ignoring the democratic trends in the country
during the early nineteenth century, South Carolina
did not allow popular choice of its governor or
presidential electors. The legislature made these
selections. An oligarchy of great planters and their
allies resisted demands for an enlarged popular voice
and a more equitable distribution of legislative
seats. This elite wanted the political process to be
generally unorganized, with a minimum of popular participation. Equating democracy with mob rule, the patri-
cians feared that political parties would organize the
white masses on a statewide level. Calhoun, whose influence was enormous, saw parties as havens for spoils-
men who would divide the state and sacrifice its
interests.[37]

Orr was equalitarian in his manners and in his
politics, even though the equalitarianism was limited
to whites. Throughout the antebellum years he consistently supported efforts to make South Carolina's
government more democratic, to give the upcountry whites
a larger voice. The young lawmaker backed an attempt
to transfer the choice of presidential electors from

the legislature to the people. The bill passed in the lower house but was beaten in the parish-controlled senate. The Andersonian also wanted to improve the free school system, under which state funds were allocated to each district for public education. In 1847 he introduced a bill to make uniform the distribution of the fund.[38]

Earlier, before he entered the legislature, his newspaper disputed Governor James H. Hammond's allegation that the free school system was a failure. Hammond, who served from 1842 to 1844, suggested the system's abolition and the substitution of one public academy in each district. The Gazette claimed that Anderson's rising generation was "better educated than the one just matured." In the large districts, the journal stated, many children would be unable to travel to the one available academy under Hammond's plan. By denying a rudimentary schooling to the indigent, the governor's scheme violated the principle that "the only guaranty which we have of the stability of a free government is based in the intelligence of the people." The Gazette expressed its democratic faith. In its words, the free school system had been established "to disseminate useful knowledge among the poorer classes and by cultivating their intellects elevate their minds, tastes and feelings; to enlighten their understandings, thereby to remove them from the influence of the tricks and chicanery of the demagogue."[39]

Orr's winsome personality and democratic outlook were great assets. In addition to being popular with his constituents, he was becoming known in the state capital. One of his friends and fellow legislators in Columbia was the low-country novelist William Gilmore Simms.[40] The Piedmont politician was re-elected in 1846 with the second biggest vote among the candidates in his legislative district. Twenty-four years of age when he won his second term, he was capable and ambitious. Much of the next two years he would spend in pursuit of a more prestigious office, a seat in Congress. Since the annual legislative session in Columbia was about one month in duration, there was ample time for his law practice, travel to the Southwest, and continued political campaigning.[41]

11

In the late spring and early summer of 1847 Orr
journeyed with his family through Georgia, Alabama,
Mississippi, and Tennessee. The quality of land, transportation facilities, and economic life of these states
held his attention. The rich and fertile lands nour-
ished by the Mississippi River impressed him, as did
the prosperous planters. The family visited some rela-
tives who had removed to Mississippi, including Orr's
father. (Larry himself might have relocated to this
area a few years later, had his 1848 bid for a Congressional seat failed.)[42]

Articles on the trip appeared in the Anderson
Gazette. One of them analyzed the impact of a railroad
upon Cass County in Georgia. Undoubtedly the writer
wanted his fellow townsmen to appreciate the value of
the Greenville and Columbia Railroad. He was deeply
interested in rail lines which would connect parts of
South Carolina as well as the different states. In the
1830's the railroad had emerged as a dynamic force in
American life. Southern leaders were eager to promote
the building of railroads which would strengthen their
region's commercial ties with the West.[43]

During the 1830's attempts were made to construct
the Louisville, Cincinnati, and Charleston Railroad.
The economic depression of the late 1830's, the fall of
cotton prices, and a terrible fire in Charleston ruined
the project. However, the enterprise was not entirely
fruitless. In the 1840's lines of the South Carolina
Railroad were completed from Branchville (in Orangeburg
District) to Columbia and Camden; thereby rail connections between Charleston and the state's middle section
were forged. In 1845 the western rail scheme, reaching
from Charleston to Memphis, was revived, with plans to
connect the South Carolina Railroad at Augusta, Georgia,
with the Georgia State Railroad. The latter line
would extend to Atlanta. By the middle 1850's links
were secured from Atlanta to points in Tennessee.[44]

Public opinion became increasingly favorable to
integrating the South Carolina up country into the
railroad network. In 1845 the legislature approved the
Greenville and Columbia Railroad charter. As originally
conceived, the route would touch Newberry and Laurensville. When the amount of the subscription fell below
expectations the railroad's future became doubtful. In
1847 Anderson and Abbeville offered financial assistance
on condition that they be added to the route.[45]

12

The initial plan required 109 miles of track; the newer scheme called for 158. In contrast, also, the newer proposal entailed heavy bridging or grading. Many people in Greenville and Laurens maintained that the financial resources were insufficient for construction on the longer route, and a spirited rivalry developed.[46]

Active in the construction effort, Orr frequently attended meetings and conventions to promote the enterprise. With his law partner, Jacob P. Reed, he spoke at the stockholders meeting in Newberry on November 19, 1847. Benjamin F. Perry was the chief spokesman for the shorter approach. The newer plan was adopted. Although many Greenville and Laurens citizens threatened to withdraw their support, a decision to start the Greenville line at Dr. Brown's station, located about ten miles south of Anderson, placated them, and work began. By late 1853 the road was built.[47]

Orr took a keen interest in the economic growth of his region. With Perry and other upcountry leaders, he wished to encourage manufacturing and industrial diversification. One of the pioneer endeavors in launching the cotton textile industry in the Palmetto state was William Gregg's mill in Graniteville. When the lower legislative house approved the bill incorporating Gregg's company by a 73 to 33 vote in 1845, the Anderson representative stood with the majority.[48]

***** ***** ***** ***** *****

Active in municipal affairs, Orr became one of the wardens on the Anderson council in September 1847. At a council meeting early in the next year he was chosen to preside in the absence of the regular chief magistrate. The local government performed numerous functions, among them keeping the roads in good condition, collecting the road tax, granting licenses to retail liquor, distributing relief funds for sufferers of fire, appointing town patrols, and preserving public order.[49]

The council's role was partly judicial, rendering verdicts in minor cases and referring more serious matters to the general sessions court. In March 1849 the town fathers heard a complaint against Mrs. Temperance Patterson and Joseph Patterson for "keeping a Bawdy House;" the defendants were ordered to appear before the sessions court. Cases on which the council passed judgment included such offenses as drunkenness,

13

assault and battery, default of road and street duty,
using indecent language, and "running an unruly and
wild horse in a buggy through the public square."
Whites usually paid for their misdeeds with money,
blacks with whippings. In May 1851 two blacks appeared
on the charge of "having spiritous liquor in their
possession." One received twenty lashes, the other
was acquitted. In the following October the council
fixed the punishment for "shooting Fire Crackers,
Rockets, Roman Candles, Raising balloons, Loud halloing
or Shouting, or any other riotous Conduct." The
maximum penalty for whites was a twenty dollar fine, for
blacks twenty-five lashes.50

When parts of western South Carolina faced a grain
shortage in 1845, a public meeting in Anderson discussed
the crisis. A central committee was directed to secure
information on what terms corn could be purchased and
delivered from other states. Orr sat on this committee.
Subcommittees were assigned to gather data on conditions
in each of the "beats" in Anderson District. (A "beat"
was a military precinct, patrolled by the state militia.)
The citizens declined to seek state assistance, choosing
to "rely upon individual capital and enterprise to supply
the demands of our District for grain." In Columbia
Orr opposed a resolution to give thirty thousand dollars
in state funds to the districts ravaged by the drought.
He deplored "the dangerous consequences which may result
from adopting the principle of going to the public
crib to supply sufferers from any and every calamity."
The young Democrat adhered to the laissez-faire
political philosophy which was widely held in nineteenth
century America.51

II. SOUTH CAROLINA CONSIDERS SECESSION, 1847-1852

During the 1840's an important change occurred in
the South's posture in the Union. Through the middle
years of the decade there was talk of economic and
political ties between the South and the West. Actively
promoting this idea, Calhoun spoke out in 1845 for
federal action to increase trade in the Mississippi
Valley. Southerners were amenable to Western demands
for homestead legislation, and Southern Democrats
anticipated Western backing for low tariffs. In both
sections expansionism was strong, with eyes on Texas
and Oregon.[1]

Much of this good will was dissipated by the end
of the decade. In the Northwest the feeling spread
that Polk had slighted that region while he favored
the South. The President was aggressive towards
Mexico and compromising with Great Britain on the
boundary between Oregon and Canada. At the South's
request the tariff was lowered in 1846, but Polk
vetoed an internal improvements bill designed for the
Great Lakes region. The Northwest reacted by voting
for the Wilmot Proviso. A resolution to ban slavery
in the territory acquired from Mexico, the proviso
was approved by the House of Representatives in 1846
and 1847 and defeated in the Senate.[2]

During the Mexican War the belief grew in the free
states that the South was selfishly seeking its own
aggrandizement at the expense of other sections.
Southerners became annoyed by Northern and Western
attempts to prohibit slavery in the territories.
Southern politicians no longer contemplated an alliance
with the West.

The controversy over the Mexican Cession strained
traditional party loyalties. The United States had a
highly developed party system; Democrats and Whigs competed in almost all of the states. By dividing the
country on sectional lines, the Wilmot Proviso disturbed
normal patterns of partisan politics. In 1848 a large
minority of free state voters cast aside their usual
allegiances and supported the newly formed Free Soil
organization. Southerners discussed the idea of a
sectional party, although it never materialized.
(Calhoun was a leader in the movement for a Southern
party. He believed that the national two-party system
worked to the South's disadvantage, giving the Northern

15

abolitionists a balance of power.) The slavery issue
was threatening the basic stability of the party
system.[3]

  While politicians pondered the question of
Southern unity, they faced the reality of the 1848
presidential contest. South Carolina Democrats disagreed about their party's nominee, Lewis Cass, and
his "squatter sovereignty" doctrine. ("Squatter
sovereignty" meant basically local option in a territory on the status of slavery.) Many party leaders
considered Cass's position more menacing than the
Wilmot Proviso. Moreover, the Whig candidacy of
General Zachary Taylor, a Louisiana slaveholder, had
much appeal. A Charleston group nominated an independent ticket with Taylor for President and Democrat
William O. Butler for Vice-President. Several Calhoun
lieutenants backed the Taylor-Butler slate, although
Calhoun himself remained aloof from the electioneering.
Despite Taylor's appeal, there was much hesitancy to
support the Whigs. Rhett's Charleston Mercury contended that the regular Democratic nominee was safer
than the Whig party, and two Columbia newspapers called
Cass's territorial stand harmless. The tide turned in
his favor, and the new legislature chose pro-Cass
electors.[4]

    *****   *****   *****   *****   *****

  In 1848 Orr and Perry, both Democrats, competed
for the Congressional seat from the Greenville, Laurens,
and Pendleton election districts. This area contained
much Whig strength, sending Whigs to Congress in the
late 1830's and early 1840's. Richard F. Simpson
captured the seat for the Democrats in 1844; in that
year the Whig party suffered for its support of protective tariffs and its ambivalence on Texas annexation.
Whig strength waned. Reelected in 1846 without opposition, Simpson chose to retire after his second term
expired.[5]

  Perry, many years older than his opponent, was a
veteran of several political campaigns. The two men,
in accord when they denounced the Wilmot Proviso,
differed on the Presidency. Perry came out strongly
for Cass, convinced that the national Whig program was
not congenial with Southern interests. In contrast,
Orr did not feel bound to endorse the Democratic nominee; he found Taylor attractive. During his 1847 trip
through the South he had noticed much good will for the

Louisianan, and he wrote Calhoun, "I am not sure that he is not the man for the South in the present crisis." While running for Congress, he endorsed Taylor, and this action worked to his advantage decidedly. Because no Whig ran for Simpson's seat, Orr's backing of Taylor drew many Whigs to him.[6]

It is difficult to judge whether the candidate's embracing of Taylor was motivated by opportunism, dislike of Cass's territorial stand, or a belief that the hero of Buena Vista would generally deal more equitably with the South than his rival. The Whig party adopted no platform for the 1848 election, and Taylor's position on the territories was unknown. Therefore, an endorsement of the Whig Presidential nominee did not imply approval of any territorial policy. The question of slavery in the West was complicated and tricky, and many South Carolinians were uncertain when confronting it. Orr assailed the Wilmot Proviso, but by so doing he was indistinguishable from Perry.

There were other issues and factors which could sway an election. Perry discussed his opponent's support of an appropriation for two New Orleans merchants, Burnley and Johnson, in 1847. The state paid these partners who supplied goods to the Palmetto Regiment, a unit which served in the Mexican War. Perry had voted against payment, charging that these two businessmen cheated the soldiers. Orr replied that the legislature had overwhelmingly approved the appropriation; he publicized a senate committee report recommending payment. In his words, Perry's pursuit of this "small game" was a sign of desperation.[7]

The younger candidate's personality worked in his favor. He loved to mingle with people, and he electioneered widely throughout the Congressional district. In the custom of Southern politicians, he generously distributed liquor to voters. Moreover, Perry believed that Calhoun and his friends, viewing the Greenvillian as too independent, exerted a "secret influence" in Orr's behalf.[8]

The election was close. In Greenville District Orr drew 423 ballots to Perry's 1,605. In Pendelton District he had 2,884 against Perry's 1,099. In Laurens District Orr received 1,147 to Perry's 1,065. The overall tally was Orr, 4,454, and Perry, 3,769. One newspaper estimated that the winner had taken a solid Whig vote in Pendleton and Laurens election

districts, while many Democrats were indifferent to the
Presidency. Perry's pro-Cass stand probably hurt him.
Rigid and uncompromising, he disregarded the advice of
friends that he avoid the Presidential question. He
would not sacrifice principles or be silent in order to
win an election.[9]

*****   *****   *****   *****   *****

South Carolina became the center of protest against
the alleged Northern encroachments upon Southern rights.
Influenced by Calhoun, the legislature in December 1848
announced its desire for cooperative action with other
slave states in opposing the principles of the Wilmot
Proviso. In the months following popular anger reached
a fever pitch. Local committees of safety were organized
and sent delegates to a state convention of Southern
Rights associations, held in Columbia in May 1849.
Orr, elected to his district's delegation, sat on one of
the key committees.[10]

The convention's work proved innocuous. Although
desiring joint action with other states, the members
did not issue a call for an interstate conference.
Heeding Calhoun's advice, they waited for another state
to take the initiative. In October Mississippi obliged,
and two months later South Carolina's legislature
accepted the invitation. Preparations began for the
regional gathering, scheduled for June 1850 in Nashville.[11]

During the early months of 1850 South Carolinians
looked forward to the Nashville convention, hopeful of
united Southern action. People spoke frequently of
disunion, yet they viewed secession as a last resort,
to be taken only if guarantees for Southern security in
the Union were not obtained. Because radical disunionists of the Rhett type did not oppose the campaign
for sectional unity, there was little discord. In the
spring delegates to the Nashville body were chosen at
public meetings throughout the state.[12]

When Orr entered Congress in December 1849 leading
Democrats and Whigs were beginning the search for an
accommodation between the sections. The country was
in a grave crisis, and in both the free and slave sections anger and distrust were on the rise. On May 8,
1850, the newcomer from Anderson delivered a Congressional speech which expressed South Carolina's perception of a hostile North. To buttress his charge that
the North had succumbed to abolitionism, he offered

concrete examples--the election of such antislavery
figures as William H. Seward and Salmon P. Chase to
major offices, endorsements of the Wilmot Proviso,
efforts to obstruct the capture of fugitive slaves,
and attempts by abolition societies to incite the
slaves to violence. Emancipation and racial equality
were the obvious goals, and the granting of Negro
suffrage in some states revealed the North's intentions.[13]

> At the last State election in New York, the
> free negroes held the balance of power be-
> tween the two political parties. Representa-
> tives upon this floor receive the votes of
> this degraded class, and the success of re-
> publican institutions is made to depend upon
> the judgment and intelligence of the free
> negro sovereigns. The aim of the Aboli-
> tionists looks first to the emancipation of
> the slaves throughout the South, and then
> is to follow their elevation to all the
> social and political privileges of the white
> man. The thick-lipped African is to march
> up to the same ballot-box, eat at the same
> table, and sit in the same parlor with the
> white man.

In the orator's mind every normal political
cleavage had dissolved in the path of the anti-slavery
storm. In his words, the mass of Northerners sympathized with the free-soil position, which was being
advanced by two groups--the Wilmot Proviso supporters
and the non-interventionists.

> Some of the northern non-interventionists
> deny that Congress has the power to pass the
> Wilmot proviso; others maintain the posi-
> tion that Congress has the power, but
> should not exercise it, and straightway
> offer the excuse to their constitutents,
> that it is not necessary to pass it--that
> the Mexican laws are in force and they
> exclude slavery. This is the opinion
> entertained by General Cass and all the
> non-intervention Northern Democrats in this
> House. Is this not a heavy tribute which
> non-intervention pays to free-soil? It
> is tantamount to saying we are in favor of
> the end which the proviso aims to accom-
> plish, viz: the exclusion of the slave

States from all the territory acquired
from Mexico--we oppose its adoption only
because we regard it as unnecessary, and
because we believe the course we propose
to pursue will most effectively subserve
the end without giving offence and producing irritation in the South.

Over the California issue, he argued, Northern party
divisions had vanished. Because this prospective new
state drafted an anti-slavery constitution, Northerners
were pushing relentlessly for admission. The North
"is making it a sectional question." Moreover, Orr
asserted, the preliminary steps taken to secure
California statehood had violated the usual procedures.[14]

He was convinced that an unfriendly Northern majority would pass unconstitutional laws harmful to
his section. Unless the North abandoned this intention, disunion would be inevitable. Because slavery
was so firmly bound to its social order, the South would
never permit its destruction. If the antislavery
agitation did not cease, the Southern people would
eventually be compelled to choose between secession
and Negro emancipation. These words expressed South
Carolina's outlook in 1850. The Anderson representative voiced the state's resentment at what it inter-
preted as Northern unfairness and moral arrogance.
Like most white Southerners, he was a racist and a
believer in slavery, and his conscience was not
troubled. He alluded to "our now happy slaves," and he
was satisfied that the Bible justified slavery.[15]

The May 8 speech contained a plea for Southern
representation at Nashville. In his view, this conference held out the possibility of a unified Southern
voice. However, he doubted that the conference would
be successful. False hopes of compromise had "deluded"
many Southerners; they were deceived by the belief that
Northern "aggressions" would cease. "I warn them to
rise from the lethargy into which they have been betrayed. I tell them now, in all candor, that I see
no returning sense of justice in the North."[16]

This address did not exclude a possible rapproche-
ment between the free and slave sections. In spite of
his grim assessment, the Representative implied that
the preservation of the Union, on terms agreeable to
the South, was desirable. He hoped that the Nashville
convention would make possible continued union.[17]

The ends of that convention were high and
holy; it was called to protect the Constitution, to save the Union, by taking such
steps as might prevent, if possible, the
consummation of measures which would probably lead to the destruction of both.
Had the purpose been disunion, those who
called that convention would have waited
until the irretrievable step had been
taken, and nothing left to the South but
submission or secession. The present is a
critical conjuncture of political affairs;
there is a propriety, nay, almost a necessity
for southern men to commune with each other.

Shortly before the convention assembled, the
nation learned of the set of proposals which became the
Compromise of 1850; in the late summer Congress enacted
them. The main parts were California statehood with
slavery forbidden, creation of the Utah and New Mexico
territories under the popular sovereignty formula, and
a stringent new fugitive slave law.[18] In most Southern
states the Compromise program had a pacifying effect.
In contrast, South Carolina was overwhelmingly displeased. Free state status for California was seen as
a clear victory for the North, while the use of popular
sovereignty for New Mexico and Utah was considered a
prelude to eventual statehood without slavery. Almost
nothing in the plan appeared as a concession to the
South.[19]

On June 3, the Nashville convention met. Three
ardent South Carolina disunionists, Rhett, James H.
Hammond, and Francis W. Pickens, were among those
present. Because Southern sentiment seemed amenable
to the proposed Congressional settlement, the Nashville
body avoided extremism. Realizing that the country
as a whole desired moderation, the delegates knew that
rashness would damage the cause of Southern unity.
The convention unanimously endorsed a resolution that
the 1820 Missouri Compromise line (36°30') be extended
to the Pacific. The assemblage adjourned on June 12,
after deciding to reconvene later in the year if Congress refused their demand.[20]

Speaking against the proposed Compromise, Orr on
June 12 upheld the Nashville stand. To the free state
Congressmen he offered an extension of the Missouri
Compromise line as "a fair and equitable division of
the territory." In the past the South had yielded to

the free section the larger share of new lands. The Louisiana territory, which was entirely slave area when purchased, was divided by the Missouri Line; the greater part was north of the line.[21]

> I do not appeal to northern men to do us justice; I hope I nevèr shall be so far lost to self-respect as to become a suppliant at the feet of power. We tender you this line to the Pacific--you can accept it or reject it; but there is one thing which it is my duty now to say: we do not intend to submit to exclusion from that territory; we will have a fair proportion of it, 'peaceably if we can--forceably if we must.'

The Andersonian repeated this argument in an August letter to a Georgia gathering. The 36°30' line was "one of extreme concession, but for the sake of harmony and the Union, the South will acquiesce in it." Lamenting California's probable admission as a free state, he noted that Georgia's legislature had made plans, in that contingency, for a state convention. The neighboring state's decision he called "wise and patriotic."[22]

In his Congressional speech of May 8, Orr had painted a dark picture of sectional relations, with the free states bent upon destroying the South. Later in the year he advocated the extension of the Missouri Compromise line "for the sake of harmony and the Union." The arrangement that he favored did not materialize. Congress ignored the Nashville declaration and passed the Compromise of 1850 in the later summer. (Orr voted against all parts except the fugitive slave bill.) Throughout the country overall satisfaction with the settlement prevailed. In most Southern states an unenthusiastic and qualified acceptance became evident.

In May Orr had remarked that hope of accommodation "deluded" many Southerners. After the Compromise became law he recognized that his section was giving its assent. If the Compromise was unjust, and if the North had succumbed to abolitionist madness, most Southern whites were apparently indifferent to the grave danger to their well being. Disturbed by this seeming apathy, the young Congressman spoke of disunion with the aim of arousing the South. He wanted security for his section, in or out of the Union.

22

When the Nashville convention reconvened in
November, the attendance was small and the spirit
dampened. In perfunctory fashion the delegates
assailed most of the Compromise provisions, reaffirmed
their preference for extension of the 36°30' line,
and called for a Southern congress. Throughout the
slave states the second Nashville meeting stirred little
interest.

At about the same time Georgia elected a solid
unionist majority to a state convention which met in
December. Its labors produced the "Georgia Platform,"
which linked acceptance of the Compromise to Congressional respect for Southern rights. Any federal
legislation which menaced the interests of the South
would, in the platform's language, justify disunion.
Georgia's manifesto reflected the section's dominant
attitude. Southern unionism in 1850 was conditional.[23]

In only two states was secession a strong possi-
bility--South Carolina and Mississippi. Unique traits
distinguished these hotbeds of radicalism. The keen
awareness of a black majority and its precarious
economic position gave the Palmetto state a sense of
desperation. The uncertainties of the overseas market, to which much of the state's prosperity was tied,
a perception of constricting opportunities for wealth
from the overworked soil, and the resulting migration
of people into the Southwest; these factors, combined
with the haughty arrogance of the ruling gentry in
the nation's most class-ruled state, contributed to
the radical milieu. Moreover, Calhoun's influence
was pervasive. His opposition to the Compromise
program, articulated before his death in March, had a
powerful effect upon the state. The Democrats were
overwhelmingly behind him, and no Whig organization
existed which could effectively oppose the cause of
resistance. Disunion feeling reached its height in
the remaining months of 1850. Local Southern Rights
associations were formed.[24]

Mississippi was the domain of a new and brash
planter elite, merchants, professional men, large
numbers of struggling small farmers, and, in parts,
formidable concentrations of blacks. In this state,
much of which was a raw frontier society, the mixture
of these restless elements produced a self-sufficient,
aggressive, and often violent spirit. Governor John
A. Quitman was eagerly pushing for disunion. An
animated contest ensued between the radicals and those
who reasoned that secession would be unwise.[25]

Decisions elsewhere in the South restrained
Mississippi. In November the unionists captured the
governorship and most seats in a state convention.
The South as a whole was agreeable to the Compromise
with the understanding that the free states would act
in good faith. Most Southerners wished to avoid confrontation, and they rejected Calhoun's view that
their section should discard old party ties. Because
of the South's minority status, a sectional bloc did
not seem to promise the best defense. Rather, most
slave state politicians preferred to affiliate with
Northerners in the national parties.[26]

***** ***** ***** ***** *****

By the autumn of 1850 it became clear that South
Carolina could expect no outside support for secession.
Nonetheless, disunion sentiment gathered momentum in
the state. Orr continued his attacks on the Compromise, speaking of eventual dissolution. Law practice
and political meetings claimed much of his time when
Congress was recessed. He addressed several gatherings,
urging membership in the local Southern Rights associations. In Pickens in April 1851 he called the Union
a curse and forecast the creation of a Southern
confederacy. In a public letter he wrote that unless
the federal government were reformed drastically, "and
I confess I see no hope of it," the history of the
United States would soon be completed.[27] The Congressman was perturbed by the North's posture on the territories, and he deplored the South's approval of what
he deemed a bad bargain. He was earnest when he
described the Union as a curse.

South Carolina encountered a painful choice between acquiescence and lone resistance. The cooperationists maintained that secession would fail without
the collaboration of other states. Orr became, with
such men as Andrew P. Butler, Robert W. Barnwell,
Christopher G. Memminger, and Langdon Cheves, one of
the prominent cooperationists. The separate secessionists, demanding immediate disunion, were led by Rhett,
Maxcy Gregg, and Governor Whitemarsh Seabrook. Only
a small minority stood by the Compromise. Among
them were some notable members of the impotent Whig
party--Waddy Thompson, Richard Yeadon, William Grayson,
William C. Preston, and James L. Petigru--and a tiny
number of Democrats, including Perry, Joel Poinsett,
and John Belton O'Neill. They had no political
organization through which they could combat the radicals.[28]

24

The separate actionists desired a state convention, and the moderates favored another Southern assemblage. The two groups compromised; in December 1850 the legislature granted both demands. Delegate elections for the state convention were fixed for February 1851, but no meeting time was set, since it would await the action of the proposed sectional conference. The legislature issued the call for a Southern congress, to meet in January 1852 in Montgomery, Alabama. Elections for South Carolina members of the regional body were scheduled for October 1851.[29]

Apathy and light voting marked the February 1851 election of delegates to the state convention. (Orr did not run for a seat.) The separate secessionists won control, stunning the cooperationists with their victory. The opponents of separate secession became more energetic as they prepared for the October delegate election for the Southern congress. Unionists like Perry backed the moderate disunionists.

In several speeches and letters during the spring and summer of 1851 Orr argued that precipitate action would harm the cause of resistance in other Southern states. As an independent nation, he added, South Carolina would suffer economically. Charleston's trade, dependent upon exports to other states, would perish, to the delight of Savannah and Augusta in Georgia. The United States ban on the foreign slave trade would preclude the sale of South Carolina's surplus blacks elsewhere, and the state would face the burden of a "redundant" population.[30]

Very likely, he believed, a federal blockade would result, cutting off South Carolina's overseas cotton and rice trade. "If our coast should be blockaded or our custom houses abolished and no government troops marched into the State, what benefit would the sympathy of individuals in other States be to us?" They would be spectators to South Carolina's isolation and destruction.[31]

Speculating about the possible federal response, Orr implied that the United States might not use coercion against a unified South. Secession by at least two or three states together "greatly reduces the prospect of the Federal Government treating secession as revolutionary." The Congressman's reasoning was cogent and persuasive. He wanted his state to be cautious, to approach secession as a matter of correct

timing. Also, he maintained, time was on the side of
resistance. Because abolitionism was still rampant,
opponents of the Compromise would soon gain the
ascendancy in the slave section and remedy the South's
grievances "either in the Union or out of the Union."[32]

His words expressed a willingness to preserve the
Union if his section could be placated. Such an outlook he considered unlikely. "The agencies now
actively at work in the free States demonstrate to my
mind that the dissolution of this Union and the establishment of a Southern and Northern confederacy is an
inevitable necessity." Orr's primary loyalties were
to his state and to the South. In 1851 he was neither
unionist nor disunionist. He was a pragmatic politician who wished to promote, by whichever means seemed
most promising, the welfare of South Carolina.[33]

The radicals controlled a state conference of
Southern Rights associations in Charleston in May.
The cooperationist leaders at this gathering were
Barnwell, Butler, and Orr, who fought the radicals'
request for an endorsement of immediate secession. By
prescribing a specific mode of redress, Orr declared,
the Charleston body would be dictating to the state
convention. He introduced a resolution asking the
Southern Rights assemblage to let the forthcoming
state convention act at its own discretion. This plea
was rejected.[34]

By their highhandedness, the radicals annoyed the
public and goaded the opposition. Stepping up their
campaign, the moderates printed and distributed the
speeches of Barnwell, Butler, and Orr. In July the
Andersonian contended that the immediate secessionists
no longer enjoyed popular support.[35]

> In such an issue, gentlemen, they will be
> beaten in the mountain districts. Our
> people here are not submissionists--nearly
> all are for resistance, and for efficient
> resistance, to the Clay Compromise--but
> they have yet to be convinced that they
> have more courage and patriotism than their
> Georgia and North Carolina neighbors. They
> have too much modesty to thrust themselves
> forward as the only champions of Southern
> rights and Southern honor. They believe
> that Georgia, Alabama, and Mississippi are
> as spirited as South Carolina, and that

there is no very startling disgrace in their
waiting for the co-operation of these States.

In the October 1851 balloting for delegates to
the Southern congress, the cooperationists and
separate secessionists vied in each Congressional
district. The cooperationists carried every district
except Rhett's. Only in the low country parishes and
middle country black area did the more extreme disunionists command majorities. In the up country,
where the whites comprised a large part of the population, and in Charleston, with considerable commercial
interests, drastic action was rejected. Orr and James
H. Irby, a Laurens attorney, were the two delegates
named from their Congressional district; they crushed
their radical opponents.[36]

The October election and the attitude of the
other states had a restraining effect. Controlling
the state convention which met in April 1852 in
Columbia, the extremists claimed the right to secede
but declined to exercise it. (The projected Southern
congress never assembled.) The state convention's
failure to act demoralized the radicals. Believing
that his leadership had been repudiated, Rhett
resigned as United States Senator.[37]

After the April convention tensions subsided, and
the Compromise of 1850 faded as an issue. The moderate
mood of the country was felt in South Carolina, and
few people continued to talk seriously of disunion.
Orr reflected this sentiment, and he bagan to reappraise
his state's position in the Union. The Congressman
had emerged from the recent secession controversy with
a statewide reputation. His ideas and arguments during
the crisis had not been original or unique, but they
had been ably presented, and they had generally typified
majority opinion in the state.

27

0772023

South Caroliniana Library

III. NATIONAL DEMOCRAT, 1852 - 1860

Emotionally exhausted by the crisis of the early 1850's, South Carolinians yearned for internal harmony. As a conciliatory mood gathered strength in the months that followed the April 1852 convention, the extreme secessionists moved to placate the cooperationists. Anticipating future conflict with the free states, they wanted to isolate the small number of unionists. The extremists helped to make possible the unanimous election of John L. Manning as governor in late 1852. Soon after taking office, Manning told Orr that he had attempted to make his inaugural address "in every respect moderate."[1]

The Anderson politician found reason to believe that the South could remain safely in the Union, and he was a conditional unionist for virtually the remainder of the decade. At the 1852 Democratic national convention in Baltimore he was a spectator. The party platform and Presidential candidate satisfied him that the country would, under Democratic rule, return to the "wise and patriotic doctrines" of Jefferson. Speaking in Congress on June 9, he praised the nominee, Franklin Pierce, as "eminently conservative" on the slavery question, a man who would respect the South's constitutional rights. The speech contained an elaborate attack upon the Whig program--protective tariffs, the distribution of revenues from public land sales to the states, and "a wild system of unjust, local, and unconstitutional" internal improvements at federal expense.[2]

The Congressional orator was lavish in his praise of Pierce. Reviewing his public career, he pointed to the nominee's unswerving support of President Andrew Jackson against the Bank of the United States in the 1830's. "General Jackson in no act of his public life exhibited so much sagacity as in making war upon the Bank; and all who sustained him in the fierce encounter with this great colossal moneyed power, richly merit the gratitude of the country." The speech, which said much of Pierce, also revealed much about Orr. He was enthusiastically and exuberantly partisan, proud to be a Democrat, proud to belong to the party of Jefferson and Jackson.[3]

The speech presented a challenge to South Carolina's practice of shunning national politics. Since the nullification controversy of the 1830's the state had customarily abstained from sending delegates to national conventions, although it regularly cast its electoral votes for the Democrats. In Congress the state delegation usually did not attend party caucuses. Now Orr wanted his state to forge close bonds with the national organization, and no longer did he regard the Northern Democrats as inseparable from the antislavery zealots. He predicted that his state would gladly support Pierce. "The nomination is far better than the people of South Carolina had hoped could be made; and although General Pierce may not believe in the doctrines of State rights and State remedies to the extent which we go, yet he is a better Republican than we ever expected to see again in nomination for the Presidency."[4]

Only with the friendship of other Southerners and conservative Northerners, he insisted, could South Carolina protect its interests. This was the position of the National Democrats, a faction which emerged in the state in 1852. Disputing their approach were those who preferred the old aloofness; members of this wing were often called Southern Rights Democrats. Uncommitted and frequently holding a balance of power between them were many Democrats. In addition, a small minority of South Carolinians entered the American ("Know Nothing") party during the 1850's.[5]

Reactions to Orr's endorsement of Pierce were mixed. His critics charged that open approval of the Democratic platform and nominee implied acquiescence in the Compromise of 1850. A letter writer in the Charleston Mercury maintained that the state would surrender its principles by indulging in the "undignified contentions and intrigues" of national politics. When the time came to vote, this person added, South Carolina would probably stand with Pierce against the Whigs. "But let it be done in silence and as a necessity. Let us not toss our caps and beat our drums as though a victory had been achieved." Whatever the outcome, the oppression of the South would continue; resistance would still be justified. "While we consider it expedient to forebear that resistance, let us quietly attend to our own business at home, develop our resources, and live in hope." The Mercury editorialized, "Shall the people of South Carolina turn about and swear fealty and devotion to the Union, and thoroughly amalgamate with the Democratic party, or shall they keep themselves

unfettered?" The Anderson Congressman replied that
this newspaper was undermining the South's friends,
and he pointed out that the Southern Whig press was
gleefully reprinting the Mercury's derisions of Pierce.
On the slavery issue he asked, "Do you doubt that
Franklin Pierce is true to the constitutional rights
of the South on that question? If not, why attempt
to excite suspicion and manufacture weapons to fight
him in the South, that General Scott may be promoted?"
(General Winfield Scott was Pierce's Whig opponent.)
The message was plain: by refusing to aid its friends,
the Palmetto state would help its enemies.[6]

From 1852 to 1860 Orr was the acknowledged leader
of the National Democrats in South Carolina. Promi-
nently associated with him were Perry, Pickens, and
Congressman Preston Brooks of Edgefield. This faction
attracted many cooperationists and unionists of the
1847-1852 controversy. At the same time many cooperationists gave the National Democrats occasional backing.
Among them were Manning, Christopher G. Memminger,
Robert W. Barnwell, and United States Senators Andrew
P. Butler and Josiah J. Evans.[7]

The Southern Rights Democrats, led by Rhett,
Maxcy Gregg, and Congressmen Lawrence Keitt and John
McQueen, would put no faith in national parties.
The more radical disunionists of the recent crisis
were found mainly in this wing. They retained their
fundamental belief that secession was inevitable, and
they assumed that the North was at heart unfriendly
to their section.[8]

With the prospects of disunion obviously diminished,
many South Carolinians wanted to cultivate the good
will of other Southern states. Such an outlook precluded isolation. The Darlington Flag admonished
against "a sullenness and an obstinacy which would
tend to stir up and excite the prejudices of our
neighboring States." The National Democrats took
advantage of this temperate mood. In late 1852 Judge
Josiah J. Evans, a cooperationist backed by Orr and
Perry, won the Senate seat vacated by Rhett. Evans'
victory was encouraging to the politicians who wanted
to move the state into the mainstream of national
politics.[9]

***** ***** ***** ***** *****

The Piedmont Congressman was prosperous and influential. In 1850 his Anderson holdings included
one hundred and ten acres of improved land, six hundred acres of unimproved land, fourteen slaves, three
horses, two mules, two cows, and twenty swine. He
grew vegetables and grain, and he produced home manufacturers valued at one hundred dollars. To supple-
ment his Congressional salary Orr depended largely upon
his law practice. When Congress was not in session he
was busily representing clients in a variety of cases,
involving such matters as larceny, bastardy, retailing
without a license, riot, assault and battery, and cow
stealing. In the equity courts much of his work concerned guardianship petitions.[10]

He found time for travel and out-of-state investments. An 1855 journey took him to Mississippi, where
his brother Jehu resided. Two years later he toured
several Northwestern states and territories and made
extensive land purchases in Minnesota and Missouri.
Ironically, in light of the developing sectional
antagonism, Southern investments in Northern lands
were considerable in the middle 1850's.[11]

Orr's family increased during the decade with the
birth of four children, James Lawrence, Jr. (1852),
Samuel (1855), Mary (1858), and Amelia (1860). Two
daughters born previously were Eliza (1845) and Martha
(1847); Eliza died in the 1850's. The last of the
offspring, Christopher, was born in 1862. Their
father was, in the eyes of a friend, "extremely tender-
hearted and devoted to his family, around the members
of which his affections were closely bound."[12]

Well known in Washington, the genial Carolinian
resided for many years at Brown's Hotel, a favorite
rendezvous for Southern politicians. He joined a
dinner group which included such persons as Senator
and Mrs. Clement C. Clay of Alabama, Lucius Q. C.
Lamar of Mississippi, and Jabez L. M. Curry of Alabama.
Orr frequently visited the Clays. Saddened by the loss
of his daughter Eliza, he would ask Mrs. Clay to play
the piano and sing for him. His favorite ballad was
"Lilly Dale," which usually brought tears to his eyes.[13]

32

Because South Carolina did not keep pace with the
nation's population growth, the delegation in the House
of Representatives was reduced from seven to six after
the 1850 census. In 1852 the legislature redrew the
Congressional districts. Until this time Orr represented the Pendleton, Greenville, and Laurens election
districts. Under the reapportionment Laurens was removed from his constituency, while Spartanburg and
Union were added. In 1853 he sought re-election against
another incumbent, Daniel Wallace of Union, whose old
constituency embraced the Spartanburg, York, Union,
and Chester districts. The Andersonian won easily,
trailing his rival only in Union. Except for this
contest, he never faced opposition when he ran for
re-election.[14]

***** ***** ***** ***** *****

In many respects Orr's Congressional positions
typified the Southern Democratic outlook. He
desired low tariffs, and he voted against the distribution of the United States Treasury surplus among the
states. He stood against homestead legislation,
designed to encourage westward expansion through land
grants to settlers. In 1855 he asserted that federal
funds should not be used to attract people from the
older states into the newer ones, thereby depleting
the older areas of their strength and wealth.
Southern politicians usually regarded homestead bills
as antislavery, aimed at populating territories which
would eventually become free states.[15]

When Louis Kossuth, the Hungarian revolutionary,
toured the country in 1852, there were mixed reactions
to his presence. Virtually all German-Americans and
many Irish immigrants, mindful of conditions in their
homelands, were sympathetic to his cause. Southerners
were mainly unfriendly to this symbol of rebellion
against established authority. Orr objected to a
Congressional resolution welcoming the Hungarian and
appropriating money for his expenses.[16]

During the early 1850's the Piedmont Representative sat on the House committee on public lands and
frequently presented its recommendations on the floor.
His record on this panel revealed his enthusiasm for
economic growth. Desirous of closer rail ties between
the South and the West, he was the only South Carolinian
who voted to grant alternate sections of public land
to the states for railroad construction. When he

33

spoke in 1852 for a bill linking the Missouri River valley and Charleston, the problem of constitutional power to donate public lands to the states did not trouble him. In his view, the authority rested upon the federal government's rights as proprietor of the public domain. Moreover, he contended, the scope and benefits of the project would be national.[17]

Acquiring a national vision and favoring the national rule of the Democratic party, Orr did not, however, advocate a strong federal government, and he subscribed to his party's traditional states' rights philosophy. When Congress debated homestead legislation he detected a tendency to make people lean too heavily upon the federal government. "It is a wrong policy. The Government should lean upon the people. It is time to stop the practice of appropriating the common funds of the Government for every conceivable purpose. It is centralizing in its tendency; and the passage of such an act as this will only serve to increase the tendency." These were the words of a Jeffersonian Democrat.[18]

His reputation after 1852 as a moderate who disliked sectional friction helped to make him popular in the nation's capital. Another major asset was his personality. John Forney, editor-politician from Philadelphia, called Orr the best-tempered Southern Congressman of the antebellum years. One newspaper, alluding to his forensic talents, noted the Carolinian's "invariable coolness and courtesy" and parliamentary dexterity. This paper added, "There is a genuine, homespun plainness, frank, open disposition and kindness of heart about him, making him also one of the pleasantest men of the day."[19]

When the Thirty-Third Congress assembled in December 1853, the Andersonian, now beginning his third term in the House, was a main aspirant for the speakership. The Democrats, solidly in control, designated Kentucky's Lynn Boyd as their nominee and elected him. In accordance with South Carolina custom, none of Orr's colleagues attended the caucus which named the party candidate. Attributing his defeat to their absence, he told Benjamin F. Perry that their "idiosyncracy" had lost the state much influence in Washington. "When will our state see the folly and absurdity of this transcendental isolation?"[20]

On the contrary, the Charleston Mercury, Rhett's
organ, did not lament the state's failure to capture
the speakership. "We thought it inconsistent with
the position of a Resistance man of 1850 to be a candidate for an office which necessarily fettered him by
a pledge of Unionism." A conciliatory figure in
Washington, the upcountry politician was controversial
in South Carolina. The charge most frequently
levelled against Orr, according to his friend William
Gilmore Simms, was that he was "simply a national man."
Francis W. Pickens remarked that "national reputation
will be his ruin at home."[21]

***** ***** ***** ***** *****

Although the National Democrats were chiefly
concerned with keeping the federal government in
friendly hands, many members of this wing had other
goals as well. They wanted the state to democratize
its political process and institute reforms, such as
the popular choice of presidential electors and a
public school system. Support for this program came
primarily from the up country and the Charleston business districts, from the yeomanry and the less prosperous whites.[22]

"The Gov. of this state is a close oligarchy,"
Pickens observed. Demands for more democracy plainly
threatened the wealthy planters and their allies who
worked shrewdly to maintain popular acquiescence in
their rule. Overrepresentation of the coastal
parishes in the state senate was the key to their
hegemony. Powerful yet self-restrained, the ruling
class governed within a democratic framework. Believing in the ideal of an aristocratic republic, but
afraid to offend the white masses, this gentry publicly
accepted and privately scorned democracy. A web of
contradictions, South Carolina's political life was
simultaneously volatile and static. The aristocrats
sensed their vulnerability to any popular outcry
against their dominance. By the middle 1850's demands
for educational, electoral, and court reform became
decidedly more abrasive, mirroring bitter sectional
and class feelings. However, the governing elite
viewed the recently-established inland planters and
businessmen as potentially more bothersome than the
white lower class. These newer men of property, the
oligarchs suspected, might agitate the dispossessed
with democratic slogans and seize power. The elite
was frightened by the ambitious and wealthy politicians
who seemed sympathetic to change.[23]

35

Proponents of reform worked energetically but made little headway during the 1850's. The populous up country obtained one additional state senator. However, the parish-controlled senate scuttled the attempt to distribute the school fund by white population. (This plan would have benefitted the western section.) Also defeated were efforts to allow popular choice of the governor and presidential electors. By the late 1850's, with national issues becoming more explosive, South Carolina put aside the reform question. Opponents of change argued successfully that tampering with the internal status quo might distract the state in the face of the external menace.[24]

Although opposed to reform, the ruling gentry often divided over South Carolina's position in the Union. The uncommitted oligarchs, affiliating with neither the National nor Southern Rights Democrats, occasionally supported Orr's faction on external matters. In 1858 the very wealthy Camden planter James Chesnut, Jr., was sent to the United States Senate. In the following year Orr commented, "I see that Col. Chesnut is soon to make known his position. I have great curiosity to know what it will be--I have never known his politics." Fear of disunion and reluctance to annoy other Southern states with "fire-eating" South Carolina radicalism--these factors contributed to the National Democrats' strength. This wing never dominated state politics, but it scored occasional victories.[25]

The aristocratic bias of the South Carolina College, located in Columbia, was an object of the reformers' scorn. The institution's emphasis upon classical studies had long been recognized as reinforcing the planter elite's social conservatism. In the legislature Perry tried futilely to diversify the curriculum in accord with different student needs. The critics obtained only limited changes. The South Carolina College made some concessions, while the first up country institutions of higher learning were established in the 1850's, in face of the College's opposition.[26]

Orr derided the curriculum which presumed that the interests and abilities of all students were identical. In his opinion, undue stress was given to ancient, classical, and mathematical subjects. He desired a wide range of elective courses useful to students, and he favored the university method of instruction, under which professors could specialize. Moreover, he wanted educational opportunities to become available to a wider portion of society. Commending the private denominational schools like Furman University, Wofford College, and Winthrop College, he urged them to request an annual legislative contribution. The state might provide funds on condition that a certain number of indigent young men receive free lodging and instruction. The recipients of these subsidies, he suggested, should agree to be teachers for a specified period.[27]

Proponents of economic diversification, many National Democrats supported a movement which had commanded much interest in the 1840's. During that decade, with an agricultural depression lingering, numerous public leaders and journalists had asked that industry and agriculture complement each other more efficiently. Factories were built, employing a small fraction of the state's manpower. The best known was William Gregg's textile mill at Graniteville. In the late 1840's the South Carolina Institute for the Promotion of Art, Mechanical Ingenuity, and Industry was organized. Orr was one of the original members.[28]

In an 1855 speech the Anderson Congressman criticized the planters' heavy concentration upon cotton production, which he blamed for an imbalance in the state's economy. "The market for agricultural labor stagnates under a superabundant supply, the market for agricultural capital is satiated." He pictured the planter who swelled his number of cotton bales, went to the provision market for his provisions, and turned to the livestock market for his animals. Little of his cotton money remained "when he has paid his merchant, his grocer, and his stock drover." The speaker maintained that South Carolina could achieve economic self-sufficiency, a goal which would require the planters to reduce their cotton acreage. The losses entailed in this shift would be absorbed by the gains, "the falling off of plantation expenses."[29]

Orr asked his listeners to estimate how much of the state's wealth, wrested from "the laborious tillage of cotton and rice in a soil once rich but now gradually impoverishing," was spent in other sections. Pointing out that much of South Carolina's soil was washed off or exhausted, he urged a more judicious use of the land. "When she has grown weary, enfeebled by long and faithful service, let her rest. She will soon acquire new strength and vigor, and bear

you on her generous bosom a teeming harvest." The
Congressman perceived that the state's prosperity was
decaying. Gullied fields and delapidated mansions
were evidence that "agriculture languished."[30]

At the same time, he observed, South Carolina's
physical geography was well suited for industry.
Columbia and the up country districts possessed ample
supplies of inexpensive water power; railroad access
was easy. Unlike the Northern states, South Carolina
did not endure harsh winters which would freeze the
streams and interrupt production. Currently South
Carolinians were denying themselves rich opportunities.
"Can a policy so obviously at war with every precept
of political economy, and so fatal to every principle
of social progress, be longer persisted in?"[31]

He noted the unwillingness of many planters and
farmers to risk capital outlays in anything new. As
investors, they demanded the certainty of a seven per
cent annual yield. Ironically, these people were
often extravagant in fulfilling their own wants and
those of friends; they were also harmfully timid.

> We transfer our surplus capital to distant
> States to grow more cotton and sugar, or, if
> it be retained here, it is represented by
> bonds and notes bearing seven per cent in-
> terest. This was the habit of our fathers,
> and any innovation upon long established
> usage or theory is resisted--hence reforms
> of old habits prove a great labor to the re-
> former.

In addition, manual labor was not sufficiently regarded,
and professional men enjoyed an unduly high esteem.
Sent into the professions by "ambitious fathers," too
many young men became unproductive. Those who in-
herited plantations were frequently ill-prepared for
their duties. Ignorant of the details of farming,
they "are deceived by their workers and duped by their
overseers. A few years reveal to them the prospect
of bankruptcy, and the overseer becomes the owner of
the estate which he lately supervised." The speaker
was censuring the planters' life style as well as
their economic priorities. Hoping that public attitudes
would change, he wanted South Carolina to attract the
skilled white mechanic.[32]

This plea for economic diversification emphasized white labor and an increased white immigration, yet it was not antislavery. Orr used the standard historical and racial arguments to justify slavery. The great empires, he observed, had systems of domestic servitude. In earlier times, when slaves had generally been vanquished enemies, no racial line had separated master and slave. In the Americas, in contrast, the slave's status was stamped by his color and an inferior intellect. Dull perceptions, indolent thought, sluggish movements, improvident habits, and feeble reasoning were, in the Congressman's words, the Negro's familiar traits. Such inferiority, "appreciated by himself, induces a prompt and cheerful submission to the authority of the master, with but little necessity to appeal to restraint or punishment."[33]

Believing that the slaves should remain in bondage, Orr did not want additional Negroes brought to America. He sharply denounced the campaign of the 1850's to re-open the foreign slave trade, illegal since 1808. A minority in South Carolina and elsewhere, the slave trade proponents were vocal and potentially disruptive. The movement's best known adherents in the state were Rhett, James H. Adams (governor from 1854 to 1856), Edward B. Bryan, Maxcy Gregg, Alexander Mazyck, John Middleton, and Leonidas W. Spratt. All of these men were known disunionists. However, many disunionists opposed the movement, fearing that it would divide the South. The National Democrats were solidly against the proposal, as were many members of the uncommitted group that stood between the National and Southern Rights wings of the Democratic party. Such politicians as James H. Hammond and James Chesnut, Jr., who were in this middle group, rejected the movement.[34]

The slave trade advocates, claiming that the South needed an abundance of cheap labor, charged that the Congressional ban unfairly restricted the supply of slaves. Consequently, they asserted, slave prices were very high, slave ownership was becoming concentrated among the more prosperous whites, and the growing number of white nonslaveholders endangered the institution of slavery. Unable to expand its population and labor supply, the slave section was falling behind the North and becoming "an even smaller and smaller minority in the Union each year." Increasingly outnumbered, the Southerners were more vulnerable to attack from their enemies in the free states. This was the basic position of the slave trade exponents.[35]

On the contrary, Orr denied that the South needed
more slaves. A new black influx, he declared in 1858,
would cause an oversupply of cotton and deflate world
prices. In addition to economic disaster, the Anderson politican forecast dire social reprecussions if
"fresh savages" from Africa were added to the presently
docile black population.

> Look to the effect it is to have on the slaves
> themselves. Will you not be placing the in-
> struments of insubordination and rebellion
> upon every plantation? Our present slave pop-
> ulation have been for several generations
> reaching that point of civilization and sub-
> ordination which they have attained; they have
> learned from their very infancy that the white
> man is their superior. . .All fears of in-
> surrection have vanished, and we sleep in the
> assurance of perfect security in the densest
> slave districts.

He offered other arguments. Raising the slave trade
question was providing the South's adversaries with
material to use in turning Northern opinion against
the slave section. The issue had already produced
discord in the South. Also, because Congress was
solidly opposed to lifting the prohibition, the slave
trade campaign had no practical chance of success.
"Is it not folly, then, to agitate the question, when
the only power than can open the trade expresses so
unanimous an opinion against it?" In 1856 Orr introduced a House resolution upholding the ban. The resolution was overwhelmingly adopted.[36]

***** ***** ***** ***** *****

When Franklin Pierce became President in 1853
the United States was growing, times were good, and
people had confidence in the future. It seemed unlikely that the sectional accord, worked out in 1850,
would be broken. Fate ruled otherwise. In the years
ahead the ugly question of slavery in the territories
was revived, pulling the country into a tragic whirl-
pool of events that led ultimately to war.

During Pierce's presidency the South enjoyed much
influence in Democratic party and administration
councils. In 1853 it appeared that Democratic control
in Washington would continue indefinitely. The Whig
party, which could not conciliate its Northern and

Southern wings, was falling apart. Externally more
united, the Democrats were also disturbed by internal
tensions. In the Northwest and Northeast Democrats
chafed under the party's Southern-oriented leadership.
Men like Illinois Senator Stephen A. Douglas searched
for policies that would please their constituents.[37]

In early 1854 Congress passed one of the most
disastrous pieces of legislation in the nation's history. The Kansas-Nebraska Bill, whose main sponsor
was Douglas, was designed to help the Northwest by
organizing two new territories. A Democratic party
measure accepted by Pierce, the bill gave the settlers
the option of permitting or banning slavery. (There
was an ambiguity in the bill. It was not clear
whether the option existed during the territorial stage
or when the settlers were applying for statehood.)
The party managers regarded the slavery provision as
innocuous; very few Congressmen expected that slavery
would take hold in Kansas or Nebraska. Virtually
nobody intended that the sectional peace should be
undone. Unwisely, politicians in Washington underestimated the free soil sentiment in the North. In
that section the response was politically thunderous.
Many Northern Congressmen who supported the measure,
mostly Democrats, were defeated in the 1854 fall
elections.

Southerners were generally passive about the Kansas-Nebraska Act or regarded it as a friendly gesture,
establishing the principle that the slave labor system
enjoyed an equal footing with free labor in the territories. Shortly after the bill's passage Orr remarked,
"Slavery, State Rights, & the rights of the South are
stronger today than they were at any preceding time."
At a Democratic gathering in Philadelphia four
months later he shared the rostrum with his "distinguished friend," Senator Douglas. The Carolinian
exclaimed that the principle of self-government, for
which the American Revolution had been fought, was now
conferred upon the people of Kansas and Nebraska.

> Is it right? Who will say it is wrong? Who
> knows best what are the wants of our fellow-
> citizens in the valley of Kansas or the Upper
> Missouri--the representatives they elect to
> their own territorial legislature or, the
> Congress of the United States, when not a
> single member, perhaps, has made a footprint
> in Kansas or Nebraska? and which would most
> likely legislate wisely for them--territorial

legislature or Congress? The statement
of the question carries the answer with
it. If a Pennsylvanian now has the
right to make his own laws here, what is
there in the atmosphere of Kansas when
he removes there rendering him less competent to do the same thing there? This
right, conferred by Congress on the Territories, is subject to but one limitation,
which all concede is just; and that is,
that their legislation shall not contra-
vene the constitution of the United States--
a limitation that exists as to the States
and should in the Territories.

In his home district he continued his defense of the
controversial law, declaring in Spartanburg that it
was all that the South wanted. He spoke of two
principles which, in his mind, the Kansas-Nebraska
Act sustained--the right of territorial settlers
to decide for or against slavery "on the formation
of States," and the premise that Congress possessed
"no right to legislate on slavery." This interpretation was widely accepted in the South.[38]

Not expecting that slavery would flourish in
Kansas or Nebraska, Southerners were stunned by the
vociferous Northern reaction. Both pro-slavery and
free-soil forces considered themselves under attack,
and a bitter contest ensued for control of Kansas.
Many Southerners, previously indifferent, resolved
that Kansas should become a slave state. Among them
was the Anderson Congressman, who declared in 1856 that
an energetic South could win Kansas for slavery. "We
are now sending aid and men to Kansas, and if we persevere, we can build up there a slave holding community." On Kansas and slavery in the territories, Orr's
position was South Carolina's position.[39]

In the wake of the Kansas-Nebraska Act the Whig
party was shattered, its Northern and Southern wings
no longer compatible. In the North free-soil fusion
movements, backed by discontented Whigs and Democrats,
provided the nucleus for the new Republican party.
In this time of party realignments, when old loyalties
were becoming unsettled, a large minority of former
Democrats and Whigs throughout the country drifted
into the nativist American party. In the South the
American party attracted many former Whigs who were
reluctant to enter the Democratic fold. The Know-
Nothings, as members of this new party were called,

42

were usually identified in the South with the old
unionist tradition of the Whigs. South Carolina did
not conform to this pattern. The small number of
Know-Nothings in the state were mainly secessionists
who sought to lure people from the Democratic party.
Best known among them was John Cunningham of the
Charleston Evening News. Many disunionist Democrats,
reasoning that competition between National Democrats
and the Americans might divide the state into two
national parties, moved against the nativist movement.
Rhett's Charleston Mercury urged all Democrats to
shun the Know-Nothings.[40]

In the three-year period from 1854 through 1856,
when the Know-Nothing movement reached its height
of influence, Orr's speeches contained numerous
attacks upon this organization. In Philadelphia
in July 1854 he pictured its secretiveness and
anti-Catholicism as menacing to the American commitment to freedom.

> I do not perceive any difference between
> Catholic Jesuitism and Protestant Jesuit-
> ism--both are intolerant. But in this
> country I protest in the name of our
> ancestors, who were all foreigners, in the
> name of the constitution, in the name of
> liberty itself, against a secret political
> organization which fears to avow its princi-
> ples, which shrinks from their discussion,
> and which makes its members, by secret
> pledge, spies in every household.

The Congressman, who took seriously his Jeffersonian
heritage, admired the late Virginian's religious toleration and friendliness to immigrants. In Anderson
and Spartanburg one year later he defended the
Catholic Church against imputations of disloyalty,
and he emphasized that the Northern Catholics were
not among the South's enemies. No Catholic priests,
he observed, joined the three thousand New England
clergymen who signed a protest against passage of the
Kansas-Nebraska Act. In the recent Boston riot caused
by the arrest of fugitive slave Anthony Burns, the
only Northerner who shed blood on behalf of Southern
rights was an Irishman. As in the past, the Representative wanted the Southerners to know who their
friends were. In the North, he claimed, the Know-
Nothings were generally of the Whig, free-soil, and
abolitionist persuasions, and none of the Northern

Know-Nothing Congressmen had voted for the Kansas-Nebraska Act. The American party was "no party for the South." In contrast, as Orr well knew, most Northern and Southern Catholics affiliated with the Democratic party.[41]

***** ***** ***** ***** *****

During the 1850's the mounting tension over slavery in the United States caused the subject of hemispheric annexation to acquire sectional overtones. Specifically, Cuba was the center of imperialist attention. In reaction to filibuster expeditions by private American citizens, Spain spoke of emancipating Cuba's slaves. Spanish officials intimated that they might free and arm Cuban slaves in order to prevent United States conquest of the island. The thought of "Africanization" in Cuba frightened Southerners, who failed to recognize Spain's threat as a weapon to discourage American filibustering. Believing that Spain was seriously planning to emancipate, they pondered the wisdom of a preventive invasion. The belief that Cuba could become "another Haiti" stirred apprehension in the North, but there the sense of alarm was not so great as in the slave states. (Negro rule had been established in Haiti in the early nineteenth century.) In addition, after the Kansas-Nebraska Act was passed in 1854, the possibility of slavery expansion into the western territories produced a Northern determination that the "slave power" should not add Cuba to its domain. Perturbed by Northern opinion, Southern imperialists became more intent upon taking the Caribbean island in order to check the antislavery forces.[42]

Orr shared the prevalent Southern desire for an aggressive Central American policy. In Spartanburg in 1854 he stated that "we must possess Cuba," and he predicted confidently that Pierce's administration would be "a Cuba-acquiring administration." In Craytonville four years later the Representative declared that the Democratic regime, at that time headed by James Buchanan, would obtain the coveted island at a "practicable" time. Hemispheric annexation was not an issue that he raised frequently. In South Carolina there was general indifference during the 1850's to questions of foreign expansion.[43]

***** ***** ***** ***** *****

Sympathetic towards the Indians, the Piedmont Congressman regularly called attention to the abuses of tribes by dishonest agents and callous government practices. "Almost everything we appropriate for them is filched by agents and attorneys," he stated in an 1852 debate. Early in the next year he criticized a plan to grant lands to white settlers before the Indian titles had been extinguished. "The Indians hold a better title than we do, for they have possession; and it would be, in my opinion, a species of land piracy to take it."[44]

Chairman of the House Committee on Indian Affairs during the Thirty-Third Congress (December 1853 through March 1855), Orr made known his belief that the country's Indian policy had been dishonorable. In the Far Western territories (Oregon, Washington, Utah, and New Mexico), he pointed out in March 1854, no treaty arrangements for the transfer of Indian lands had ever been made. In Oregon and Washington, where about sixty or seventy thousand whites were settled, Indians had been "driven back from valley to valley, and from plain to plain, until they are now, in many instances, compelled to take refuge and seek homes upon the mountain tops." In this region many tribes had given up their lands after being promised that the United States would compensate them fairly; the promises were never redeemed. In the future, the Carolinian prophesied, the United States would regret its record of mistreatment.[45]

It is vain and idle, Mr. Chairman, to hope that these people will always continue to submit patiently and quietly to the wrongs which we have been perpetrating upon them. They are feeble, it is true. We have it in our power, with all the men and money at our command, to destroy--to annihilate them. But, occupying the position towards them that we do, great as we are, wealthy as we are, powerful as we are, magnanimity and generosity requires that we should deal liberally towards these red men of the forest.

Orr's ideas formed the basis of a committee report of April 1854. He proposed, on an experimental basis, to domesticate the Indians in the projected Kansas and Nebraska territories and elsewhere in the Osage and Kansas tribes. Each Indian head of

45

family would receive a permanent homestead. If the
settler cultivated his land industriously for two
years, he would obtain "the high privileges of a
citizen of this great republic." Failure to meet
the specified conditions would carry a penalty.

> If he should, however, cling to
> his early habits, and refuse to obey the
> divine command to till the earth, and earn
> his bread by the sweat of his brow, per-
> sist in wandering over the land, and lead
> the life of a vagabond, the President is
> empowered to withhold his annuity arising
> from the sale of his land until he shall
> return to his home and resume the pursuits
> of industry.

Envisioned also was the permanent settlement, in the
midst of the Indians, of a virtuous pioneering white
population. Orr intended that the Indians should
abandon many of their customs and absorb the white
man's culture.

> The white man will erect school-houses and
> churches; and the Indian, when he learns
> the superiority of his white neighbor, in
> all the duties of life, from his superior
> intelligence and education, will become
> the patron of the school-house and the
> regular attendant of worship at the church.
> His traditions of the power and attributes
> of the Great Spirit will melt before the
> teachings of divine revelation; the Sabbath
> will be consecrated to the service of the
> Great Chief, and no more desecrated by the
> war whoop or the sharp crack of the hunter's
> rifle.

In the following months the Carolinian offered a bill
to domesticate the Chippewas and extinguish their
land titles in Minnesota and Wisconsin. This measure
incorporated the main features of the April report.
The bill became law, and the treaty between the
United States and the Chippewas conformed with its
terms.[46]

*****   *****   *****   *****   *****

Stalwart in his defense of slavery, Orr was also
a compassionate person who could view a black man
with kindness and pity. In 1851 Noah C. Hanson, a free
Negro, was convicted in a District of Columbia court
of harboring three fugitive slaves, the property of
South Carolina Representative William Colcock. He
was fined over one thousand dollars and ordered to
remain in jail until the fine was paid. Gerrit Smith,
the New York abolitionist, became interested in the
case and had interviews with all of the South Carolina
Congressmen. None of them, including Colcock, objected
to the New Yorker's effort to obtain Hanson's pardon.
Showing a special concern, Orr met with President
Franklin Pierce to plead for the prisoner's release.
In 1854 Hanson was freed.[47]

***** ***** ***** ***** *****

Rural isolation pervaded much of the Old South.
In this region the masses of white people enjoyed
long speeches and political rallies; they enthusiastically attended testimonial gatherings for their
spokesmen. Such an occasion was the dinner given for
Orr in Anderson on July 25, 1855. Hundreds of people
arrived by train for the festivities, which included
music from the local brass band. Guest speakers
were Congressman Preston S. Brooks of Edgefield
and the poet William Gilmore Simms.[48]

Orr spoke of the "repose" which the country was
experiencing under President Pierce, noting also that
the South's security as a slaveholding section was
"so far as statutory legislation was concerned, greater
than she had enjoyed since 1787." The Kansas-Nebraska
Act was good for the South, "so much so, that almost
every Representative from the North who supported it
has been laid upon the shelf, and an Abolitionist
returned in their stead." In this analysis there
were incongruities. What was good for the South, the
Kansas-Nebraska Act, was admittedly objectionable to
large numbers of Northerners. The Northern election
results contradicted the Congressman's remark that
the South's position was secure. The turmoil in
and over Kansas belied his statement about a repose
in the country.[49]

Wishing to avert dissolution, the guest of honor
stood by the Georgia Platform, which epitomized
Southern conditional unionism. In the 1850 manifesto
the neighboring state announced that it would resist

47

any anti-slavery restriction in the territories or
repeal of the fugitive slave laws. Resistance to
such measures would be carried, as a final resort, to
severing Georgia's ties with the Union. Orr wanted
the South to unite upon this platform and be prepared
to act upon it "when our Northern friends deserted
us or were hopelessly prostrated."[50]

The Charleston Mercury spotted the flaw in Orr's
commentary, questioning his assumption that the South
was secure. "If so, whence arises the fearful antici-
pation of coming trouble, that disturbs the patriotism,
and points the language, of every Southern statesman
who has spoken to the country?" The claim of security
in terms of statutory legislation came under fire.
The Fugitive Slave Act, the Mercury noted, had been
nullified by some states and disregarded everywhere.
This paper knew that the Kansas-Nebraska Act was a
curse which had destroyed its Northern supporters.
What security did the South derive from the ambiguous
sections of this "imbecile enactment?" Furthermore,
what price had the South been forced to pay for the
law's recapitulation of constitutional right?
"Constant agitation; bitter denunciation--wanton out-
rage--every difficulty, danger and humiliation this
side of civil war."[51]

In following weeks additional speeches reiterated
the chief points stressed in Anderson. These
addresses marked the opening of the Congressman's
drive for South Carolina's presence at the 1856
Democratic national convention in Cincinnati. With
Perry, Pickens, Brooks, and other associates, he
was asking the Palmetto state to depart from its custo-
mary noninvolvement in national politics. Since the
nullification crisis of the 1830's the state's posture
towards national parties had been one of studied
aloofness; no delegation had ever attended a national
nominating convention. Temporarily reconciled in
1855 by the Know-Nothing threat, the National and
Southern Rights Democrats disputed the question
of the national convention.[52]

Expecting the 1856 Presidential election to be
crucial for his section, Orr believed that only a
unified Democratic party could defeat the Republicans
and Know-Nothings. Therefore, he maintained, it was
imperative that the South stand with its friends
throughout the nation. Following their setback in
1854, the Northern Democrats had made striking gains
in some recent state elections. These results, the

48

Representative believed, showed that the anti-slavery hysteria was subsiding. On the contrary, should this assessment prove incorrect, he reasoned that concerted Southern action in Cincinnati might be excellent preparation for future cooperationist action. If the anti-slavery fanaticism should sweep the North, "then what initiative step towards a southern Union, for the last resort, can be more effective than to unite all the South on the Georgia platform and instructions."[53]

Orr had no doubts that Democratic party defeat would bring disunion, a possibility which he feared greatly.

> Are we prepared for it? And if yea, will we not be grossly derelict to humanity if we neglect to use all the effots in our power to avert the catastrophe, so long as we can preserve the Government consistently with our own safety and rights?

He forecast that disunion would bring bloodshed, anarchy, the unhinging of a seemingly stable society. Yet, unwittingly, he contributed to the coming of the Civil War. Every Southerner who continued to defend the Kansas-Nebraska Act was pushing the country down the road to war. While advising South Carolina to maintain the friendship of its "conservative friends" throughout the nation, Orr insisted not only that the South assert its rights in Kansas. He advocated an aggressive effort to make Kansas a slaveholding territory. Thereby, he and many other Southerners were placing their Northern friends in a politically awkward position.[54]

Assuming the inevitability of disunion, opponents of the convention movement argued that closer ties with the national party were pointless. According to Lawrence Keitt, who represented one of the state's eastern Congressional districts, the whole North was abolitionized, and the Northern Democrats were undependable allies. Largely because of an ingrained dread of dissolution, Keitt's argument did not prevail. Representation at Cincinnati won the backing of many people who normally did not affiliate with any party faction. Throughout late 1855 and early 1856 the convention campaign gathered momentum. Perry spearheaded the drive to organize local meetings which would elect delegates to the state Democratic convention, scheduled for May in Columbia. Perry's labors were fruitful; proponents of representation at the national conclave won control of the state body.[55]

***** ***** ***** ***** *****

When Congress met in December 1855, sectional tension was building up. For over a year Kansas had been a battleground between proslavery and anti-slavery forces. In Washington the reverberations were felt. The new House, elected in 1854, had no majority party or coalition. As Democratic, Republican, and Know-Nothing candidates vied for the speakership, attempts to organize the lower chamber were inconclusive for several weeks. In late January 1856 Orr was sub-stituted for William A. Richardson of Illinois as the Democratic nominee. He remained in the running for a short time and withdrew in favor of his fellow South Carolinian, William Aiken. The Democrats de-cided that if Orr proved unpalatable to the Know-Nothings who backed the Kansas-Nebraska Act, they would replace him with Aiken. On the 133rd ballot the contest was won by the Republican Nathaniel Banks of Massachusetts, after the House agreed that a plurality would decide the election.[56]

Before the deadlock was broken a statement about Orr in the Charleston Mercury was mentioned on the House floor. The object of the newspaper's derision replied that the attacks upon him were without just cause. "I care not for its assaults, as I do not read them. I would rather it should be against me than for me." Rhett's organ did not wish to see its adversary preside over an assembly that would presumably be abusive towards the South. In the speakership, this paper suggested, a Southerner would be perpetually compromising himself and his section. "These federal honors are snares, rather than rewards, to the public men of the South." While the Mercury displayed its irritation, the Andersonian accepted invitations to speak in the North.[57]

He was one of the leading Southern Democrats in Congress, with a reputation for forceful and articu-late oratory. He was also recognized as a steadfast administration man, one that Pierce could turn to for help. In February 1856 he joined Mississippi's Representative John Quitman before a New York City gathering. "I come to speak to you of democracy and of democratic principles, and to see if the democracy of New York stands on the same platform as the Demo-crats of South Carolina." He scathingly attacked the

Know-Nothings. When he mentioned the "Black Republicans," someone in the crowd yelled "the nigger worshippers." Hisses followed. An address in Concord, New Hampshire, followed in the same month. Asking for equal rights for all sections, the Carolinian described the North as the main beneficiary of federal bounties. In contrast, the South received a small share of Congressional appropriations. "Ours is an agricultural people. We till the soil, and have but little commerce, and but few manufacturers. Our importunity is to be let alone." As on previous occasions he lambasted the Know-Nothings and pointed out the danger of injecting religion into politics. The New Hampshire speech was made at the request of Pierce, who also prevailed upon Georgia's Howell Cobb to speak there. With a state election approaching, the President badly needed help to insure Democratic victories in his home state. The effort failed.[58]

In early May Orr was at the South Carolina Democratic convention in Columbia. With John Farrow, he was named one of the two delegates from his Congressional district to the Cincinnati convention. Among the four delegates-at-large sent to the national meeting were Pickens and former Governor John L. Manning. The convention upheld the "principles" of the Kansas-Nebraska Act and endorsed Pierce for renomination.[59]

Orr spoke in defense of the state's presence at the national convention. Observing that a two-thirds majority was required to pick the Presidential nominee, he noted that sixteen votes would be needed to "neutralize" South Carolina's eight. "Ought not this power to be exercised? We are certain to vote for the nominee of the Cincinnati convention, and why should we not be there to take part in his selection?" Believing that South Carolina had a duty to sustain Pierce, he spoke amicably of Senator Douglas and James Buchanan, the other main aspirants.[60]

The Northern Democrats drew his praise for accepting the doctrine of Congressional non-intervention in the territories. "But for the Northern Democracy, Kansas would this day be closed against the South." He was pleased to observe that the Northern Democrats were recovering ground that they had lost in the previous two years. The Congressman turned to the Kansas-Nebraska Act, which enabled the territorial legislatures to enact laws "of local necessity consistent with the Constitution." In his words, the legislature could

51

not ban slavery, because Congress, lacking such
authority, could not delegate it to a territorial
government. The question "must be left until the
people come together to form a State Constituion."
In addition, he called for a spirited Southern push
to win Kansas for slavery. "We are now sending aid
and men to Kansas, and if we persevere, we can
build up there a slave holding community."[61]

In Cincinnati the Palmetto state delegation voted
for Pierce, then for Douglas, and finally joined
the whole convention in nominating Buchanan. They
acquiesced in the platform upholding the Kansas-
Nebraska Act and non-interference with slavery in the
territories. (This national platform was ambiguous
about popular sovereignty in the territories.)[62]

A sudden attack of neuralgia in early June prevented Orr's attendance at the Cincinnati convention.
Convalescing in Washington, where the attack occurred,
he endorsed Buchanan in a public letter. Equating
continued Democratic control of the Presidency with
continued union, he wrote that the country could not
survive if the Republican party, the party of "wild
fanaticism," gained power. This opinion reflected
the general consensus in South Carolina that the slave
states could not tolerate Republican rule.[63]

On May 22, an event occurred in Washington which
greatly exacerbated the sectional tension. South
Carolina's Representative Preston Brooks entered the
Senate chamber and severely caned Charles Sumner,
Republican of Massachusetts. Two days earlier Sumner
had used offensive language against South Carolina and
its absent senior senator, Andrew P. Butler. The
assault brought much condemnation of "Bully" Brooks
in the North and congratulations in the South. His
home state stood solidly behind him. After resigning
from Congress he was overwhelmingly re-elected.[64]

In the capital Brooks stood trial and was fined
three hundred dollars; Orr was one of his attorneys.
In the House on July 9, the Andersonian stated that
Sumner's venomous language had provoked the assault;
the senator was beaten because he insulted South
Carolina and defamed Butler. Because no Congressional
rules protected men from "the foul-mouthed slanderer,"
the recipient of invective had to seek his own retri-
bution. He charged that the uproar about the caning
was politically inspired, that the Republicans were
exploiting the incident to inflame public sentiment.
As he spoke passions were rising in the country.

Violence continued in Kansas, and the 1856 presidential campaign was in progress, the first in which the new Republican party competed.[65]

After Congress adjourned in late August the campaign moved into full swing. In early September Orr was present at a mammoth Buchanan rally on the Tippecanoe battlefield near Lafayette, Indiana. Among the party dignitaries in attendance were Douglas, Senator Jesse Bright of Indiana, and Vice-Presidential nominee John C. Breckinridge of Kentucky. Returning to his home state, the Anderson representative looked somberly to the approaching election. In Union in early October he cited recent Republican gains in the Maine, Vermont, and Iowa state elections, omens of possible success for that party nationally. Should his worst fears be realized, he expected dissolution to occur between the November balloting and the transfer of power in March 1857. He still anticipated an uncertain future if Buchanan won, although there would be peace for another four years. The speech in Union closed on a militant note. "The people of the South are more united than ever; and if the contest must come, we will be prepared to meet the enemy, undivided."[66]

By a narrow electoral vote majority and a popular plurality, Buchanan defeated his Republican and Know-Nothing competitors, John C. Fremont and Millard Fillmore respectively. Working in Buchanan's favor were the general fear that Republican victory would mean disunion, the belief that the Democratic nominee was a competent man who would deal fairly with territorial matters, the superior Democratic organization, and a momentary receding of violence in Kansas. In South Carolina the results were unsettling. Fremont's impressive showing in the free states disheartened the moderates, while many Southern Rights men claimed that the Republicans could not be denied the presidency indefinitely. However, in December 1856 the legislature declined drastic action. The National Democrats resisted radical demands that the state push for the creation of a Southern confederacy.[67]

***** ***** ***** ***** *****

Orr returned to Washington in late 1856 with hopes that South Carolina would be represented in the new President's cabinet, and he asked Buchanan to offer Pickens an appointment. What better token of the

53

National Democrats' success in bringing the Palmetto state into the stream of national politics? Finding the President elect noncommittal, he sensed that South Carolina's influence with the incoming administration would be slight, and he confided to Pickens that the cabinet might be "not entirely acceptable to us." The Congressman was also uneasy about Buchanan. "I fear that 'Buck' is too unprincipled, and many of those having his ear are, I know, unprincipled and unworthy." Later in 1857 Pickens became minister to Russia.[68]

As the upcountry legislator returned to the capital, he also found a scandal brewing, and he was named, with three others, to a select committee which probed charges of corruption. At issue were reports of unethical ties between several Congressmen and a Minnesota land company. Maryland's Henry Winter Davis and Orr were the panel's most active members. The investigation resulted in formal accusations against four representatives, three of whom resigned.[69]

After the Thirty-Fourth Congress adjourned in March 1857 Orr returned to South Carolina to work on his law practice. In late April or early May he embarked on a Western journey that included Tennessee, Missouri, Kansas, and Minnesota on the itinerary. In Memphis he spoke at a railroad jubilee, praising an Arkansas citizen, R. W. Johnson, for his work in promoting federal aid to Southwestern railroads. The lure of investments took him on this trip, the main fruits of which were real estate purchases in Minnesota and Missouri. At the same time the Congressman's presence in the West led to insinuations that the travel was, in part at least, politically motivated.[70]

By the summer of 1857 Kansas had become, once again, the scene of strife between proslavery and antislavery forces. Robert J. Walker, newly appointed territorial governor, sent by Buchanan and initially regarded as pro-Southern, assumed his duties in May. Walker perceived that while the territory could become a Democratic state, the great majority of inhabitants did not want slavery. In vain he urged the free-soil settlers to choose delegates to a constitutional convention which would prepare for statehood. Viewing as fraudulent the Lecompton-based government, which Walker headed, most free-soilers boycotted the June election. Proslavery men controlled the convention which was slated to meet in September. The governor's plea for the free-soilers' participation

in the balloting angered the South, as did his statement that if the new Kansas constitution were not submitted for popular approval, Congress should reject
it. (The proslavery group planned to present their
constitution directly to Congress without seeking
popular ratification.) By July Walker was under
attack in many South Carolina newspapers, one of
which bewailed his "treachery to the South." Unless
Buchanan disavowed the governor's policy, the Charleston Daily Courier pronounced, "he, too, will stand
chargeable with infidelity to the South." However,
until the late fall the President gave the impression
that he backed Walker.[71]

Orr's appearance in Kansas during the summer gave
rise to suspicions that he was helping Walker to
make Kansas a free state and, thereby, courting
Buchanan's favor. His critics could not indicate with
certainty his attitude towards the territorial
governor. The Newberry Mirror stated that it did not
know, but if the Anderson politician did not support
Walker "how can he call himself a National Democrat?"[72]

The Anderson Gazette and Advocate stated "by
authority" that Orr did not see or communicate with
Walker. This statement was probably correct. He
was ambitious to become speaker of the House when
Congress convened in December, and unnecessary in-
volvement in the Kansas mess would have hurt his
candidacy. Privately he told Howell Cobb, a Buchanan
cabinet member, that Walker "has made no public
opinion in Kansas but only conformed to what was
public opinion among our friends when he got there."
Regarded by Washington politicians as friendly to
Buchanan, the Carolinian was considered the administration candidate for the speakership in the next Congress.[73]

In October the Kansas convention, controlled by
proslavery men, decided not to submit its constitution
for popular approval. Instead, it allowed a choice
between the Lecompton constitution with slavery and
the Lecompton constitution without slavery. Even
if the latter option were taken, slave ownership
would continue until 1864. In December Buchanan
endorsed this procedure and urged the Kansans to participate in the scheduled referendum. The President's
decision precipitated a terrible split in his party.
Many Northern Democrats joined Douglas in opposing
the action of the proslavery convention.

*****   *****   *****   *****   *****

Shaken in 1854 by the Northern reaction against
the Kansas-Nebraska Act, the Democrats made solid
gains in the 1856 Congressional elections and seemed
likely to control both chambers. When the Thirty-
Fifth Congress assembled in December 1857, Orr was
the leading candidate for the speakership. Months
before the new Congress convened members from several
states pledged him their votes. He worked to line up
commitments in the doubtful state delegations. In
August he asked John C. Breckinridge for help in
securing Kentucky, advising the Vice-President to
move quietly "so as not to arouse hostility from
other aspirants."[74]

In addition to a host of friends and acquaintances,
his reputation for moderation and competence was a
great asset. William F. Russell of New York, not
personally acquainted, commended the Carolinian's
"pacific Union sentiments" and offered his vote.
Orr wrote privately that he would not be "the candidate of the administration or any clique. I shall
look only to the support of the party--& my personal
friends." Buchanan favored him, and the Douglas
followers were friendly. There were murmurs of
Southern protest against his rumored backing of Walker
in Kansas, but these reflected a feeble minority.
A bargain with the Douglas men, whereby James C. Allen
of Illinois was slated for clerk, assured victory.
Buchanan lieutenant Jehu Glancy Jones of Pennsylvania
nominated Orr. The balloting followed party lines,
as 128 Democrats faced 92 Republicans and 14 Know-
Nothings.[75]

Presiding officer of the House, the Andersonian
was at the height of his antebellum prestige. Two
worthwhile benefits came from the election--a higher
salary and the companionship of his family in Washington. Prior to becoming speaker, he resided at Brown's
Hotel, a leading establishment which catered to
Southern politicians. With his family the new speaker
moved into the Stockton Mansion, an imposing three-
story white brick house on Lafayette Square. His
wife, active in the capital's social life, was pictured by a friend as "tall and lithe in figure, of
a Spanish type of face." The couple entertained
guests frequently and attended important social
functions.[76]

56

In late 1857 the Kansas controversy reached its boiling point. In October a proslavery convention met at Lecompton and prepared to seek statehood under a proslavery constitution. When this charter was submitted to the voters, the antislavery settlers boycotted the referendum. This boycott, plus many irregularities, insured proslavery victory. In December Buchanan asked Congress to accept Kansas' statehood application under the Lecompton constitution. This endorsement triggered a deep rupture in his party. Northwesterners like Douglas knew that pro-Lecompton voting would bring political suicide in their home constituencies. Douglas himself worked against the President's recommendation.

In January 1858 Orr wrote privately, "The Kansas matter I fear will give us trouble though I hope the state will be admitted under the Lecompton Consti-tution. Douglas' defection imperils the measure very much, though I can hardly believe that he intends to join the Republicans." Knowing that the Kansas question was fraught with danger, the Carolinian stood by his section. He was willing to gamble on the attempt to make Kansas a slave state.[77]

The House was closely divided when it took up Buchanan's message in February. Georgia's Alexander Stephens, an administration man, headed the Committee on Territories, which normally dealt with statehood petitions. Knowing that a motion to refer Buchanan's recommendation to Stephens' committee would meet stiff objections, the pro-Lecomptonites proposed the creation of a special committee which the speaker would appoint. The committee was authorized, but with the power to investigate, a feature not desired by the administra-tion camp. Orr stacked the panel with pro-Lecompton members, and the committee waited for the Senate to act.[78]

The House rejected Senate moves to admit Kansas and Minnesota together, and to hold a new plebiscite in Kansas on the Lecompton constitution. In May, finally, the chamber agreed to submit the Kansas issue to a Senate-House conference committee. The vote on setting up this committee was tied, 108 to 108; Speaker Orr broke the deadlock. The fruit of the conference committee's labors was the English Bill, which provided for a referendum. The Kansans would decide upon immediate statehood under the Le-compton charter or continued territorial status. Congress approved the bill, and in August the

settlers voted overwhelmingly against statehood with
slavery. Kansas dealt the proslavery forces a sting-
ing defeat.[79]

***** ***** ***** ***** *****

When the South Carolina legislature filled two
United States Senate seats in 1857 and 1858, neither
the National nor Southern Rights Democrats triumphed.
James H. Hammond and James Chesnut, Jr., winners of
these elections, were not identified with either wing;
their views on parties and South Carolina's future
in the Union were not publicly known. Sending these
men to the Senate, and holding the balance between
the two main factions, were many uncommitted Democrats.[80]

The Palmetto state's temper during these years
was calm, but the Buchanan-Douglas rift over Kansas
hurt the Democratic party and left a residue of bitterness. In its aftermath Southerners became more uncertain about the trustworthiness of the Northern
Democrats. Consequently, even though South Carolina's
spirit was mild, the Southern Rights faction gained
momentum. If the present climate of opinion seemed
inauspicious for extremism, coming evenings would
give plausibility to Rhett's contention that disunion was inevitable.[81]

After Buchanan sanctioned the Lecompton constitution, there was little division in South Carolina
over Kansas. Moderates generally did not associate
with Douglas, who was now widely viewed as a renegade.
While moderates and radicals found themselves in
agreement over Kansas, a small minority of the latter
agitated the slave trade question. Most Southern
Rights Democrats were opposed, apprehensive that the
issue would divide the slave states. Because the
demand for legalization had attracted little interest in recent years, some editors abandoned their
earlier support. Nonetheless, the issue was prickly,
capable of exciting intense feelings. Former
Governor James H. Adams, leader of the so-called "Con-
go party," bitterly detested Orr for opposing the movement.[82]

In July 1858 Hammond made a speech at Beech
Island that perturbed the Southern Rights men while
it gratified the National Democrats. Contending that
the South could successfully fight its battles in the
Union, he urged the section to affiliate cordially
with its Northern friends. In his words, disunion
per se was not desirable. Orr was delighted and
told the senator, "I am glad you made a 'conservative
speech.'"[83]

On August 5, soon after Hammond's Beech Island
address, the Andersonian spoke in Williamston. Citing
the Kansas-Nebraska Act and the Democratic party's
adherence to states' rights principles, he claimed
that slavery was better protected than ever before
during the past thirty years. Should the Democratic
party go down, the slave states would have to accept
Republican rule or "dissolve the Union in blood."
Looking to 1860, the Congressman predicted an easy
Democratic victory in a three-party contest against
Republican and Know-Nothing opponents; otherwise the
election might go into the House of Representatives.
This statement implied outright pessimism regarding
Democratic prospects in a two-party competition against
the Republicans. There was an incongruity in the
speaker's analysis. Slavery was presently more secure
than ever before, yet in 1860 the Democrats would
probably encounter formidable opposition from the
Republicans.[84]

In Craytonville one week later he further expounded
his views. The Kansas referendum, mandated by the
English Bill, had recently been held, and Orr noted
that scattered returns indicated a substantial defeat
for the proslavery forces. In 1854, he recalled,
very few Southerners had expected slavery to take
hold in Kansas. The "impertinent interference" of
the antislavery Emigrant Aid Societies had changed
Southern opinion, by promoting free-soil settlement
and thereby challenging the South to respond. Nonetheless, he dismissed Hammond's appraisal of the Kansas-
Nebraska Act as "a cheat and a humbug." Admitting
that the law brought no concrete gains, he insisted
that a valuable principle was established for the
South. Here was the blind spot in the Congressman's
thinking. He defended a law which fueled the flames
of distrust between sections, in order to uphold a
principle that admittedly secured no benefits.[85]

The speaker asked his listeners to spurn the slave trade cause, which he deemed divisive and hopeless, and ponder the advantages of remaining in a Democratic-controlled Union. The Democrats had passed the Fugitive Slave Act; they would, he was confident, acquire Cuba in the near future. Although many Democrats in the country opposed slavery "in the abstract," they respected the South's constitutional rights. Orr earnestly hoped that his party would remain dominant and that disunion would never occur.[86]

> When this Government is destroyed, neither your nor me, your children, or my children, will ever live to see so good a government re-constructed. A government that gives such ample protection to all the rights of a person and property at home and abroad, and requires so little from its citizens in return.

Because Douglas had lately been combatting the Republican doctrines, he offered forgiveness. He wished the Illinois senator success in his campaign against Abraham Lincoln, "who proclaims the equality of the negro with the white man, and who avows his purpose to overthrow the Supreme Court of the United States, because the Dred Scott decision is distasteful to him." The speaker saw the Democratic party, even with Douglas as its head, as the only shield against dissolution. He predicted that South Carolina would vote for that party's presidential nominee in 1860, "however objectionable he may be," because he would be "safer" than a Republican or Know-Nothing.[87]

***** ***** ***** ***** *****

Expressing the need for "rest and recreation," Orr announced his decision not to seek another Congressional term in the 1858 election. "The long neglect of my private affairs imperiously demands my presence at home." Evidence that the legislator did not enjoy good health may explain, at least partially, his retirement from public office. Returning to private life in 1859, he engaged busily in law practice. His successor was John Ashmore of Anderson, whose political outlook was very similar.[88]

On a November evening in 1858 some friends entertained Orr at Brown's Hotel in Washington. Jovial and
expansive, he uttered this sentiment:

> I hope there will always be found conser-
> vatism and patriotism enough to put out the
> fires of sectional strife, and that con-
> cord and harmony will again be restored
> to the country. We ought to be one people;
> we were incorporated into an independent
> government under the auspices of as pure
> and patriotic men as ever lived . . .
> permit me, in addressing you perhaps for
> the last time, to conclude with a quota-
> tion from the great Webster: 'Liberty and
> Union, now and forever, one and inseparable.'

These remarks caused misunderstanding in his home
state, inducing him to declare that "with the Constitution maintained, and administered upon its true
principles," Webster's words should not offend South
Carolinians. By quoting Webster, the Piedmont
representative revealed the depth of his affection
for the Union. In the following April he told a
gathering in Laurens that the United States government
was "the best under the sun." Unhappily, he added,
the sectional quarrel was making him less hopeful
of the future than previously.[89]

***** ***** ***** ***** *****

Although Kansas receded as an issue after the
August 1858 referendum, the subject of slavery in
the territories continued to stir heated discussion
throughout the country. Especially disputed was
the idea of popular sovereignty, embraced in the
Kansas-Nebraska Act. The 1854 law did not specify
whether the settlers decided the slavery question
during the territorial stage or when they applied
for statehood. Orr argued the Southern position that
the option was available only when settlers obtained
statehood. In Congress in December 1856 he scorned
the doctrine, entertained by some Northern Democrats,
that territorial legislatures could legally introduce
or ban slavery.

I see no authority in the Constitution of
the United States which authorizes Congress to pass the Wilmot Proviso or any
anti-slavery restrictions in the Territories;
and I do not apprehend how Congress, not
having the power itself, can create an
authority and invest a·creature with greater
power and authority than it possesses itself.

He belittled as inconsequential the question of
whether "squatter sovereignty" existed. In every
slaveholding community slavery would be valueless without the safeguards of local legislation and police.
The discretion to provide such safeguards belonged
to the territorial legislature. If the legislature
declined to provide the protection, its failure to
act would be decisive.[90]

We think they ought to pass laws in every
Territory, when the Territory is open to
settlement, and slaveholders go there, to
protect slave property. But if they de-
cline to pass such laws, what is the remedy?
None, sir. If the majority of the people
are opposed to the institution, and if they
do not desire it ingrafted upon their Territory, all they have to do is simply to de-
cline to pass laws in the Territorial legislature for its protection, and then it is
as well excluded as if the power were invested
in the Territorial legislature, and exercised by them, to prohibit it. Now . . .
what is the practical importance to result
from the agitation and discussion of this
question as to whether squatter sovereignty
does not, exist? Practically, it is a matter
of little moment.

During the 1858 Illinois campaign Douglas asserted
that a territorial legislature could effectively prohibit slavery by unfriendly legislation. One year
later, in a widely publicized magazine article, the
senator justified territorial authority. By creating
territorial governments with executive and judicial,
as well as legislative branches, Congress conferred
power which it did not itself possess. Such power,
Douglas stressed, related to domestic affairs only;
national policy was not involved. This was the true
"dividing line" between federal and local authority.

62

Orr rejected Douglas' position, observing that recently uncovered material refuted all claims for territorial supremacy in local affairs. "Poor old St. Clair was removed by Jefferson from his gubernatorial office in the Northwest for holding the doctrine."[91]

Early in 1859 Senator Albert Gallatin Brown of Mississippi called for a federal slave code for the territories; Southern radicals embraced this demand. South Carolina moderates regarded the proposal as unnecessary and divisive. Orr reasoned that such legislation would violate Calhoun's non-intervention doctrine and place the South on the ground "occupied in 1847 by the abolitionists and free soilers and from which they have been driven." In practice the code would be useless. He asked if the measure would be "worth a pinch of snuff when that code had to be executed by the courts and juries of a territory whose refusal to pass a code had rendered such a code necessary by Congressional enactment."[92]

The upcountry politician sensed that the entire debate over the territories was detached from reality. He asked Hammond, "Has it occurred to you that the legislation and policy of this country must be about completed when our people all over the union become excited in discussing as naked an abstraction as the territorial question now is?" Earnestly hoping that no crisis would provoke dissolution, he was troubled and uncertain. In Pickens in April 1859 he spoke of the Northern party which, "we fear, would triumph in the Presidential election of 1860." In September he wrote privately, "We can beat Seward and no one else." (William H. Seward, controversial New York senator, was widely regarded as the leading Republican spokesman.) Orr worried that the Republicans could not be kept out of power indefinitely, but he clung to his hope that somehow the Democratic party would remain predominant, that the Union which he loved would not fall apart.[93]

Conditional unionism was an important force in South Carolina during the 1850's. This unionism rested upon the assumption that most Northerners were fundamentally conservative. Any sign that Northern conservatism was eroding could throw the assumption into doubt. Most South Carolinians were willing to preserve the status quo under Democratic party rule. For this reason conditional unionism was appealing, albeit vulnerable to the shock of unfavorable developments. Hammond caught the general mood when he observed in

1858 that the vast majority "goes with the Union until it pinches them & then for dissolving it."[94]

In October 1859 an event occurred which shook the already fragile confidence which South Carolinians placed in the good will of the North. John Brown's raid on Harper's Ferry in Virginia, aimed at inciting slave insurrection, had an explosive effect upon the Palmetto state. Many people became skeptical that the North could withstand the abolitionist surge. Moderates were distressed, while disunionists became bolder in advocating extreme action. However, the hope that Southern rights could remain secure in the Union did not collapse. Public apathy and an awesome dread of revolution still militated against precipitate measures.[95]

Meeting in December, the legislature hesitated to take drastic steps towards getting secession underway. The members were angered by signs of Northern approval of Brown, yet they were reluctant to act independently of other slave states. The legislature refused to disallow the state's presence at the 1860 Democratic national convention, and it declined to make provisions for calling itself into special session in the event of Republican victory. The lawmakers approved a resolution which invited a meeting of slave states to discuss united action. To implement this resolution Governor William H. Gist dispatched its chief sponsor, Christopher G. Memminger, to Virginia.[96]

Memminger's mission, undertaken in January 1860, bore no fruits, and its failure demoralized many South Carolinians who had placed their trust in cooperationism. Disunionists became more sternly convinced that secession must ultimately depend upon the initiative of a few states. Moderates clung desperately to their hope that the Democratic party would win another Presidential election.[97]

Uncertainty characterized South Carolina politicians in the early months of 1860. Radical leaders generally settled upon a posture of watchful waiting. Their passiveness enabled the moderates to control the state Democratic convention which would meet in April. Unlike many extremists, Rhett foresaw the possibility of disruption at the Democratic national convention, and he reckoned that South Carolina's presence might inadvertently aid the disunionist

64

cause. Anticipating the withdrawal of Alabama and
Mississippi over the slavery plank, the old firebrand
calculated that their departure might galvanize other
states, including his own, into a spontaneous show of
support.[98]

Since John Brown's raid the "Convention party" had
grown in numbers, attracting many new followers who
sensed that 1860 would be an unusually critical year.
There were National Democrats, conditional unionists
who had never regularly aligned themselves with any
party faction, unionists who had seldom been active
politically, and a small number of radicals who expected that the Republicans would capture the Presidency. Still, these radicals wanted the Democratic
party to nominate the best available candidate, one
who would offer the country a clear choice between conservatism and "Black Republicanism."[99]

Talk of a Southern Presidential candidate became
common among slave state politicians. Virginia's
Robert M. T. Hunter was highly esteemed and frequently
mentioned. In South Carolina Orr was put forward by
his friends. He made no moves on his own behalf,
believing that an active campaign would be self-defeating. The former Congressman did not want his state
to vote for him on the early ballots at the national
convention. If Douglas should lose, he reasoned, the
man supported by South Carolina might be regarded as
anti-Douglas. He told Perry,

> He will have power to defeat any man he
> chooses and though our delegation may vote
> against him and for some Southern man other
> than myself it would be no reason why his
> friends should assume an attitude of hos-
> tility to me. They would have the same
> reason of complaint against every other
> delegation in the South and if so for whom
> could they vote in the South . . . If the
> convention would with tolerable unanimity
> express a preference for me coupled with a
> declaration that the delegates should go to
> Charleston free to cast their votes without
> instructions I think it would have a good
> effect.

On the whole South Carolina opinion was unfriendly to
Douglas, the leading Northern contender for the nomination. While Orr did not associate himself with the

Douglas candidacy, he wanted his state to avoid any
gesture which might antagonize the Douglas followers.[100]

The Anderson lawyer presided over and addressed
the state party convention in Columbia in April. Can-
didly declaring that the Republican party was gaining
strength, he warned that its triumph would compel South
Carolina to "strike a blow." To avoid such an occasion,
the speaker favored moderation and prudence, because the
issue of resistance could not be met by South Carolina
alone. Rather, "thirteen or fourteen other sovereignties"
would have to join the state in combatting Republican
supremacy. For this reason South Carolina's policy would
have to promote Southern unity.[101]

In view of the Republican threat Orr advocated
reconciliation with those Northern Democrats who upheld "squatter sovereignty." He noted that many of
them had gallantly opposed the Wilmot Proviso and the
doctrine of Congressional intervention. Moreover, the
1856 Cincinnati platform and the Dred Scott decision
sustained the Southern position.

> The Supreme Court has pronounced in our favor,
> and I cannot, therefore, perceive why it is
> that there has been so much alarm manifested
> in certain quarters, or why it is that we
> have been so frequently cautioned by our
> opponents within the last few weeks as to
> the threat of our falling into the heresy
> of Squatter Sovereignty.

Regarding the Douglas Democrats' attachment to "squatter
sovereignty" as harmless, he wanted to keep the door
open for harmony between Southerners and pro-Douglas
Northerners.[102]

The body endorsed Orr for the Presidency, reaffirmed the 1856 Cincinnati platform, and rejected
Alabama's demand for federal protection of slavery in
the territories. Delegates to the national convention
were named. One of them, J. P. Reed of Anderson,
denied the allegation that many people present were
Douglas supporters. He added,

> I do speak for Col. Orr, knowing him as well
> as I know myself, and I say that, in politi-
> cal sentiment, so far as the great question
> of the day is concerned, he does not concur
> with Judge Douglas in his territorial views

in any particular. He is, however, or has
been, a warm personal friend of Douglas, and
many of Douglas' friends are his friends, not
on account of any political affinities, but
on account of the character which he possesses,
and which will draw all men to him who know
him as well as I know him.

After the main business was completed Orr spoke again,
prayerful that the free section would restrain the
hands of fanaticism. Saddened by the peril of dissolution, he cited examples of past confederacies that
had disbanded. The historical record showed "a series
of petty tyrants, springing up" whenever disunion
occurred. The results were the destruction of civil
liberty and "the wiping out of every vestige of civili-
zation." In closing, he asserted that the Southern
people would resist any invasion of their rights. In
defense of its liberty, his section would "strike with
all its might."[103]

As he presided over the state party convention, Orr
was the acknowledged leader of the National Democrats
and of the "Convention party." Among disunionists
there was respect for his influence, mixed with fear
and suspicion. The Andersonian was pictured as the
compromising politician, the "trimmer" who would bargain
away the state's interests, the seeker of federal honors,
the agent of the "spoils party." Besides, he was perceived as a threat to the patrician values of South
Carolina's ruling gentry. In 1858 Maxcy Gregg wrote,
"Mr. Orr is the leader of the National Democratic
Party in South Carolina, and I look upon him as the
most pernicious of the enemies of our old States Rights
Faith, and of our State Constitution." In 1860 an
intimate of Governor William H. Gist spoke of his
animosity towards Douglas. "Orr only has more of his
hatred." Hammond's appraisal of the Piedmont leader,
also uttered in 1860, was more revealing of state
opinion than the sentiments of Gregg and Gist. The
senator told Charleston's disunionist Congressman
William Porcher Miles, "I think there is a vast deal
in him that the state should cherish. I think him an
able, brave, & true man. I would not taunt him into
doing wrong. Let 'Orrism' & all that be dropped &
meet him when he brings forward an unsound measure with
reason & firmness."[104]

67

Harper's Weekly, Feb. 27, 1858

IV. SECESSION AND THE COMING OF WAR

The Democratic national convention met in Charleston in late April 1860. Orr, not a delegate, was present in the city. His personal features caught one reporter's attention. "Passing along, we find a tall portly man in glossy black, with a bad stoop in the shoulders, a new stove-pipe hat retaining in places the original shrine, a bright red face out of which look brilliant eyes, carrying in his right hand, as if it were a mace, a huge gold-headed cane."[1]

The convention broke up before a nominee could be chosen. After the body rejected the Southern position on slavery in the territories, thirteen of South Carolina's sixteen members joined Alabama, Mississippi, and Louisiana in withdrawing. These departing South Carolinians declared that the party had negated the principles of their state convention. This assertion was inaccurate; the state convention had repudiated the Alabama Platform. Two factors explain their withdrawal. By leaving, the Carolinians joined other states in cooperative action; the appeal of Southern unity was great. The state's delegates were also swayed by the passions of the hour. People who had previously been passive were swept away by the emotional tide.[2]

The Southern bolters agreed to meet in Richmond in June. South Carolinians generally favored the state's presence at this forthcoming conclave, but disagreement arose over the selection of delegates. The radicals insisted upon a new slate to replace the moderates who had attended the Charleston convention. An openly disunionist delegation, led by Rhett, was sent to Richmond. There South Carolina was the lone dissenter when the decision was made to seek admission to the national convention, scheduled to reconvene in Baltimore. After the national body denied the request, another Southern Democratic meeting was held in Richmond in late June. This second Richmond gathering nominated John C. Breckinridge for the presidency; the Baltimore convention chose Douglas.[3]

Not active in the post-Charleston maneuverings, Orr did not attend the second state convention which met in May. He was told, "Your friends complain that you have not taken position and used your talents and influence far enough in the party." Saddened by

69

the drift of events, the former Congressman criticized
the Palmetto state's withdrawal in Charleston as "unwise and impolitic." In his view, Douglas, "who was
so justly obnoxious to the South," could never have
been nominated by a full convention. On the contrary,
he believed that Breckinridge would have won at
Charleston had the Southerners remained. The election
of Breckinridge, as the candidate of a united party,
"would have been a certainty."[4]

The party that had achieved so many victories
"over federalism, abolitionism, and consolidation" was
now shattered. The leader of the state's National
Democrats resigned himself to the likelihood of
Republican victory. Although supporting Breckinridge,
he called for mutual toleration between the Breckinridge and Douglas followers in the slave section,
perceiving that they might soon be waging war on the
same side.[5]

Personal tragedy came in July. Orr's wife was
suddenly stricken with paralysis, about five weeks
after giving birth to a child. She became confined
to a wheelchair, and she recovered her speech. While
she was recuperating, her husband spent part of his
time building a large mansion for their family.[6]

In July the Piedmont leader publicly committed
himself to secession as the proper response to
Republican ascendancy.

> I believe that the honor and safety of the
> South, in that contingency, will require
> the prompt secession of the slaveholding
> states from the Union, and failing then to
> obtain from the free States additional and
> higher guarantees for the protection of our
> rights and property, that the seceding
> States should proceed to establish a new
> Government. But whilst I think such would
> be the imperative duty of the South, I should
> emphatically reprobate and repudiate any
> scheme having for its object the separate
> secession of South Carolina; if Georgia,
> Alabama and Mississippi alone--giving us
> a portion of the Atlantic and Gulf coasts,
> would unite with this State in a common
> secession upon the election of a Black
> Republican, I would give my assent to the
> policy.

70

He left the path clear for possible negotiations
between the slave section and the Union. At the same
time he implied that "guarantees" for the South would
probably not be secured, because the Republican party
was relentlessly hostile to slavery.[7]

In another public letter dated August 16, he predicted that the Republicans would mobilize the entire
governmental machinery to harass the slaveholders.
"If the South should think upon this subject as I do,
no Black Republican President would ever execute any
law within her borders, unless at the point of a
bayonet, and over the dead bodies of her slain sons."
The former Congressman expressed hope that the impending showdown might be averted, but he stated that such
hope probably "will never be realized."[8]

His announcement for secession provided succor to
the longtime disunionists, who recognized his considerable influence. One historian has written that
"no man in the state was more feared by secessionists
than Orr. As always, that fear involved not only the
power to divide the state on disunion, but also to
challenge the traditional political system." His
secession stand did much to unify statewide opinion
and assured the radicals that bitter division was
unlikely. The conditional unionists of the past now
spoke of disunion. The hardcore unionists, of whom
the best known were Perry, James L. Petigru, and John
Belton O'Neall, were a small minority.[9]

The question of separate secession or cooperation
was the overriding issue as the presidential election
approached. Through the late summer and early fall
the Palmetto state's mood was quiet. Many prominent
politicians were not certain that the sister states
could achieve the unity sufficient for revolution.
Hammond and Chesnut avoided making any public pro-
nouncements for secession until after the election.
Hammond especially doubted the possibility of a
unified seceding South.[10]

In Greenville in late October Orr warned that
South Carolina should not withdraw alone. He proposed
the appointment of commissioners who would consult with
leaders in other states "so that there might be a
concert of action." Like other important South
Carolinians, such as Congressmen Miles, Boyce, and
Keitt, the Anderson lawyer wanted his state to take
the initiative in promoting secession, but in his mind
taking the initiative did not require separate secession.[11]

In early November, before the election results were known, he declared again that concernted Southern action would be necessary, because of the common interests which these states possessed. The Spartanburg Carolina Spartan summarized his outlook:

> He would be willing for South Carolina to go out of the Union with any two or three of the Southern States. When out of the Union, he would favor the sending of delegates from the seceding States to Congress; and perhaps the sober thought of those in power might induce them to give additional guarantees to the South that her rights would be respected.

At this point the up-country leader did not view the disunion process as irreversible. He contemplated negotiations between the South and "those in power" after secession was accomplished.[12]

J. Johnston Pettigrew, former legislator and National Democrat, privately suggested a Southern convention which would bargain with the Republican-controlled Union. Anderson's Representative John Ashmore held similar thoughts. The most ardent disunionists sensed that the state's unity was brittle, that the idea lingered that a secession decision need not be irrevocable. For this reason the Charleston-based revolutionary managers, among whom Isaac W. Hayne, Robert N. Gourdin, and William D. Porter were the key figures, wanted to avoid delay in getting secession underway. (This group had seized the leadership reins from Rhett, the major voice in the state's delegation to the Richmond conventions in June.) By the late summer the Hayne-Gourdin-Porter cabal was directing propaganda and vigilante efforts aimed at moving public opinion irresistably towards dissolution. After Lincoln's election became known this clique worked intensely to pressure any wavering politicians.[13]

In early October Governor William H. Gist dispatched his brother to several other states with the request that one of them commence the secession movement. The replies were discouraging. Gist concluded that no other state would take the lead; none of them could match South Carolina's one-party system and apparent internal unity. The governor reckoned that a bold gesture by his state might activate the disunionist forces elsewhere. Besides the mission by

Gist's brother, there was much additional correspondence with leaders in other states. The impression grew that the sister states would react affirmatively if South Carolina forced the issue. Proponents of separate secession contended that the old distrust of the Palmetto state had died out.[14]

When the legislature met in November reports that Georgia, Mississippi, Alabama, and Florida would follow South Carolina's lead placated the cooperationists. Moreover, popular excitement was giving tremendous momentum to the campaign for immediate action. After initially scheduling a convention for January 1861, the legislature yielded to pressure for an earlier date. December 17 was set as the opening day of the convention, December 6 for the election of delegates. It was clear that South Carolina would start the secession drive.[15]

At an Anderson meeting in November Orr termed the signs of cooperative action unmistakable, and he called for the formation of military companies. If the South ever intended to resist, "now is the time." In Pendleton the former unionist described the future for nonslaveholders in the Union--emancipation, competition between white and black workers, and reduced wages for white labor. Present wages would be driven so low that many whites would be driven to the poor house or flee the country. Furthermore, in his words, the white man would absolutely never accept equality with the black, at the ballot box, the jury box, or the witness stand. The speaker insisted that he would not even argue the subject of equality between the races. This was the logic of most white South Carolinians. Republican rule would bring emancipation and, ultimately, racial equality. Ashmore, who was reluctant to leave the Union, concluded that "Lincoln could not be conservative if he would."[16]

Soon after assembling in Columbia on December 17, the convention moved to Charleston. (Reports of smallpox cases in the capitol city prompted the relocation.) Elected from Anderson, Orr was nominated for president of the body. One of the major contenders, he was defeated by the Barnwell planter David F. Jamison on the fourth ballot. He sat on the committee assigned to draft the secession ordinance, which was unanimously adopted on December 20.[17]

***** ***** ***** ***** *****

When the convention chose three commissioners to negotiate with the Buchanan administration about the federal property in South Carolina, it drew from its own ranks. Orr was named, with Robert W. Barnwell and James H. Adams. Barnwell had been a cooperationist during the 1850's. Adams, governor from 1854 to 1856, had been a militant Southern Rights advocate.[18] Arriving in Washington on December 26, they consulted William H. Trescot, the South Carolinian who had just resigned as Assistant Secretary of State.[19]

Buchanan, denying the right of secession, would not surrender the forts in Charleston harbor. He agreed to meet the commissioners "as private gentlemen of the highest character," without recognizing them as emissaries from an independent nation. Initially arranged for December 27, the interview was postponed until the next day. An unexpected occurrence caused the delay. On the morning of the 17th it became known that Major Robert J. Anderson, federal commander at Fort Moultrie, had secretly moved his force to the more formidable Fort Sumter. In South Carolina and in Washington the tension mounted. The Palmetto state diplomats were stunned.[20]

On the 18th the commissioners urged the president to remove all federal troops from the Charleston waters. Because of Anderson's move, they maintained, the continued presence of United States forces prevented amicable negotiations and endangered the safety of Charleston. Barnwell cited the "gentlemen's agreement" of early December under which both sides had promised to observe the status quo. Now Anderson's unauthorized occupation of Sumter had broken the pledge. Barnwell exclaimed that the president's "personal honor" obligated him to undo Anderson's deed. Annoyed by this pleading, Buchanan declined to act and requested time to consider the matter.[21]

Replying on December 31, the president was unyielding. South Carolina's recent seizures of Forts Moultrie and Pinckney, he indicated, had made any federal abandonment of Sumter impossible. Buchanan denied that there existed any danger to Charleston. He further maintained that Congress, rather than the executive branch, possessed the authority to determine the relations between the federal government and South Carolina.[22]

Embittered, the diplomats answered that the president had promised no aggressive measures against their state; the occupation of Sumter they termed a hostile act. "You have resolved to hold by force what you have obtained through our misplaced confidence, and by refusing to disavow the action of Major Anderson, have converted his violation of orders into a legitimate act of your executive authority." In their words, Buchanan's policy precluded any withdrawal of troops from Sumter; it signified a determination to reinforce the federal garrison in the Charleston harbor. "By your course you have probably rendered civil war inevitable. Be it so."[23]

Their mission a failure, the three men reported to the Charleston convention on January 4. Orr's diplomatic labors were not completed. On January 2, before his return, the convention named him commissioner to Georgia, where a vote on secession was imminent. Howell Cobb, prominent Georgia politician, wanted to have a forceful South Carolina agent in his state, and he voiced his preference for the former Piedmont Congressman.[24]

At the Georgia convention in Milledgeville, which commenced on January 16, 1861, the majority favored secession. Speaking on the first day, the South Carolinian urged representation at the proposed Southern convention in Montgomery, Alabama, in February. As the basis of a provisional Confederate government he suggested an amended federal constitution.[25]

The commissioner understood that timing was the key question. On the opening day he wired South Carolina Governor Pickens that the Georgians were debating whether to secede immediately or on March 4, the date of Lincoln's inauguration. Orr expected immediate action. On the next day, January 17, he reported, "Temper good. Majority will reach 40 we hope, or more." Two days later Georgia became the fifth state to leave the Union.[26]

Excitement reigned in Anderson on Monday, January 21, when South Carolina's emissary reached his home town. The train that carried him brought the news of Georgia's secession. In the evening he addressed an enthusiastic crowd at the court house, announcing that "the position, power, and weight of Georgia is pushing onward the cause of Southern independence." Georgia, with its strategic location, was pivotal, and its

decision meant that a unified Southern nation could
soon exist. The sister state's action was a cause
for celebration. The firing of cannon followed the
commissioner's speech.[27]

***** ***** ***** ***** *****

The spring months of 1861 found the Anderson
attorney busily engaged in his law practice. In a
murder case which gained attention in the locale he
was the defense counsel. Church affairs also continued to interest him. When the Episcopal diocesan
convention met in June, Grace Church of Anderson was
represented for the first time. Orr was one of four
deputies representing the parish at the conclave in
Abbeville.[28]

After the Fort Sumter showdown of April ignited
armed conflict, volunteer military companies formed
throughout the state. Orr issued a call for a regiment
and drew a highly positive response. Confidence in
the organizer was so great, observed the Charleston
Daily Courier, that he was obliged to refuse admission
to many companies. The group became known formally
as the South Carolina First Regiment (Rifles) or,
more familiarly, as Orr's Rifles. By early summer it
was fully organized. The founder was elected colonel,
and his brother-in-law, J. Foster Marshall of Abbeville, became lieutenant-colonel. The regiment
comprised ten companies, each with about one hundred
men, coming from Anderson, Pickens, Abbeville, and
Marion Districts.[29]

Governor Pickens, an old political ally of the
commander, supported the regiment's request for an
active combat role. Because the members came from
some mountain districts, Pickens told President
Jefferson Davis, "they can be safely spared." In
July the regiment was mustered into Confederate
service. One soldier recalled the general impression
that hostilities would last from six to twelve months.
"Some of us were afraid it would be all over before
we reached the front." In the same month the men
encamped at Sandy Springs, near Anderson, and in
September they moved to Sullivan's Island on the coast.
Davis decided to retain this regiment as a reserve to
safeguard the Charleston area. There the group was
stationed when Orr won a Confederate Senate seat. He
resigned his commission and in February 1862 was
succeeded in command by Marshall.[30]

76

On the morning of February 1, as he took leave
of his regiment, a scene occurred which revealed the
warmth of his personality. Many residents of Sullivan's Island gathered, and the companies were assembled
before the Moultrie House. Marshall announced that
the meeting would adopt resolutions expressing the
regiment's sentiments. In his remarks, the departing
commander declared that he had been torn between a
desire to engage in combat and the call of the state
to serve in the national councils. He could not ignore
the voice of his state, and he resolved to work for
the independence of the South. One reporter observed
that "many a tear dimmed the eyes of the manly and
noble forms that were before him." After being dismissed for two hours, the regiment reassembled at
Orr's headquarters and escorted him to his boat.
After he reached the deck of the boat, every officer
and soldier came to bid him a personal farewell. The
newspaperman called this "one of the most interesting
and impressive scenes that it has ever fallen my
lot to witness."[31]

***** ***** ***** ***** *****

Unanimity existed at the South Carolina convention
on secession in December 1860, but other matters sparked
disagreement when the body reconvened in March 1861.
The more moderate delegates preferred, as the Confederacy's organic law, the old United States Constitution with slight modifications. Another group,
led by Rhett, wanted major revisions in accord with
their ideal of a slaveholding, free-trading republic.
Moderates, fearing that stringent demands might annoy
other states, insisted that changes could be made in
due time, and their position generally prevailed.
Consistently moderate, Orr voted against most proposals
for specific amendments. Deletion of the "three-fifths"
clause, by which five slaves were counted as three
persons in fixing the population basis of representation; exclusion from the Confederacy of any state
that banned Negro slavery--these drew his opposition.
He did, however, favor amendments imposing limits on
tariff duties and requiring all such duties to be
uniform. The Andersonian also opposed the call for
a Southern constitutional convention. Its proponents
wanted such a gathering soon after the new government
went into operation.[32]

The convention adjourned on April 10, after resolving that its president could order another session before the year's end. On December 14, Jamison called for a meeting on December 26. The crisis caused by federal occupation of much of the coast, and mounting dissatisfaction with Governor Pickens, who had been elected in 1860, induced the summons.[33]

After the fall of Port Royal in November, the Hayne-Gourdin-Porter group, which had previously managed the secession campaign, decided to assert itself. Confusion on the coast, alleged incompetence in the governorship, and the state's inability to provide troops for coastal defense--these factors moved the Charleston-based clique to take strong measures. Before the convention reassembled, they contemplated revisions in the state constitution, whereby the executive authority could be taken from Pickens. This cabal spoke of transferring the executive power to a council or to another person who would be more effective than Pickens. The man chiefly in mind was Orr.[34]

When the body reconvened in December, the Andersonian had recently been elected to the Confederate Senate. He had also been active as the commanding officer of his regiment. He did not attend any meetings after the convention reassembled; in early January 1862 he was granted leave of absence "on account of military duty."[35]

The convention enjoyed much public confidence when it gathered in Decmeber 1861. The Hayne-Gourdin-Porter group successfully broadened its base of support and drastically revamped the state administration. The governor's powers were absorbed by a five-man executive council, comprising the governor, the lieutenant-governor, and three members named by the convention. Pickens and Lieutenant-Governor W. W. Harlee were joined by Hayne, Chesnut, and Gist as the council members.[36]

The council acted vigorously, establishing military conscription, imposing martial law in certain areas, impressing slave labor, and taking several other strong measures. Despite determined efforts, the council did not achieve its goals in 1862. Its attempts to evacuate the coastal areas failed; its defensive policy suffered from insufficient support from Richmond. Around the council raged South

78

Carolina's most heated wartime political controversy.
As popular acquiescence waned, Pickens' indignant
friends, resenting the obvious insult, became bolder
in attacking the council.[37]

After creating the council in early 1862, the
convention provided for its own reconvening by Jamison,
at his own discretion or at the request of twenty members. The body then adjourned. By the summer the
public outcry against the convention and council
had intensified. To many people the council seemed
the embodiment of arbitrary power. In spite of urgent
pleas that reconvening was imperative to pacify the
public, Jamison would not issue the summons on his
own initiative. It became difficult to acquire the
twenty delegate requests that could force Jamison to
issue the call. Finally, the twentieth delegate
letter was obtained by August 21. The twentieth
signature was Orr's.[38]

Meeting in September, the convention arranged for
its own dissolution in December; the council's status
it put at the option of the legislature. In accord
with public sentiment, the new legislature, elected
in October, dismantled the hated directory. Pickens,
who had regained public confidence, had much good
will in the legislature. His friends, wishing to
vindicate him, hoped that a Confederate Senate seat
might become vacant. There was talk of electing Orr
to the governorship and sending Pickens to the Senate.
Remaining aloof from the convention-council enbroilment,
the Andersonian enjoyed the trust of the Pickens
followers. He declined to seek the governorship,
responding that he could best serve the state in
his present capacity. Pickens retired to private
life, succeeded in the governor's chair by Edgefield
Congressman Milledge Bonham.[39]

V. CONFEDERATE SENATOR

The Anderson politician sat briefly in the
Provisional Congress, named by the South Carolina
legislature to replace a delegate who resigned. He
took his seat on February 17, 1862, the provisional
body's last day in session.[1] On the following day,
when Congress organized under the permanent frame
of government, Orr was still representing his state.
In the previous December he had been elected, with
Robert W. Barnwell, to the Confederate Senate.

The competition for South Carolina's two Senate
seats was lively, in progress since July 1861. In
Charleston during much of the year, commanding his
regiment, Orr was well positioned to conduct his
campaign. James Chesnut, Jr., who had the backing
of the Hayne-Gourdin-Porter faction, was expected
to win. By failing to join forces with another
leading candidate, Chesnut's friends blundered. In
contrast, the Barnwell and Orr followers coalesced and
carried the election.[2] Ironically, the state that
initiated the secession movement chose as its senators
two conspicuous moderates of the pre-war years.

The two served in Richmond until the war's end.[3]
Barnwell was friendly to Jefferson Davis, while his
colleague became one of the President's sharpest
critics. Although frequently in the minority when
important roll calls were taken, Orr was respected
by the other members. He headed the foreign affairs
committee and at various times sat on the commerce,
finance, and printing committees. In debate he was
logical, concise, and often sardonic. He could also
be petulant and cantankerous.

On one occasion the Senate considered a bill to
give Congressmen certificates enabling them to travel
through the Confederacy without annoyance. The Piedmont senator complained that he and two other legislators, on their way to Richmond, were almost ejected
from a train carrying soldiers. The incident occurred
when a provost-marshall and a guard had tried to "carry
out their absurd and tyrannical instruction." Orr
delivered a blistering tirade against the abuse of
military power, stating that there was not "the sha-
dow of authority" for any provost-marshalls beyond
the limits of a camp or army. At one point he
characterized the military draft as despotism. Louis

Wigfall of Texas called the affair accidental, caused by an official who had neglected to list "members of Congress" as the only non-military personnel who could occupy the train. The Texan was sorry to see his friend take the matter so seriously.[4]

The Confederate soldier exemplified the Southern mores, with its democratic and individualistic temper. One historian has called him a "liberty-loving individualist; his Union counterpart became a cog in a vast machine."[5] The rebel soldier was more inclined than the Yankee to personalize his relations with an officer, to be more familiar and less disciplined. This equalitarian heritage was manifest in the custom of allowing men in the ranks to elect their officers. While professional military men disliked the elective system, politicians who were sympathetic to the soldier's outlook defended it. Such a politician was Orr. In September 1862 the Senate debated a bill which specified that when vacancies occurred, and the officer elected or next in line for promotion was declared incompetent, the President could appoint the successor. James Phelan of Mississippi stated that many units had picked the least intelligent men as leaders. Orr responded that he hoped such instances were rare. Laughter broke out when he remarked that any group that elected a fool or a thief knew better than an examining board or the President who was the proper man to lead them.[6]

Orr was one of the Senate's staunchest exponents of the traditional rights of individuals and states. He was among the five senators who voted against the conscription law of April 1862. Before its passage he suggested a conditional draft, a system of requisitions upon the states; his proposal was rejected.[7]

The Carolinian valued highly the government's honorable dealings with individuals. On August 27, 1862, the Senate discussed a proposal to empower enrolling officers to seize persons subject to conscription wherever they might be found. Orr was indignant. "Because a few unworthy persons might seek, by flight, to escape their share of the dangers of this war, it was no reason for passing this sweeping act, which would harrass a great number of our most loyal citizens."[8] He also opposed the enrollment of persons whose substitutes had deserted. Such action he called retroactive, violating an agreement between the government and the principals. "The Government had accepted the substitutes without condition. If a substitute deserted, the remedy of the Government was against the substitute."[9] The senator had contempt for those persons who had presented substitutes, but he would not tarnish the government's honor in order to penalize them. The Senate majority took a less tolerant attitude, especially as the war picture became more critical. On December 30, 1863, approval was given to a House bill that denied exemptions to those men who furnished substitutes. Orr and Herschel V. Johnson of Georgia were the only dissenters.[10]

On the exemption question the Carolinian favored leniency. On September 9, 1862, when the Senate pondered exemptions for justices of the peace, he declared that the Confederate government had no right to touch state officers. There were rumors, he noted, that North Carolina might appoint all of its citizens state officers and thereby exempt them from military service. "Can it be, sir, that already, when this Government is scarcely a year old, it has become so distasteful to the State governments that they would take measures to keep their citizens out of its service?" He hoped not, but he believed that such action would be legal.[11]

Several days later Orr tried to secure exemptions for all men exempted by state convention ordinances. Such an arrangement, he argued, would avert collision between the Confederacy and the states. Moreover, he doubted that the states would withhold more men than were needed for their internal maintenance and police systems. Mississippi's James Phelan observed that South Carolina's convention was still in existence; that state would enjoy a special advantage. Orr replied that his state's exemption ordinance had been passed before the Confederate draft law was enacted.[12]

The exemption law of October 1862, which he supported, exempted state officers except those specified by a state as subject to militia duty. In addition, the act benefitted either the owner or the overseer on a plantation employing at least twenty blacks; or one exemption was allowed on any plantation where state law required a white man's presence. The overseer provision gave rise to the slogan "rich man's war and poor man's fight." On February 12, 1863, Orr denied that class favoritism had been intended. If so, the measure "would never have received a vote in the Senate." The law had been passed only to safeguard

83

"the great interest of the country."[13]

When revised and stricter draft laws were passed he remained in opposition; he never relented in his efforts to obtain liberal exemption policies. The Senate almost unanimously approved the conscription act of September 1862; Orr and Williamson Oldham of Texas cast the only negative votes. Each new law broadened the age groups of men subject to the draft; the range of occupations and state officers eligible for exemptions was narrowed.[14]

Impressment legislation had his support. However, he opposed national regulation of the railroads, a measure which attracted growing support as the war progressed. Not until February 1865 did Congress finally authorize national supervision of all transportation facilities. Although Congressmen understood the difficulties that railroad operators faced in running their lines efficiently, they hesitated to intrude upon private enterprise. (A number of railroads were under state as well as private ownership.) In April 1863 the Senate approved the partial Confederate operation of any road in an emergency; if the owners were uncooperative, the secretary of war could seize the road completely. The government could also transfer rolling stock or rails to other areas. Orr criticized this plan, which became law in May. He observed that one provision allowed seizure of the railroads, in certain contingencies, and their supervision by the quartermaster-general, "who may compel the continued presence, employment and work of all its officers, agents, employees, and operatives," whether or not they were conscripts. The senator feared that these men might be treated as slaves. His main objection, moreover, was that the roads would not be managed as capably as under private direction. Under the quartermaster-general they would "soon break down entirely."[15]

On November 15, 1864, Orr introduced a bill to exempt stateowned vessels from Confederate restrictions upon exports and imports, and on December 2, he asked that such an exemption cover any vehicle or vessel in which a state had any interest. Robert M. T. Hunter of Virginia pointed out that this measure would enable the states to control all exporting and importing. The Senate never acted upon the bill.[16]

***** ***** ***** ***** *****

Orr consistently voted against the suspension of the habeas corpus writ, and he opposed a bill to define and punish conspiracy against the Confederacy. On December 15, 1864, debate flared over an amendment authorizing Confederate district courts to try conspiracy cases. The Carolinian did not participate in the deliberations, but his vote reflected his usual fear of national encroachment upon states' rights. The Senate dismissed the contention, made by John Watson of Mississippi, that the states would be denied "their proper jurisdiction" in criminal cases.[17]

The creation of a Confederate supreme court was contemplated in early 1863. The question arose as to whether adequate talent could be obtained with low salaries. Louis Wigfall believed that low salaries would enable only the rich to hold office; yet he feared an overbearing court with brilliant men who would work to expand its powers. If the tribunal would not seek to arrogate supervision over the state courts, the Texan remarked, it would have little business and would not require exceptionally gifted judges. Orr joined the majority which voted for salaries not likely to attract intellectual giants. His vote also prevailed when the Senate moved to deprive the supreme court of appellate jurisdiction over state judiciaries. Many legislators were apprehensive that a domineering high court might subordinate the states to the Confederate government. Orr did vote to establish a supreme court. The court was never created, because the two houses of Congress could not agree upon its jurisdiction.[18]

The question of Senate seats for cabinet ministers was debated in March 1863. Favoring the proposal, Orr maintained that the cabinet members would enforce the laws more diligently if they were held accountable to questioning in Congress. William Yancey of Alabama warned that this practice would bring into the cabinet "great dialecticians and men cunning at intellectual fencing," who would take advantage of the senators. Orr had no fears of cabinet members overwhelming the Senate "by the force of their intellect." Yancey replied that he did not allude to the present cabinet. The opportunity to interrogate cabinet officers on the Senate floor never materialized.[19]

On June 6, 1864, the Senate considered a bill
allowing the quartermaster-general to provide forage,
fuel, and lights for the President, who was commander-
in-chief. Robert W. Johnson of Arkansas scolded Orr
for raising constitutional objections. Congress had
been generous to itself and to others, Johnson pointed
out. Moreover, he added, the President could not live
in the required style on his salary. The Carolinian
answered that the Constitution specified the President's
salary, prohibited any increase during his tenure,
and declared that a residence should be provided. In
his words, Congress could not "get rid of" the constitutional problem.[20]

In February 1865 the Senate took up a bill allowing
the War Department to employ a solicitor. In Orr's
opinion, the bill "dissipated too much the responsibility"
of the secretary of war, to whom there was "little
enough responsibility" attaching already. Besides, the
bill created another office, and he wanted to hear some
justification for it. Tennessee's Langdon C. Haynes
asserted that the War Department's immense legal business warranted the appointment of a solicitor.[21]

*****   *****   *****   *****   *****

Most South Carolina Congressmen were partisans
of General Pierre G. T. Beauregard, whose relations
with Davis were strained. During much of the war the
Louisianan was in charge of the Charleston defenses.
Beauregard and Charleston's Representative William
Porcher Miles, chairman of the House military affairs
committee, were intimate friends. Miles, Orr, and
Representative William W. Boyce of Winnsboro were
among the general's most enthusiastic admirers in
Richmond. Anticipating a Union attack, Beauregard in
early 1863 sent requests to Orr, Barnwell, Secretary
of War James A. Seddon, and others for reinforcements,
particularly of artillery. On February 6, Orr introduced a bill to increase the strength and efficiency
of heavy artillery for coast defense. Congress passed
the bill, which sought to reorganize and increase the
size of the companies in the South Carolina infantry
and artillery units. Davis vetoed the bill on the
grounds that such reorganizations were under the
executive's jurisdiction. The House sustained the
President's veto.[22]

In 1863 the controversial Creole arrested the chief commissary for South Carolina, Major Henry C. Guerin, but Secretary of War Seddon released him, since he had received no formal complaint. Orr, meeting with Davis, explained that Beauregard expected the court in his district to hear the case. It was appropriate, the President replied, to hold the trial in Richmond or in another military district. After this interview the senator told Beauregard that he had acted indiscreetly by not sending the charges against Guerin promptly to the War Department. Orr advised him to be more prudent, and he also expressed confidence that the general would vindicate himself. "If you come out of the impending struggle before Charleston with a triumphant banner unfurled to the breeze as I have no doubt you will, then you will have such a record as that envy, jealousy and malignity will cower before the storm of popular indignation."23

General Braxton Bragg, one of Davis' favorites, was frequently the target of Orr's wrath. In September 1862 the Carolinian asked the Senate military affairs committee to examine accusations that Bragg had unjustly executed some soldiers. Alabama's Clement C. Clay, Mississippi's James Phelan, and others stated that the publicity given the charges might undermine any discipline. Orr retorted that an investigation would assure the soldiers that their rights would be protected. If Bragg could abuse his power with impunity, he asserted, other commanders of lesser stature might act similarly. The Senate approved a rephrased resolution which avoided mention of any specific person.24

Orr was sympathetic to General Joseph E. Johnston, commander of the Army of Tennessee from December 1863 until his removal in July 1864. In November the senator submitted a resolution calling for the general's official report on the Army of Tennessee operations under his command. In the following month, on his motion, the privileges of the Senate floor were extended to Johnston. On February 3, 1865, during deliberations on another subject, Orr digressed into an attack upon Davis for dismissing Johnston, claiming that only disaster had followed his departure. On the next day he was one of fifteen senators who signed a letter to General Lee, urging him to recommend Johnston's reinstatement.25

Complaints about impressment procedures were often colored by Congressional dislike of Commissary-General Lucius B. Northup. Orr, one of his critics, deplored "the arbitrary, unjust, and needless impressment" of provisions under his orders.[26] The senator was hostile to two other administration officials, Secretary of the Navy Stephen Mallory and Secretary of State Judah P. Benjamin. In January 1863, when the Senate was questioning Mallory's jurisdiction over naval courts martial, he charged that the secretary had exceeded his authority.[27] In February 1865 the Senate split on Wigfall's resolution demanding Benjamin's retirement from the cabinet. Orr favored the resolution, which stated that the cabinet minister had lost the nation's confidence. The motion failed.[28]

Concerned about the medical care of soldiers, Orr desired legislation which would regulate hospital discharges more efficiently. When the Senate considered a measure in April 1863 it accepted his amendment that no furlough should be granted if, in the judgment of the examining board, the patient's life or convalescence would be imperiled. On another occasion the senator drew attention to the callous treatment which many wounded soldiers received in consequence of disputes among doctors.[29] The welfare of prisoners of war also interested him. In November 1864 he requested information about Confederate prison camps. Specifically, he asked whether the commissary-general had suspended the issue of meat rations to captives. He wanted to know, in that contingency, what substitute had been provided.[30]

***** ***** ***** ***** *****

In 1863, with Union advances in Mississippi and Alabama keenly felt, newspapers in those states raised the subject of black soldiers. When the Alabama legislature petitioned Davis to enroll Negroes, the President was unreceptive. The Confederate government, recognizing that black enlistments might lead to eventual freedom, was reluctant to act.[31]

A prelude to action on black troops was the decision to employ Negro laborers in the army. In March 1863 Congress passed an impressment act, which Orr supported, allowing for the induction of black laborers. On January 30, 1864, Orr presented a bill to use free Negroes as cooks, teamsters, and laborers, and on February 13, the Senate approved a House bill to employ free blacks and slaves in certain noncombatant capacities.[32]

In early 1864 General Patrick Cleburne revived
the issue of black soldiers at an officers' meeting
in the Army of Tennessee, suggesting the promise of
freedom. In spite of government attempts to suppress
Cleburne's proposal, news of it circulated widely.
Fears that whites would leave the ranks if blacks
entered did not hinder the movement for arming the
slaves. Many soldiers had left the army for various
reasons, and the steady inroads of Grant and Sherman
by the fall of 1864 made conditions more desperate
than ever. In October the governors of five states
recommended black enlistments, and in the next month
Davis gave his endorsement. As the military situation
deteriorated public opinion shifted towards acquiescence. The enormous prestige of General Lee, whose
support was publicized in early 1865, was important
in breaking down resistance.[33]

In February 1865 Congress revised the legislation
on free blacks and slaves in noncombative army tasks.
Debate erupted over a resolution to set a numerical
ceiling of 30,000 east and 10,000 west of the Mississippi
River. Urging a restriction, Orr stated that the use
of black laborers had aroused the public to the
possibility of black soldiers. If no limitation
were imposed, he was sure that the protest would be so
vehement that the army might fall apart. The senator
turned to the likely impact upon the slaves. When the
Yankees first occupied Southern land, he noted, blacks
flocked to the Union lines; the exodus ceased when the
enemy began to enroll the blacks as soldiers. Although
viewing the Negroes as naturally cowardly, he was convinced that they would overwhelmingly join the Yankees
if forced to choose between Union and Confederate
military service. Should the blacks perceive that "we
designed putting them into our armies they would leave
by thousands."[34]

The Carolinian insisted that the country would
regard the unrestricted use of black laborers as the
opening wedge to slave enlistments. Emancipation, the
"necessary concomitant" of arming the blacks, would
inevitably result and bring disaster to the country.
After Augustus Maxwell of Florida advanced a similar
line of reasoning, Waldo P. Johnson of Missouri charged
that the real issue had been confused. In his words,
the question was restricting the number of black
laborers, not arming the slaves. By a 9-10 vote the
Senate defeated the effort to remove the limitation.
Soon after this balloting Orr asked that the vote be

reconsidered, possibly hoping for a more decisive
result. After further discussion the Senate reversed
itself, and later in the month Congress authorized
unrestricted numbers of black workers.[35]

At the same time the legislators prepared to arm
the slaves. On March 8, the Senate accepted a House
bill which left emancipation to the option of the
states, and on March 13, Davis signed the measure into
law. The Senate tally was close, 9-8, with Orr opposed.[36]
The Carolinian believed that the Confederacy could
find a sufficient number of whites to meet its needs.
While the bill was being discussed he wrote, "If we
could get the white men back who are now absent without
leave and the skulkers it will make us as large an
army as we can feed."[37]

***** ***** ***** ***** *****

As chairman of the Senate foreign relations
committee, Orr frequently submitted resolutions asking
the President to supply papers pertaining to foreign
policy. In November 1864 he presented a tersely worded
set of resolutions demanding firmness in response to
the Florida incident in Brazil. A Confederate steamer
had been seized and captured by the United States Navy
in the Bay of Bahia. Protesting this "flagrant out-
rage" against Brazil's sovereignty and the Confederacy's
rights in neutral waters, the foreign relations panel
asked Davis to bring the affair to the attention of the
European governments.[38] The committee's usefulness was
confined mainly to writing reports and resolutions; it
played no significant role in Confederate diplomacy.
Congress itself exerted little influence in foreign
policy, and Davis did almost nothing to enlighten the
legislators about international diplomacy.[39]

The Piedmont senator joined the Congressional
majority which balked at the conscription of aliens
residing in the Confederacy. In May 1862 Attorney-
General Thomas H. Watts ruled that all foreigners
permanently domiciled in the South were subject to
military duty. Orr asked Secretary of State Benjamin
if "domiciled foreigners" were, under the attorney-
general's definition, persons who had avowed their intention of becoming Southern citizens. This interpretation he found unobjectionable. On the other hand,
if the administration planned to draft all resident
aliens, he warned, conflict with foreign nations might
occur. Such a policy he termed a reckless violation

90

"of the usages of civilized nations."[40]

In the pre-war years Orr had favored a larger influx of white laborers into the South, with the aim of promoting industrial growth. During the war he spoke against any restriction upon white immigration. The Confederacy retained the United States naturalization laws and made changes only to allow aliens in the army to become citizens. Attempts to repeal the laws failed.[41] When repeal was proposed in April 1863 Orr was enraged. After the war, he predicted, the Southern need for foreign mechanics would be more acute than ever. After he cited the Irish and Germans who had fought for the South, Alabama's Clay remarked that many foreigners were in the Union army. Clay speculated that many of them would migrate to the Confederate border states after the war and, if not excluded from the suffrage, become a powerful anti-slavery force. Oldham of Texas contended that the Confederate government could not force citizens upon the states against their will. He added that the naturalization laws made the foreigner think that his main allegiance was to the general government rather than his state. It was not on constitutional grounds that Orr, normally a proponent of states' rights, favored retention of the naturalization laws.[42]

Alternating periods of optimism and gloom marked his perception of Southern diplomatic prospects. In May 1863, before the pivotal battles of the coming summer were fought, Orr reckoned that the Union would soon concede the South's independence. "If we can prevent the enemy gaining any decided advantage over us for the next four months I think we will have peace before Christmas." A series of federal disasters would, he believed, place the Northern peace party "in the ascendant this fall." Consequently Lincoln's government would collapse.[43]

He was among the small number who initially signed an "Address to the People of the Confederate States," adopted in December 1863 and eventually endorsed by the entire Congress. Upholding the right of secession, this manifesto contained an overture for peace negotiations. Should the Union rebuff efforts to achieve a settlement, the document stated, the South would insist upon its independence as a condition for peace. Copies were distributed in Europe as well as throughout the South.[44]

By early 1864 Orr's mood was mixed. Writing to
Hammond in January, he reviewed the South's misfor-
tunes--military reverses of the past year, the loss
of Kentucky and Missouri, enemy occupation in
Tennessee and Arkansas and penetration elsewhere.
A huge debt had accumulated, and in the army straggling
and desertions were rampant.

> A weak incompetent President and an imbecile
> cabinet to sustain him. A general surrender-
> ing more than thirty thousand of our veteran
> troops and not only no court martial of in-
> quiry to inquire and pass upon his incompe-
> tency or treachery, but the same general
> tendered another corps in another army. Add
> to this a truculent and indecisive Congress
> and you have a picture which is gratifying
> neither to our hopes or pride.

One bright note appeared--foreign affairs were
"looking better" than ever before; soon "one of the
leading powers" would probably recognize the Confederacy. Declining to give any "particulars," he believed that a sequence of events favorable to the
South was imminent. In addition, the senator
expected a vigorous buildup of the army to facilitate
a military breakthrough.[45]

While making this assessment, Orr joined his
colleagues in looking to a Mexican connection. On
January 5, the Senate unanimously adopted resolutions
calling for negotiations with Emperor Maximilian, a
puppet of Napoleon III. Alabama's Clay encountered
a negative response when he stated that the South
should not negotiate a treaty of alliance with Mexico.
Orr opposed Clay's stand.[46]

By the following month the Carolinian's analysis
of international affairs had changed. On February 7,
he admitted, "I do not perceive any probability that
England or France will help or that we can hope for
any help elsewhere than our own strong arms & brave
hearts." He did not despair. Southern troops were
reenlisting enthusiastically, he noted, and morale
seemed to be high. He also forecast an energetic
Union drive in the months ahead.[47]

By the spring of 18t4 Lee's victories at Spotsyl-
vania and in the Wilderness encouraged the opinion
that the North might accept Southern independence.[48]
Several legislators, among them Senators Orr, Herschel
V. Johnson of Georgia, and William A. Graham of North
Carolina, and Representative William W. Boyce of South
Carolina, met in the quarters of Mississippi Senator
John Watson. They agreed to offer resolutions calling
for negotiations. On June 2, Orr introduced the Sen-
ate resolution, which failed by a 5-14 vote. The
House motion, presented by Tennessee's Henry S. Foote,
was tabled.[49]

In November, after Lincoln's re-election in the
North, Davis addressed Congress abou the enemy's goal
of forcing the South's unconditional surrender. While
the President and most Southerners were determined
to continue fighting, peace agitation persisted.
The most vocal peace proponents were in the House,
where several resolutions based upon Southern independence were put forward but rejected. In early 1865
the unofficial mission to Richmond of Francis P. Blair,
a prominent Northern politician, spurred talk of a
diplomatic solution. The interest stirred by Blair's
visit probably influenced Davis' decision to send
delegates to a meeting with Lincoln.[50]

At the Hampton Roads conference on February 3,
Vice-President Alexander Stephens, Senator Hunter,
and Judge John A. Campbell faced Lincoln and his
secretary of state, William H. Seward. The Union
leader, promising a generous use of the pardon power,
demanded reunion and abolition. The effort was
abortive. Davis, insisting upon Southern independence,
was able to show that negotiations had been attempted;
he shrewdly undercut the peace advocates. The dominant Southern sentiment was a stiff resolve to continue
the war.[51]

Orr subscribed momentarily to this prevailing
outlook. On February 17, he wrote to Perry that if
Beauregard could restrain Sherman, "then our cause
is on the topmost wave if not our affairs will
become gloomy in the extreme. The humiliating terms
of peace tendered us by Lincoln has nerved the heart
and braced the arm of Lee's army. The army has never
been so resolute & defiant since '62." By early
March the senator's mind had shifted; he now estimated
that the Union forces could not be checked. He adhered to the minority appraisal described by Texas

Senator Williamson Oldham, "Already conquered, they were willing to accept the terms of the conqueror."[52]

The Senate named Orr, Hunter, and Graham to consult Davis. The three recommended negotiations on the basis of reunion. The President asked them to prepare a Senate resolution, which he would answer promptly. After the interview Graham stated that "at a proper time" he would introduce the resolution. The "proper time" never came. Accurately gauging the public spirit, Davis once again had outmaneuvered the peace proponents.[53]

On March 18, the Senate adjourned <u>sine die</u>. Orr returned to Anderson and suffered from typhoid fever during the closing weeks of the war. With federal troops in the vicinity, there was danger to his personal safety. His residence was sacked by soldiers who took much of the furniture and clothing.[54]

Writing to Francis W. Pickens on April 29, he blamed Davis for the South's predicament, and he alluded bitterly to the President's refusal to work seriously for a peaceful settlement.

> I was anxious last winter that negotiating should have been opened with the enemy to ascertain upon what terms the war could be closed. Davis as now was too obstinate and supercilious to entertain the proposition. I fear now that we will not be allowed to retain slavery--if at all it will only be temporary, but even with that great loss and humiliation it is to be preferred to a hopeless and desperate prosecution of an impossible war.

Much of the South was in enemy hands, Orr noted, and continued fighting would only devastate the country. The surrender of Lee's army, "the only real army we ever had," had doomed the Confederacy.[55]

Under wiser leadership, he maintained, the South could have won independence without sacrificing the civil liberties of whites or arming the slaves. In his mind Jefferson Davis' failure of statesmanship made the difference between victory and defeat, between the retention of slavery and abolition. The abuses of military power, the inefficient government practices, and the often blundering conduct of the war--all of these seemed unnecessary and avoidable. Orr joined the Congressional peace movement when he became convinced that Davis' policies would lead to disaster. He was in the minority that understood the folly of continuing the war. The Carolina senator was a fighter, but he did not like to fight for a lost cause.

VI. MISCALCULATING THE SITUATION

Orr was a realist who knew that continued warfare by guerilla fighting would be destructive to his side. On May 10, 1865, he declared that South Carolina should accept "in good faith" the authority of the United States. He suggested that Governor Andrew Magrath convene the legislature and, before its meeting, order all state troops to disband.[1]

There was much distress and confusion as the fighting ceased. Uncertain about Washington's position, Southern politicians hoped to placate the conqueror and gain acceptance of their governments. Therefore, they sought to present the North with the reality of operating state governments. Orr's plea for a conciliatory stance, and his proposal that Magrath convene the legislature, exemplified this tactic. Aware of the Southerners' ploy, the federal authorities dissolved the existing regimes and instituted martial law. In South Carolina Magrath and other state officials were arrested, as military rule took effect.[2]

In May 1865, one month after entering the presidency, Andrew Johnson moved towards a mild restoration program and the speedy creation of civil governments in the South. He offered pardons to most Southerners who would take an oath of allegiance to the United States; persons who owned property valued at $20,000 would have to secure special pardons. The president appointed provisional governors, who were instructed to call conventions in their states. These conventions were expected to repeal the secession ordinances, repudiate all Confederate debts, abolish slavery, and draft new constitutions. After this work was completed, the people would elect new governments and send Congressional delegations to Washington.[3]

Johnson's program entailed the appointment of civil provisional governors and continued military rule. On June 27, Secretary of War Edwin Stanton announced that a military commander would be assigned to each former Confederate state. The relationship between provisional governors and military commanders was vague and undefined, but Johnson assumed that the military personnel would acknowledge the primacy of the civil officials.[4]

On June 30, Johnson named Benjamin F. Perry provisional governor of South Carolina. In addition the president designated Major-General Daniel E. Sickles military commander for the Carolinas. Shortly after his appointment Perry conferred with Johnson in Washington. Orr and four others accompanied him. Johnson suggested that white population alone should be the basis of representation in the South Carolina convention. Orr supported the president's recommendation. Perry, however, decided upon an equal ratio between population and property, used since 1808 in the state house of representatives. The provisional governor, for many years one of the leading advocates of reform, was reluctant to effect drastic changes in the political structure on his authority only. When he issued the convention summons, he asked his fellow citizens to accept the president's amnesty offer and choose delegates. Only whites who held pardons could vote and serve as delegates. It was made known that pardons would be granted to persons who backed the convention call. This information induced many prominent persons to become delegate candidates.[5]

Johnson was hesitant to pardon well known ex-Confederates, especially anyone whose restoration to political rights would offend the North. At one time Perry inquired about Orr, saying that the former Confederate senator could be helpful in promoting Johnson's policy. "The President told me the Northern editors were watching him like hawks," the governor recalled. Johnson promised a pardon when he took a seat in the state convention. The Anderson politician was elected and received his pardon. The president and his cabinet were sympathetic, viewing him as an original opponent of secession who had reluctantly gone along with his state.[6]

Perry's appointment as governor meant that South Carolina's political system could be democratized. The provisional governor, as the president's agent, was granted unprecedented authority. Perry, prewar unionist and National Democrat, was a longtime critic of the seacoast aristocracy. To the forthcoming convention, he announced, each election district would send as many delegates as it had representatives in the lower house of the legislature. This arrangement assured the middle and western districts of an enlarged voice. In the past the coastal dominance had been based upon overrepresentation in the senate.

The convention assembled in Columbia on September 13. Among the better known members, in addition to Orr, were Pickens, former Confederate Congressman John Farrow, State Senator Franklin J. Moses, and Confederate military officer Samuel McGowan. For convention president Orr nominated C. W. Dudley of Bennettsville, a close Perry ally for many years, and the Charleston delegation presented Judge David Wardlaw of Abbeville. Wardlaw won and named Dudley chairman of the committee on constitutional amendments. Up country members filled most of the other chairmanships.[7]

Proclaiming the end of slavery was potentially contentious. Orr wanted the convention to comply with Johnson's requirements and avoid any rancor which might annoy the North. He therefore deemed the question of phraseology unimportant, so long as the declaration was innocuous. After one delegate offered an amendment which sought federal compensation in return for emancipation, the Andersonian remarked that South Carolina should not imply that it was negotiating with the Union. (He did, however, express confidence that compensation would come.) The amendment was tabled. The body approved a perfunctory statement that slavery was forever dead, but the point was made that federal coercion, not the state's free choice, had doomed the institution.[8]

The convention repealed the 1860 secession ordinance, but it ignored Johnson's request that the state repudiate its rebel war debt. Perry failed to recommend repudiation. The governor also upheld the "white man's government" concept in his message to the convention. Although privately amenable to a qualified black suffrage, he believed that a large black vote would give the great planters "a most undue influence in all elections."[9]

Only a handful of delegates, among them Wade Hampton, favored a qualified Negro suffrage. White opinion in South Carolina was solidly against enfranchising any freedmen. However, there is evidence that White House pressure could have secured some black voting. The delegates did not feel compelled to provide black suffrage in order to placate the North, because Johnson let them think that readmission into the Union did not require such a step.[10]

In addition, the convention refused to count the
blacks in determining representation in the legislature, thereby denying the heavily black low country
of an obvious advantage. The low country delegates
spoke against too drastic a change from the old system.
A. P. Aldrich of Barnwell asked that three-fifths of
the Negroes be counted in fixing the lower house
representation, but the up country members were unyielding.
Orr argued frankly that only white people should be
counted, because the state should have a "white man's
government." In his words, the time had not come to
enfranchise the blacks. "They are not prepared to
receive that privilege, and by bestowing it upon
them the best interests of the State must suffer."
The Andersonian suggested that the lower house be
apportioned by white population, and the senate based
upon white population and taxation, with at least one
senator from each judicial district. Edgefield's
George Tillman wanted to use white population and
taxation in alloting seats in the house of representatives, while giving each judicial district one
senator. By a close vote Tillman's formula was
accepted, with the added provision that no district
should have more than twelve representatives. This
rule was designed to limit Charleston's allotment.[11]

The up country was determined to overthrow the
old oligarchical rule, which had been based upon low
country control of the senate. Under the "Compromise
of 1808," added to the 1790 constitution, the house
of representatives was apportioned by white population
and taxation, while each election district, including
each parish, held one senate seat. However, the new
system was scheduled to take effect with the second
election after the convention. The legislature chosen
in 1865, the only legislative body under the 1865
constitution, was elected under the 1808 plan.[12]

Efforts to democratize the governmental structure
met moderate success. The governor, lieutenant-
governor, and presidential electors, all heretofore
named by the legislature, would be popularly chosen.
The governor would have a qualified veto and serve
for four years, although he could not succeed himself,
as Orr had desired. The convention accepted his
suggestion that viva voce balloting be used in the
legislature, and property qualifications for election
to the legislature were discarded. However, the
popular election of such state officers as treasurer
and secretary of state, which Orr recommended, was

rejected. There were limits to the willingness to
institute reforms. The fear of "unmixed" democracy
remained strong, evidently cutting across sectional
lines. One Northern reporter observed, "Dozens of
delegates have said to me that it isn't well to
allow people to elect their own rulers." Nonetheless, the convention significantly altered the
political system. Even without black suffrage or
representation, the new legislative apportionment
based upon white population was more democratic than
ever before.[13]

     At this time Andrew Johnson was reinforcing the
Southern impression that the path to reunion would
not be difficult. Orr was cautiously optimistic
that the country would approve the president's
program, yet he recognized the need to conciliate
Northern opinion. On one hand he voiced his "white
man's government" conviction, on the other he urged
discretion in proclaiming the end of slavery. Stating
that Johnson was shielding the South from the "fanati-
cal crowd" of Radical Republicans, he wanted the
convention to satisfy the president's conditions.
The Anderson delegate subscribed to a general consensus.
The members desired peace, were resigned to the death
of slavery, but were deeply skeptical about the freedman's capacity to labor and survive. Uncertain about
the Negro's future, they authorized the provisional
governor to name a commission to frame a "black code."
Instituting the code would be a task for the new
legislature. The delegates also instructed the
legislature to establish "district courts" which would
hear all civil cases involving blacks and all criminal
charges against blacks.[14]

          *****   *****   *****   *****   *****

     Emotionally and physically stunned by the dislo-
cation of war, the Palmetto state did not experience
normal divisions of political opinion in 1865.
Throughout the South, with the exception of Louisiana,
there existed a resolve to avoid party organization
in choosing convention delegates, state officials,
and legislators. Editors and politicians recognized
that partisan activity might annoy the Republican
Congress. Moreover, at this critical time there was
a desire to present a united front to the North. In
three states--South Carolina, Georgia, and Mississippi
--governorship nominations were made by members of the
constitutional conventions. The shortness of time

between convention adjournments and election dates mainly accounts for this. In all of these states offers were tendered to well known figures who had not been prewar disunionists. The South Carolina delegates favored Wade Hampton, original opponent of secession and highly esteemed Confederate general. Believing that his election might displease the North, Hampton declined the bid.[15]

Almost unanimously the delegates signed a petition asking Orr, their second choice, to seek the office. The men who endorsed him represented, according to the Charleston Daily Courier, "nearly every political sentiment and interest" in the state. He was a familiar and respected politician, credited as one of the prime movers in the democratization of the state. The Columbia Daily Phoenix praised the Andersonian as the dominant person in the convention, while Perry remarked privately that he had "popularized the Constitution."[16]

There existed much resentment against the convention's action in establishing the popular governorship election and then naming one of its own members as a candidate. Hampton's friends undertook a campaign on his behalf, and only the general's stern refusal to run enabled Orr to win. In spite of his pleas, Hampton's backers amassed 9,185 votes for him against Orr's 9,927. The result was in doubt for several days after October 18, when about one-third of the eligible voters cast ballots.[17]

The immensely popular Hampton would have been elected easily if he had sought the office. In the public mind he was regarded as more fervently devoted to the Confederate cause than Orr. As the only announced candidate the Piedmont lawyer wondered if he had been repudiated by the large number who had preferred Hampton or declined to vote. Perry and former Congressman Armistead Burt of Abbeville dissuaded him from the notion of refusing to serve. Without enthusiasm the war-weary people accepted him as their chief magistrate. One reporter observed that the new governor was not beloved, not a Calhoun, rather he was looked to as "the man to manage a difficult problem among sharpers in politics." Here was a competent and experienced man who would work to protect his state's interests. In 1865 Orr was one of the few well known figures who could have been

satisfactory to both his own state and to the North.
The Republican Harper's Weekly declared that his
election would "afford gratification to the loyal
people of the country."[18]

***** ***** ***** ***** *****

On October 25, soon after the state elections,
the legislature convened in Columbia. The lawmakers
ratified the anti-slavery Thirteenth Amendment,
elected Perry and former Governor John L. Manning to
the United States Senate, and prepared to enact a
"black code." Obeying the convention's mandate,
Perry had appointed a committee to submit recommendations to the legislature.

Before the freedmen's law was passed, the new
governor took office. In his inaugural address he
urged kind treatment and full legal protection for
the blacks.

> The Convention and the Legislature,
> both recently elected by the people, have no
> doubt faithfully represented the sentiment
> of their constituents on this subject, and
> it cannot be doubted that, since the slave
> is emancipated, it is the fixed purpose of
> the people to secure to him his rights of
> person and property as a freedman -- that a
> just renumeration shall be paid him for his
> labor, and that he shall be protected against
> the fraud and violence of the artful and the
> lawless. . .They must be restrained from
> theft, idleness, vagrancy and crime, and
> taught the absolute necessity of strictly
> complying with their contracts for labor.
> They must be protected in their person
> and property; and, for a few years at least,
> some supervisory power should be established
> to ratify their contracts for labor, until
> their experience and increasing knowledge
> may teach them to guard against the craft
> of the unscrupulous.

To safeguard both the freedman and society, he asked
that the rules of evidence be modified to permit the
Negro to testify in all cases involving his rights.[19]

Taking a condescending but benign attitude, Orr
stated that the freedman's moral and intellectual
elevation should be promoted. As time passed he
became a leading advocate of public education for the
blacks. He spoke frankly of the need to treat them
decently, since they performed many vital tasks.

> The labor of every negro in the State
> is needed, if not to till the soil, in some
> other useful employment--for the culture
> of cotton and rice; and, in all menial
> occupations, it is very doubtful whether
> any laborers in this country or in Europe
> can supply his place. His long and thorough
> training in these employments give him a
> certain skill and aptitude which a stranger
> can only obtain by experience. It is, there-
> fore, of the first importance that such a
> policy should be adopted as will enable the
> farmers and planters to employ the negro,
> and that he should remain cheerful and
> contented.

In this address he spoke of the need for black labor,
but three weeks later he wrote privately that he
would accept colonization. "If you would advocate
the proposition to colonize the african race now in
this country, and make them a homogeneous people
apart from the whites I would concur with propriety."
In his private correspondence he noted that "thought-
ful people" doubted the possibility of whites and
blacks living together upon terms of "social and
political equality." They feared that such coexistence
would prove "degrading" to the white race.[20]

The Andersonian differed from many white Southern
leaders and opinion-makers in his position on colonization. Many conservative whites saw the Negroes as
an indispensable source of cheap labor to exploit.
However, the governor shared the widely held assumption that the freedmen were not prepared for the
responsibilities of free adults in society. In his
inaugural address he implied that the experience in
slavery had denied them such preparation. Because
the freedman had been recently relieved from the
restraints of slavery, his ignorance was excusable.[21]

He has been born and reared among us, and while
he has, unfortunately, qualities that stamp
his inferiority to the white man, he possesses
others that invite our respect. As a class,
during the war, their loyalty to their owners
and to society was worthy of the highest
commendation. In no single instance, even
where the slave population preponderated
over the whites as a hundred to one, was
there an outbreak or insurrection.

Soon after taking office Orr signed into law his
state's "black code." This statute reflected the pervasive opinion that the Negro lacked the self-disci-
pline necessary to survive in a free society. In 1865
and 1866 almost all of the former Confederate states
passed "black codes," the most severe being those of
South Carolina, Florida, and Mississippi. The Palmetto
state's code was drafted by Judge David Wardlaw and
former Congressman Armistead Burt, both of Abbeville,
members of the commission named by Perry. The freedman's legal rights were outlined, among them rights to
sue, make contracts, and hold property. Special district courts were created to hear all civil cases involving blacks and all criminal cases in which the
accused was black. Expensive licenses were required
to pursue work other than as farm workers and domestic
servants. One provision contained elaborate "Regula-
tions of Labor on Farms." Disobedience or disrespect
towards an employer, "vagrancy and idleness" were
among the offenses which could warrant judicial proceedings and punishment. Racial intermarriage was
banned.[22]

The "black code" provoked bitter denunciations
from the state's freedmen and from the North. Orr and
a minority in the legislature perceived that passage
of the code had been unwise. On December 10, he vetoed
a bill to amend the old patrol laws, asserting that the
abolition of slavery had rendered them obsolete; amendments would imply that the law still functioned. (This
was the first gubernatorial veto since the last royal
governor left office during the Revolutionary era.)
In January 1866 Sickles complied with his request that
enforcement of the "black code" be suspended. The
governor and the military commander had been friends
in prewar days as Democratic Congressmen, and their
relations were cordial.[23]

In his inaugural speech Orr had spoken kindly of the freedmen, and he came to recognize the unwisdom of the "black code." He did not, however, want them to think that society owed them a living or any special favors. In a proclamation of December 30, he admonished those Negroes who possessed neither land nor capital "to make contracts at once" for the year ahead. "They may be assured that the government will not give them lands, stock, or agricultural implements, nor will any food hereafter be furnished to those who are able to work." The blacks could elevate themselves and become respectable only by "sobriety, industry, economy and honesty."[24]

Although the Negro had to become self-sufficient, he could not, in Orr's judgment, be left unwatched and unprotected from his own baser instincts. In December the governor and many others voiced alarm over rumors of imminent Christmas day black insurrections. He told Sickles that while he did not anticipate trouble, he was disturbed by the likelihood of blacks congregating "in large numbers at the villages and towns where they will get liquor." He suggested that local garrisons be alerted.[25]

Orr also complained to Sickles that many blacks, expecting the government to divide the lands and stocks of the whites among them, were refusing to make contracts. Responsible for this expectation, he said, was the Freedmen's Bureau, which had given many blacks "a quasi land warrant for fifty acres, etc., on the Islands and perhaps the main land, and all expect to be recipients of the same bounty." He advised that the Freedmen's Bureau instruct the blacks to make contracts promptly. Those who failed to contract by mid-January and lacked visible means of support, he suggested, should then "be treated as vagrants and put to work by the United States authorities on public works, etc."[26]

In his famous Field Order Number Fifteen of January 1865, General William T. Sherman had set aside for the freedmen's use the Sea Island lands abandoned by their owners. The Freedmen's Bureau law of March 1865 allowed the blacks to pre-empt forty acres of the abandoned land, rent them for three years, and eventually purchase them. In September 1865 Johnson had ordered that all the confiscated lands, except those condemned for taxes in the Port Royal area during wartime, be restored to their former holders. The Freedmen's Bureau, under the leadership of Brigadier-General Rufus B. Saxton, its head in South Carolina, and Oliver Otis Howard, the national head, had been intentionally dilatory in enforcing Johnson's decree. Saxton and Howard worked against the former owners who tried to reclaim the lands. Orr viewed this situation as unfortunate, encouraging many landless blacks to believe that land grants were forthcoming. In the lower part of South Carolina "scarcely a contract has been or can be made." In his words, the contested area was looked to as "a land of promise for every indolent freedman in the State." In January 1866 he wrote Johnson that the Sea Island lands should be restored to their former holders. In the following month, however, he proposed to Francis W. Pickens that the planters in the state ought to divide their lands into forty and fifty acre sections which the blacks could occupy and till.[27]

Orr's values were those of an individualistic and competitive society, and also of a racist democracy. Within the traditional white supremacist order he wanted the freedmen to be treated kindly, but he was determined that they should earn everything that they received. His attitude contained elements of both compassion and contempt. He did not want the black population to be increased. In antebellum days he had opposed revival of the African slave trade, and in 1865 he was agreeable to colonization. This up country spokesman retained his dream of a more diversified economy, based upon an enlarged white population.

He wanted an enterprising spirit and the self-help values to animate both races. As one newspaper commented, the governor was imbued with "the progressive spirit of the age." At the 1865 convention he was quoted as saying privately, "I am tired of South Carolina as she was. I covet for her the material prosperity of New England. I would have her acres teem with life and vigor and industry and intelligence, as do those of Massachusetts." In his inaugural address he noted that the mechanic, the manufacturer, and the artisan had not been encouraged to enter the state, nor had the native people pursued these employments sufficiently.[28]

Our first great want is enterprise and
industry--if we will them we command them.
Our next great want is skilled labor--this
must come from the North and from Europe;
it will not come if we do not invite it
and extend the hand of friendship to the
immigrant.

During the early Reconstruction years a number of
politicians, journalists, and planters urged the im-
portation of white labor. Some reasoned that the free
black workers would not survive and that white immigrants should be available to replace them. Others
hoped that incoming white laborers would impel the
Negroes and native whites to work harder. This movement to promote white immigration, which reflected
a general pessimism about the Negro as a free laborer,
proved inconsequential during the Reconstruction
period. However, during his governorship Orr entertained hopes for its success.[29]

In his inaugural speech he predicted that Southerners would soon regain all of their rights in the
Union, and he believed that Congress might compensate
the former slaveholders for the manumission of their
slaves. His optimism, shared by other Southern
leaders, was based upon the expectation that Andrew
Johnson would triumph over his Republican antagonists.
In the absence of pressure from Washington Orr and
most white Southerners were reluctant to make concessions to the freedmen. The issue of black
suffrage provides an example. In August 1865 provisional Governor Perry had declared that Johnson
regarded suffrage as a strictly internal question, to
be determined only by the states. Perry's statement
attracted much attention and interest throughout
the country. When black voting was defeated in
several Northern states and territories in 1865,
many Southerners concluded that this was not a popular
cause in the North.[30]

In December 1865 Orr wrote privately that he would
consider Negro suffrage, but he wanted it on the
South's terms, not on the conqueror's. He expressed
his thoughts to Republican Congressman William D.
Kelley of Pennsylvania, who wanted to enfranchise the
freedmen by federal legislation. The governor contended that Kelley's plan would deny to the South a
traditional right of states in the Union, "the right
to make their own laws." He wanted the suffrage

108

matter left exclusively to the states. "Where all or
a portion" of the blacks were qualified "by experience
education & moral elevation" to vote, they would not
be kept from the ballot box. The South Carolinian
belabored Kelley for inconsistency, noting that in
Pennsylvania arbitrary standards were set, "founded
no doubt on good reasons," while the Congressman
would not permit another state to establish its standards.

> You preclude women of the highest intelligence
> from the privileges of the ballot box. You
> say that your own sons--though they may have
> received the degree of M.A. at your highest
> seats of learning shall not exercise the
> elective franchise till they attain the age
> of twenty one. . .

> But you do not wish to allow us who
> are brethren in the same union the same
> privilege. You are for enfranchising them
> if they can read. The ability to read
> furnishes you no knowledge of the princi-
> ples morals or worth of the person. Look
> to the prison houses in the whole country
> & see how many of the convicts who can read
> & write have perpetrated the most enormous
> crimes against society.

In effect he rebuked Kelley for favoring a criterion
in the South which was not used in his own Northern
community. He observed that South Carolina had been
among the first states to grant universal white
suffrage, yet he would not support it for blacks. He
implied that the Negro must prove his fitness by education and moral character to vote, although the whites
in his state had never been required to undergo testing
for literacy and character.[31]

The governor resented the idea of outside interference in his state's domestic affairs. Who, he
asked Kelley, is more interested in making South
Carolina's Negroes honest, industrious, intelligent,
and moral--the white South Carolinians or the Congressman's constitutents in Pennsylvania? "If he is vicious,
idle or desperate who are to suffer most? If he is
dishonest whose property does he prey upon?"[32]

***** ***** ***** ***** *****

At this time, in December 1865, the Republican-controlled Congress had recently refused to seat the Southern delegations. The Republicans maintained that the South was not acting in good faith towards the Union and the freedmen. The belief persisted that Johnson's restoration procedures did not require of the South sufficient guarantees for the Negro's welfare. Enactment of "black codes," the elections of former Confederate leaders to Congress and state offices, and indiscreet statements by several Southern politicians, raised suspicions. (Many Northerners feared that Southern mistreatment of the freedmen might encourage black migrations into the North.) The majority party in Congress would not yield to Johnson, the South, and their likely allies in the Northern Democracy the controlling voice in restoration policy.[33]

During the early months of 1866 the gulf between Johnson and the Republicans widened. Many moderate Republicans, not inclined towards harsh reconstruction measures, were dismayed by Johnson's vetoes of the Freedmen's Bureau Bill and the Civil Rights Bill. (Congress overrode vetoes of both bills, although an initial veto of the former was sustained.) The Civil Rights Bill became the nucleus of the first section of the Fourteenth Amendment, which Congress passed in June and sent to the states. The amendment's first section restated the Civil Rights Bill. The second section reduced the Congressional representation of states which disfranchised any adult male citizens. Black suffrage was left at the option of the states, which could reject it at the cost of reduced representation. The third section barred from federal and state offices persons who, having previously taken an oath to the United States Constitution, supported the rebellion. (By a two-thirds vote Congress could waive this disability.) The fourth section empowered Congress to enforce the amendment.

By the spring of 1866 the amendment was the leading issue in reconstruction. The Republicans demanded Southern ratification as the price for readmittance. When Johnson urged the South to reject the amendment, the lines were drawn between the president and his Republican adversaries in the critical election year of 1866.

Watching the developing contest, Orr was regularly advised by William Henry Trescot, his agent in Washington. The general picture that Trescot conveyed was of a fluid political situation. South Carolina's governor expected that the president would be sustained in the Northern elections. Working for his state's representation in the National Union convention, he anticipated a strong coalition of Johnson supporters throughout the country.[34]

The president's Northern backers had organized the National Union Club in March, and by the late spring the various pro-Johnson clubs in Washington were merged with the National Union Club. A convention was planned in order that a national party could be established, holding all the Republicans except the Radicals and absorbing the Northern and Western Democrats. Southern support was expected. In the North the movement attracted many men whose status in the major parties was anomalous--marginal figures in the Republican party, and War Democrats who detested the Copperhead influence in the regular Democratic organization.[35]

With mixed feelings Southern politicians looked to the national meeting, scheduled for mid-August in Philadelphia. Inactive in national politics since the war's end, they were sympathetic but initially aloof. As they gained the impression that the convention might be successful, they moved towards participation.[36]

Launched in early July, the campaign to promote South Carolina's representation drew a mildly favorable response. The press was restrained but agreeable. In early August the Charleston _Daily Courier_ observed that public opinion was adverse to any participation aside from "an earnest but _quiet_ endorsement of President Johnson."[37]

On July 4, Orr issued his call for South Carolina's representation. In his words, the Philadelphia meeting provided the first opportunity in five years for communication between the South and other sections. He was confident that most Northerners and Westerners would sustain Johnson and concede to the Southerners their status as equals in the Union.

The compact organization of the conservative men is a necessity to meet successfully
the well-organized bands of the radicals, and
every man who disapproves of the tyrannical
and unwise policy of the latter, should join
in this national patriotic league to defeat
them.

We are without representation in both
houses of Congress; neither our opinions nor
conditions can be officially known to the
country; unjust and discriminating taxes are
imposed on us--a people sadly impoverished
by the calamities of the last five years--
and we are allowed no voice of protest even
in the councils of the nation. Our loyalty
to the Government of the United States is
impugned in the face of our oaths of allegiance, taken solemnly and in good faith, and
the poor privilege of an official denial is
withheld. We are threatened with disfranchisement and being remanded to a   territorial condition, and we are to be denied
all the rights and privileges dear to an
American, and consecrated by the blood of
the heroes of 1776, until we subscribe to
terms too degrading and humiliating to be
entertained by a free man for a single
moment.

The "degrading and humiliating" terms were the provisions of the Fourteenth Amendment. This opinion
was held by other Southern leaders, who suspected that
acceptance of the amendment would not satisfy the
Republican Congress. The notion existed that further
demands, such as unconditional black suffrage, might
be imposed.[38]

Later in the year Orr confided to Alexander H.
Stephens that he could tolerate the amendment's second
and fourth sections, which dealt with the suffrage-
representation question and rebel war debts. However,
he insisted that approval would be foolish, leaving the
South vulnerable to more pressures. He asked what
assurance existed that ratification "would secure us
even our shorn representation?" In his words, favorable
statements about any part of the amendment would involve
"a shameful abandonment of President Johnson & his
policy."[39]

On August 1, the Conservative Union convention of
South Carolina assembled in Columbia, with only a
few districts in the state not represented. Orr,
chosen president of the body, admitted that the movement might fail, but "it is neither wise nor philoso-
phic to cower before the calamities by which we are
overtaken." He entertained no doubts about the Radical Republican designs. Besides attempting a "speedy
seizure" of the judiciary, they sought dominion over
the legislative and executive branches. They would,
if victorious in the fall elections, move to impeach
Johnson. Should the National Union campaign be
effective, the president's foes might lose their two-
thirds majority in Congress, and Johnson's vetoes
could prevail against their "obnoxious legislation."
The Columbia body named delegates to the national
gathering. The governor was one of them.[40]

On Monday evening, August 13, before the
national assemblage convened, Orr addressed a Democratic rally in Philadelphia. In his opening remarks
he spoke of his friendship with Stephen A. Douglas.
The late Illinois senator had been the Northern
Democrats' presidential choice in 1860, and by referring to him, the South Carolinian sought to present
himself as a moderate. His main purpose was to per-
suade his listeners that the South wanted peace.
The issues of the war had been irrevocably settled,
he declared, and surely the dreadful contest would not
be renewed.[41]

> This is my Government; it is to be my children's
> and grandchildren's Government. As a partici-
> pant in the rebellion, I am now for this Govern-
> ment, and its honor is my honor. I desire
> it to stand before all nations of the earth, in
> all its glory and pride and prosperity of a
> great nation of the world. Fellow citizens,
> we have been knocking at the door for eight
> long months asking Congress that the best of
> the intellectual and the leading men of the
> South shall be admitted into Congress to repre-
> sent us there. If we are not to be trusted
> now, when are we? Is it just or right that we
> should be excluded from these privileges? No;
> for the right of representation is regarded as
> one of the most sacred rights in this country.
> Is it just, or fair, or generous that we
> should be excluded from legislation while taxes
> are imposed upon us without our consent?

113

On the following day the Massachusetts delegates, composed entirely of Democrats, called upon the South Carolinians and suggested that they enter the convention hall together. As they entered, the presiding officer, Alexander Randall, announced their appearance "arm-in-arm." This incident attracted attention, as delegates and spectators rose to cheer. Orr and General Darius Couch of Massachusetts led their states in an entry which gained for the body the designation of "arm-in-arm convention."[42]

The delgates encountered a thorny problem in the presence of Copperheads. So bitter was the feeling against Clement L. Vallandigham, prominent anti-war Ohioan, that some states contemplated withdrawal if he were admitted. The Southerners were asked to oppose the seating of Northerners who had been stigmatized because of their wartime stand. Orr responded affirmatively to this appeal. On Sunday, August 12, he was persuaded to approach Vallandigham and urge him not to take his seat. Perry reluctantly agreed to accompany the governor, who told the Ohioan that his withdrawal would promote harmony in the convention. The Copperhead replied that his voluntary removal would be an implicit confession of dishonor. He challenged the right of Southerners to attend while Northerners who had sympathized with the South were barred. Perry was impressed by these arguments. Orr, in contrast, viewed him as ambitious and selfish, and he suggested that South Carolina abstain from voting should the Vallandigham issue be raised. Perry vehemently objected, but the majority consented. Before this unpleasant matter could be brought to the floor, however, Vallandigham withdrew.[43]

The attitudes of the two South Carolinians revealed basic differences in political temperaments. When Orr proposed that the state abstain from voting on an exclusion motion, Perry protested that "sooner than see Vallandigham treated so unjustly, the convention might break up and go to perdition." He thought it impolitic and ungrateful for Southerners to act against this true friend of theirs. Rigid and tactless, Perry would not compromise for the sake of accommodating Northern opinion. Between the two, Orr had the keener sense of public relations. More flexible and conciliatory, he was subjected throughout his career to the charge of opportunism--a charge that could never have been levelled against Perry.[44]

114

The convention's pro-Johnson platform upheld the right of all states to Congressional representation, acknowledged the invalidity of rebel war debts and the death of slavery, and denied that Congress could regulate the suffrage in the states. Southern reaction to the convention was favorable, and the participation of the section's leaders helped to turn opinion against the Fourteenth Amendment.[45]

***** ***** ***** ***** *****

Upon returning from Philadelphia, Orr called a special legislative session, which began on September 5. His recommendations embraced repeal of the "black code" and the establishment of uniform law enforcement procedures for both races. Convinced that the federal military authority would disallow district court jurisdiction over the freedmen, he had not commissioned any judges. He criticized the law that barred Negro testimony in cases in which blacks had no direct interest. This discrimination he termed indefensible, having its foundation in "a prejudice against the caste of the Negro." In civil cases the black's testimony would often be necessary to secure a just verdict.[46]

> In criminal cases, these considerations weigh
> with peculiar force. The negro is readily
> deceived and corrupted, and becomes an easy
> prey to the machinations of depraved white
> men; and past experience teaches that he is
> employed to execute the most dishonest pur-
> poses, and with impunity to the principal,
> because of his exclusion as a witness from
> the Courts of Justice . . . will the law of
> the State continue to offer a reward to the
> dishonest to further tempt and corrupt the
> negro? The well-being of the State materially
> depends upon the elevation of this class of
> our population, and if there was no other
> argument in behalf of their accessibility
> to our Courts, the tendency of such a measure
> to elevate their moral and intellectual
> character would be sufficient.

In September and at the regular December session the lawmakers' response to this advice was generally affirmative. New legislation specified that Negro testimony would be heard in all cases, and the district courts became inferior tribunals for civil and criminal cases involving blacks and whites. In October General

115

Sickles, who had previously suspended enforcement of
the "black code" and the operation of the district
courts, permitted the civil courts to function. Orr
was satisfied that his state had adequately complied
with the North's demands, and he regarded continued
Republican insistence upon the Fourteenth Amendment as
unreasonable. He told Alexander H. Stephens,[47]

> The legislature of this state at its extra
> session passed every law with reference to
> freedmen that is demanded by the most ex-
> acting interpretation of the Civil rights
> act. They are not permitted to go to the
> ballot box nor to intermarry with whites but
> all other rights of person & property are
> secured and enforced before the same tri-
> bunals as whites.
>
> They are allowed to give evidence in
> all cases and at the present fall courts
> where many of them have been sworn the
> impression is universally favorable to
> the change admitting them.
>
> What then can we do? Will any
> Northern republican have enough of patrio-
> tism and sense of justice to propose in
> Congress this winter a material modifica-
> tion of the amendment? I fear not and it
> seems to me that sound policy & true dig-
> nity demands if we are to be pursued with
> other degrading exactions that we should
> require its imposition by others and not
> do the deed ourselves. Self respect at
> least will then be preserved.

The National Union movement failed to turn the
North against the Republicans, who emerged from the
1866 fall elections with their Congressional majorities
increased. As the elections approached Southern politicians were privately discouraged, although they
generally believed that Johnson's campaign tour, rather
than the Philadelphia convention, had damaged their
cause. In October Orr told Georgia's Governor Charles
H. Jenkins that whatever good resulting from the convention had been "dissipated" by the president's trip
in the West.[48]

116

The election returns did not deter the Southern leaders from their opposition to the Fourteenth Amendment, and they still believed that the North would eventually repudiate any severe reconstruction program. South Carolina's governor expressed this view, telling Jenkins that the Republican majorities in the next Congress were not "overwhelming." If Johnson would stand firm, the Radicals would not attempt impeachment, "and if they do they will fail or produce a revolution at the North." He repeated this point to Georgia's Herschel V. Johnson, predicting that the more moderate Republicans would restrain the Radicals. He forecast a Radical attempt to impose black suffrage, nullify the present Southern governments, and establish "territorial or military" regimes.

> Provide for the calling of new State conven-
> tions--authorize the negroes to vote and
> exclude every white man who bore arms or in
> any other way aided the Southern Confederacy
> during the war. There will be a section of
> the party who will be contented to do no
> more than exclude us from representation in
> Congress and if they are as strong as I
> anticipate they will be it is probable that
> we may be spared the anarchy which the more
> extreme men would willingly precipitate in
> the country.

> We are powerless to help ourselves in
> this hour of our greatest need.

Orr continued to oppose ratification of the Fourteenth Amendment, advising that the South agree to no further conditions offered by the conqueror. The more sub-missive his section became, "the more exacting, tyrannical, and humiliating to us become their demands."[49]

He did not interpret the Republican election vic-tories as precluding continued Southern attempts to manipulate the reconstruction process. His outlook reflected the considerable fluidity in the 1866 political picture. Because the national cimate of opinion was difficult to assess, differing appraisals of the Northern elections seemed plausible. In the face of Republican victories, many Southerners believed that a settlement could be bargained for on their terms. They doubted that the Fourteenth Amendment enjoyed substantial support in the North. In their minds its defeat was

117

certain if the South spurned it. The Charleston
Daily Courier predicted that numbers of Northern
people would leave the Radical ranks. "They will
tolerate no extreme measures, such as impeachment,
confiscation, negro suffrage, etc., and care not a
straw for the constitutional amendment." One historian,
Avery Craven, concludes that few Northern voters in
1866 understood precisely what their vote implied.
Nonetheless, most Northerners accepted the Fourteenth
Amendment, which represented their section's commitment to protect the freedman's rights, and they wanted
an end to reconstruction.[50]

Opening the regular legislative session on November 27, Orr praised the new law authorizing black
testimony in all cases, and he spoke of the freedman's
honesty on the witness stand. This law was important
in elevating his "moral sense." The Negroes he
described as invaluable to South Carolina's productive
resources; he wanted to discourage them from migrating
to other states. About one year ago, in December 1865,
the governor had been privately amenable to black
colonization. Now he was publicly asking them to remain.

> If the Negro remains here, his labor must be
> made sufficiently renumerative to subsist
> and clothe him comfortably. Schools must be
> established to educate his children, and
> churches built for his moral training.

> The experiment of free labor, whilst it
> has not been entirely satisfactory, is far
> from proving a failure. Where the blacks
> have been adequately compensated and kindly
> treated, they have generally labored faith-
> fully.

At this time there was a westward movement among Southern
blacks, who were lured by the hope of better wages and
richer lands.[51]

The legislative message contained a scathing attack
on the Fourteenth Amendment. The third section, the
disabling clause, would "necessarily result in perjury
on the part of those who attempt to fill such offices,
or to anarchy, if they are not filled." The first and
fifth sections he saw as subverting "the theory and
practice of the Government since its foundation." Congress would have absolute power, Orr declared, to deter-

mine who should be citizens of the respective states,
eligible to vote, and able to enjoy all the rights of
citizenship.

> With this amendment incorporated in the
> Constitution, does not the Federal Govern-
> ment cease to be one of "limited powers" in
> all of the essential qualities which con-
> stitute such a form of Government? Nay,
> more; does not its adoption reverse the
> well-approved doctrine, that the United
> States shall exercise no powers, unless
> expressly delegated by the Constitution?

As in the past, he asserted that ratification would
carry no guarantee that Southern representatives would
be seated in Congress. Rather, there were "unmistakable indications" that they would be excluded.[52]

Johnson's continued opposition to the amendment
stiffened Southern resistance to Republican demands
for approval. By the end of 1866 most of the section's
legislatures, including South Carolina's, had defeated
the amendment. Southern politicians looked ahead to
a period of bargaining between themselves and the
Republican Congress. They believed that the crucial
issues of reconstruction and black suffrage were
still negotiable between the victor and the vanquished.[53]

VII. "ACCEPTING THE SITUATION" 1867

By late 1866 the Congressional Republicans had
reached an impasse over Reconstruction policy. Moderates favored approval of the Fourteenth Amendment as
the quid pro quo for Southern restoration. Radicals
refused to commit themselves to the amendment as the
final condition. Northern moderates and conservatives
generally agreed that Southern acquiescence in the
amendment would have been sufficient. Against heavy
Congressional backing for the amendment, Johnson remained obdurate, and the South stood by its strategy
of "masterly inactivity." From the president and the
Northern Democrats, the former Confederate states received assurances that Congress could not make the
restoration process more drastic than it already was.[1]

When some Southerners entertained second thoughts
about the amendment, Johnson advised them not to bend.
In December 1866 South Carolina legislator T. C.
Weatherly conferred with leading Republican Congressmen,
who informed him that acceptance of the amendment would
secure his state's representation in Congress. Weatherly
also consulted Johnson, whose position was unchanged, and
South Carolina stood by the president. In the following
month Alabama Governor R. M. Patton asked his state to
reconsider. Johnson's opposition was publicized, and
the legislature reaffirmed its earlier refusal. Taking
their signals from the president, the South held the
line against ratification.[2]

Perturbed by this intransigence, the Republicans
attempted to forge new legislation. Pennsylvania's
Thaddeus Stevens wanted reorganized Southern governments with universal male suffrage. John Bingham of
Ohio suggested recognition of the incumbent governments on condition that they approve the amendment
and institute impartial suffrage. In early 1867, while
the Stevens and Bingham wings bickered, several Southern
leaders journeyed to Washington to present an alterna-
tive. Satisfied that the Fourteenth Amendment faced
slim prospects of success, they were confident of
their power to bargain. These men overestimated
Johnson's strength against Congress, and they misjudged
the temper of the majority party.[3]

In January Orr went to Washington and conferred
with several leading Republicans. He then joined
other Southern spokesmen, among them Governors
Jonathan Worth of North Carolina, R. M. Patton of
Alabama, and former Governors William E. Sharkey of
Mississippi and Lewis Parsons of Alabama. In con-
sulation with Johnson and some Northern conservatives,
they decided that North Carolina should take the
initiative by offering a constitutional amendment:

Section 1. The Union under the Constitution
is, and shall be perpetual. No state shall
pass any law or ordinance to secede or withdraw from the Union, and any such law or
ordinance shall be null and void.

Section 2. The public debt of the United
States, authorized by law, shall ever be
held sacred and inviolate. But neither
the United States nor any other State shall
assume or pay any debt or obligation incurred
in aid of insurrection or rebellion against
the government or authority of the United
States.

Section 3. All persons born or naturalized
in the United States, and subject to the
jurisdiction thereof, are citizens of the
United States, and the States in which they
reside. No state shall make or enforce any
law which shall abridge the privileges or
immunities of citizens of the United States;
nor shall any State deprive any person of
life, liberty, or property, without the due
process of law, or deny to any person within its jurisdiction the equal protection of
the laws.

Section 4. Representatives shall be apportioned among the several States according
to their respective numbers, counting the
whole number of persons in each State,
excluding Indians not taxed. But when any
State shall, on account of race or color,
or previous condition of servitude, exclude
from voting at any election for the choice
of electors for President and Vice-President
of the United States, Representatives in
Congress, members of the Legislature or other
officers elective by the people, any of the
inhabitants of such State, being twenty-one

years of age and citizens of the United
States, then the entire class of persons
so excluded from the elective franchise,
shall not be counted in the basis of
representation. No State shall require
as a property qualification for voters
more than two hundred and fifty dollars
worth of taxable property, nor as an
educational qualification more education
than enough to enable the voter to read
the Constitution in the English language
and write his own name.

In addition to an amendment to the United States Constitution, the "North Carolina Plan," as this proposal was called, embraced an amendment which each
state would add to its constitution:

Every male citizen who has resided in
this State for one year, and in the country
in which he offers to vote six months
immediately preceding the day of election,
and who can read the Constitution of the
United States in the English language, or
who may be the owner of two hundred and
fifty dollars worth of taxable property,
shall be entitled to vote at all elections
for Governor of this State, members of the
Legislature, and all other officers elective
by the people of the State: provided, that
no person shall, by reason of this article,
be excluded from voting who has heretofore
exercised the elective franchise under the
Constitution and laws of this State, or
who, at the time of the adoption of this
amendment, may be entitled to vote under
said Constitution and laws.

This plan differed from the Republican-sponsored Fourteenth Amendment by providing for impartial suffrage
and by its omission of a disabling clause. It did
not, however, offer universal amnesty.[4]

With this program the Southern leaders were
abandoning "masterly inactivity" in dealing with
Congress. They sought to capitalize upon Republican
divisions, negate the 1866 election results, and
unite the North behind Johnson. Persuaded that the
proposal had a reasonable chance of success, the
president gave his support. Copies of the North

Carolina Plan were sent to all of the Southern governments, with a letter from its chief sponsors, who
declared that the way was open to a final reconstruction
settlement. Johnson sent telegrams to the Southern
legislatures still in session, urging adoption, and
Senator James Dixon of Connecticut, a conservative
Republican, submitted the plan to the Congressional
Joint Committee on Reconstruction.[5]

The sponsors erred in thinking that an appreciable
number of Republican moderates would back the plan. In
the North it failed to arouse interest, and the Democratic press was mostly silent. The South was initially
friendly to the program, since its managers were prominent Southerners and Johnson had endorsed it. However,
as support for the plan failed to materialize in Congress, the Southern legislatures and press dissociated
themselves from it. The section's dominant opinion was
that "masterly inactivity" would be less painful than
the humiliation of a rebuff. Newspapers that spoke
out raised the matter of "honor."[6]

Returning to South Carolina in early February, Orr
was not aware that his labors had been fruitless, and
he expected to convene the legislature after North
Carolina acted. In a Charleston speech on February 13,
he discussed his private conversations with several
moderate Republicans, who had expressed the desire for
"a perfect and complete settlement." Then some of
these same men delivered Congressional orations "of
the most violent character." If North Carolina adopted
the program and other Southern states did likewise,
he predicted, such action would impress "a considerable
portion of the Radical party, and save the South from
many of the proposed Radical measures."[7]

The governor scolded those people who would fold
their arms, remain passive, and rest upon "dignity."
In his judgment, the defeated states had to take positive steps to assure Congress of good intentions towards
the Union and the freedmen.[8]

I have believed in our doing something for
ourselves. I have believed in indicating
to this people that there is no sullenness
at least on the part of the people of the
South, that we were prepared to give them
all honorable guarantees to secure their
rights in the Government, and when we did
so, we at least challenged the respect of
the honest portion of that party.

Moreover, in his view, the protection of Southern interests required representation as soon as possible. He made this point at a Negro meeting in Charleston on February 14, citing the federal cotton tax as a harmful measure; Southern representation in Congress would combat such legislation. The North Carolina Plan, he believed, would secure the necessary representation on terms satisfactory to the South. He was agreeable to impartial suffrage for both races as the price for representation.

> One of the features of this programme, recently published, provides that the Legislature of North Carolina shall call a Convention, and that Convention shall provide, by an amendment to its Constitution, to give to every male citizen able to read and write, of all classes, the privilege of voting, but if not able to read and write, then it is proposed that every one worth $250 shall have that privilege. That proposition has received the sanction of some of the most distinguished Southern gentlemen in this country . . . I trust that we will be able to secure representation. I am prepared to stand by the colored man who is able to read the Declaration of Independence and the Constitution of the United States. I am prepared to give the colored man the privilege of going to the ballot box and vote.

Although desiring Negro and white approval of the North Carolina Plan, with impartial suffrage, Orr did not want the blacks to expect universal suffrage. Presently, he maintained, the average freedman was not sufficiently educated to benefit from the vote. Moreover, the Negro should be too busy working to concern himself with politics.

> Do not trouble yourselves upon the subject of politics. I think your people might profit very much by the experience that some of us white people have had in South Carolina. I think the more you work and look after your own business and economise your own time the better.

> Do not stand at street corners idling away a half hour talking politics, but go to work. You will find it much more to your interest to work and keep clear of politics and all such subjects.

125

There was an incongruity in this speech. He wanted
the South to recognize the connection between Congressional representation and the protection of its
economic interests (e.g., opposing the federal cotton
tax). At the same time he did not want the Negro to
notice any connection between politics and his personal welfare.[9]

The chief executive encountered disappointment.
In North Carolina the compromise plan was received
unenthusiastically and withdrawn after being introduced in the legislature. The sentiment existed that
backing the proposal would bring defeat and loss of
self-respect. Governor Worth, one of the original
framers, became pessimistic. He wrote Orr that there
was almost no objection to a limited black suffrage,
but he feared that the Negroes would construe the
North Carolina Plan as granting them the right to
hold public office. It might appear that the states
were restrained "from denying to a negro any privilege
accorded to a white man." Elsewhere in the South and
in Congress the plan died.[10]

Frankly displeased, Orr maintained that prompt
acceptance by North Carolina, and its return to
Washington by mid-February, would have influenced
Congress favorably. "The delay however has enabled
the Extremists to prepare measures and force the
moderate radicals to vote in favor of the revolutionary
propositions emanating from Williams, Elliott, and
Stevens." His talks in Washington had satisfied him
that a sufficient number of moderate Republicans would
have broken with the extremists. In his view, a better
managed Southern effort would have won over enough
moderate Republicans to achieve success. He especially
regretted Alexander Stephens' absence from Washington
at a critical time.[11]

> Your presence and counsels would have proved
> invaluable in reaching a solution of our
> difficulties, favorable to the South. Many
> of the Radicals were in a good frame of mind
> to be impressed by moderate counsels, but
> we had so few Southern men in the city at
> the time, that the opportunities for doing
> good were partially lost.

In reality the situation was not so fluid as he had anticipated. Developments in early 1867 had actually pushed the Republican party into a more rigid stance. On January 28, many House moderates had, by votes and abstentions, helped to table Thaddeus Stevens' bill which looked to land confiscation. At the same time they considered the Fourteenth Amendment a fair settlement, and they were perturbed by the South's rejection of it. The South's apparent intransigence disillusioned many Northerners who wished only a minimum of coercion against the former Confederates. Moreover, reports that Southern unionists and blacks were being mistreated affected Northern opinion adversely. Now the Congress would have nothing less than compulsory black suffrage and greater federal interference in Southern political life than the Fourteenth Amendment had specified.[12]

Uncertain about the future, Orr saw "nothing left for us but to bear with courage and fortitude, such enormities as the heartless conqueror may choose to impose." The conqueror's terms were outlined in the Reconstruction Act of March 2, 1867, and in subsequent laws passed on March 23 and June 19, 1867, and March 11, 1868. The ten "unreconstructed" states were divided into five military districts. (The two Carolinas comprised one of these districts.) The military authorities were directed to register the eligible voters, including all blacks and excluding those persons disqualified by the Fourteenth Amendment. The voters would decide in a referendum whether to hold a constitutional convention. If the majority of eligible voters spoke positively, a convention would be held. If the majority failed to vote affirmatively, the state would remain under military rule indefinitely. The new constitution had to provide universal black suffrage. After the state ratified the Fourteenth Amendment, and the Congress approved its new constitution, representation in Congress would be restored.[13]

As the Reconstruction Acts took effect, the civil government in South Carolina became provisional, existing on the sufferance of the federal military commander. Sickles, who retained his post in the two Carolinas, permitted the state governments to continue in office. In the previous fall he had expressed satisfaction with the administration of civil affairs in these states, and in March 1867 he announced that there would be as little change as possible. Orr would occupy the governorship until a new regime could

be installed; thereafter he was disqualified from
holding office. The military authorities prepared to
register the eligible voters for the referendum,
scheduled for November.[14]

***** ***** ***** ***** *****

In early 1867 the Southern leaders had reasoned
that Republican divisions or Congressional stalemate
would work to their advantage. When the first Reconstruction Act was passed, they knew that their cal-
culations were discredited. The strategy of "masterly
inactivity" was an obvious disaster. Revising their
assessments, the Southern spokesmen knew that the new
legislation would be enforced. In late February
Georgia's former Governor Joseph E. Brown, returning
from a Washington trip, declared that his region must
accept the Congressional program or face sterner
measures. This message was echoed throughout the
South during the spring. In states with large black
populations, like South Carolina, Mississippi, and
Louisiana, the wisdom of compliance seemed clear. In
March Wade Hampton and black leader W. Beverly Nash
told a Negro meeting in Columbia that the races should
strive for harmony and political equality. At the
same time the South Carolina press was giving solid
support to acquiescence in the Congressional policy.[15]

Orr's position mirrored the new realism. Disliking
a universal black suffrage, he nonetheless urged the
eligible white voters to approve the Congressional program. With a black majority looming, he realized that
white opposition would be futile. For the next two
years, he pointed out in Charleston on April 2, Congress
was secure in its power. He would not dispute, in
the United States Supreme Court or elsewhere, Congressional authority to pass the Reconstruction Acts.
He also warned that harsher penalties, possibly confiscation, might be inflicted upon a defiant South.[16]

> Looking, therefore, to the interests of the
> great mass of the people of South Carolina,
> and believing that the threat of confiscation
> will not be carried into effect if we accept
> the terms of this bill; and believing that
> confiscation will follow if we do not; knowing
> also that we shall be benefitted by its accep-
> tance, I say that, as my humble judgment, in-
> terest and wisdom dictate that we shall concur
> in the measure proposed by Congress.

In his view, the state's economic life would remain paralyzed until "political relations" were reestablished with Washington. While he considered disfranchisement unwise, excluding many able people from public affairs, he would bear it. Especially distasteful to him was the bestowal of universal black suffrage, with the prospect that many Negroes would be swayed by evil men. In contrast, he believed, a qualified suffrage would have induced prospective voters to become educated and, consequently, better citizens.

> It is, therefore, to our interest to give
> them an intellectual character; and it is
> your interest further that the black man
> shall vote with you in the common election.
> I have heard a great deal said of controlling
> the vote of the black man. It has been
> supposed that his vote will be controlled by
> personal influences, and notwithstanding his
> convictions of interest, but you are mistaken.
> That vote is destined to be controlled not
> by personal considerations, but by going to
> the black man and talking to him in private
> conversation, and proving to him that his
> interest in South Carolina is your interest.
> I think it can be shown to any rational
> black man that it is to his interest to make
> his friends here rather than in the State of
> Massachusetts.

Not by intimidation could the Southern whites control the Negro votes. Rather, Orr maintained, the whites had to convince the blacks that their common interests required unity.[17]

In his view, racial harmony in South Carolina had to be attained outside of the two national parties. The Democrats, he contended, had tried to make selfish use of the 1866 National Union convention. Then, after advising the South to reject the Fourteenth Amendment, they had played a role in passing the Reconstruction Acts. The governor opposed the Republicans as well, blaming them for the oppressive cotton tax. This outlook was common among Southern politicians. Much feeling existed that Andrew Johnson and the Democratic party had been untrustworthy friends of the former Confederate states. The opinion existed that the region should pursue neutrality between the two major parties until the reconstruction question was settled. In Columbia in late April, Orr suggested

that the South "go back into the Union, holding the
balance of power, and then both parties will court us."
He wanted the blacks and whites to form a non-partisan
alliance which could bargain with the national parties.[18]

Fearful that the illiterate blacks would become
a formidable political force, the governor did not
want the whites to lose influence by default. In
Anderson on June 3, he urged the whites to support
the convention call and elect delegates. Only in
this way could they prevent the ignorant, and consequently the barbarian and tyrant, from gaining power.
Because of the black numerical preponderance, he
argued, the whites could not defeat the convention
call or protect themselves in any direct contest with
the Negroes.[19]

During the spring and early summer of 1867 the
belief was widely held in the South that conservative
whites would command the freedman's political
allegiance. It was expected that the blacks would
turn to native whites, with whom they were familiar,
rather than to outsiders. Several conservative white
politicians made overtures to the Negroes, stressing
the theme of mutual interests between the races. The
highly respected Wade Hampton asked the freedmen to
shun the outsiders and follow their former masters.
He asked the blacks to choose as convention delegates
"men whom you know to be honest and trustworthy, and
who are identified with the State." If an unsatis-
factory constitution were drafted, Hampton observed,
the freedmen had the option of rejecting it and
calling another convention.[20]

Counteracting the conservative white bid were
the Union Leagues, political clubs which worked to
recruit the blacks as Republicans. The Republican
party, which became organized in the state in the
spring, presented itself as the champion of emancipation and Negro rights.[21]

Another challenge to the Orr-Hampton approach
came from former Governor Benjamin F. Perry, who took
the lead in urging the whites to oppose a convention.
Perry publicized his stand in a series of letters
printed in newspapers throughout the state. By remaining under military rule, he argued, South
Carolina might "sonner or later" be restored to the
Union with its suffrage policy unchanged. He would
wait for an anti-Radical reaction to crystallize in
the North, citing a recent Democratic victory in

Connecticut as the beginning of such a trend. Perry
dismissed the threat of confiscation as a penalty for
defeating a convention. On the contrary, he thought
land division more likely if a Radical state government were formed. He mocked the assumption that the
whites and blacks had common interests and should work
together politically. Led by Radical emissaries, the
freedmen would oppress and plunder. They would demand
the right to serve on juries and mix with whites in
hotels and other facilities. Perry thought most of
the Negroes unfit for voting, likely to be duped by
clever men. (He was, however, amenable to a qualified
black suffrage.) Race warfare would occur, with the
"weaker and less intelligent" facing extermination.
By voting for a convention, the whites would volun-
tarily surrender political power to a black majority.[22]

To Orr the wisdom of holding a convention was more
of an academic question, because it was inevitable.
He hoped the whites and blacks would not divide into
opposing camps. Such polarization could only hurt
the whites. From this assumption stemmed his plea
for racial collaboration. He implored the whites to
accept a difficult situation, and he spoke in a
friendly way to the blacks. His personal manner was
cheerful and ingratiating. At a Negro meeting in
Columbia he spoke humorously about "controlling" the
black vote. He remarked that bad men might sway the
black voter by exploiting his love for whiskey or
tobacco. The crowd roared when he added that some
blacks also had a weakness for "a pocket handkerchief
or a clean shirt."[23]

He questioned the Republican party's claim to the
Negro's loyalty. In his words, the Northern blacks,
not the Republican party, deserved the chief credit
for the wartime emancipation measures.

When the recent struggle commenced, it was
not to set you free; and until two years
elapsed, and it was found necessary to make
use of the colored man as an element of
military strength in conquering the South,
your manumission was scarcely thought of.
You owe to the efforts of your own race at
the North, therefore, quite as much as you
owe to any party.

131

Several Northern states barred Negro voting. In
addition, the federal tax of two-and-one-half cents
upon cotton hurt both races. He reiterated his theme
of mutual interests.

> They cannot be separated and prosper. The
> same legislation which injures the white
> man, injures the black. If one is depressed,
> so is the other. Whatever affects or impairs
> the industry and usefulness of one race,
> equally disturbs the entire community. You
> will be mistaken, therefore, should you yield
> to the seductions of false teachers, who will
> endeavor to make you believe that your in-
> terests are in any way different from those
> of the white man; and for this reason I again
> warn you against attaching yourselves to any
> existing organization of a national character.
> Look first to your State affairs. Get your
> constitution right. Secure those laws which
> you need every hour in the day.

By supporting the Democrats, the governor stated, the
blacks would offend the Republicans. By entering the
Republican party, they would alienate "thousands upon
thousands of friends" to whom that organization was
anathema.[24]

Orr advised the freedmen to use their political
strength to obtain legislation beneficial to them--
free schools, homesteads, and the abolition of imprisonment for debt. He suggested that they secure
pledges from delegate candidates in the elction, but
he warned them not to be too exacting.

> You are interested as much as we are in pre-
> serving harmony between the two races. You
> desire to remain here. I desire to remain
> here. When I saw hundreds and thousands of
> your people seeking new homes in the West
> and Southwest, it filled my heart with regret,
> because I felt we could not afford to spare
> a single arm from South Carolina and the
> work of regeneration which we are called upon
> to perform.

I say to you frankly, that if you make
unjust exactions, you may succeed in South
Carolina, because there are more black people here than white; but it is not the case
in North Carolina, Georgia, or Florida, or
Alabama. In Mississippi and Louisiana, there
are a few more; but do you not perceive that,
if you are extravagant in demanding more than
you are really entitled to, and you succeed
in arraying the white race against the black,
and creating prejudices which, happily, do
not now exist--do you not perceive that the
same injustice which you attempt to visit
upon the white man in South Carolina will be
visited upon the colored man in North Carolina
and elsewhere?

The governor expected that many large tracts presently
owned by planters would be divided and sold at low
prices. White immigrants with greater financial
resources than the blacks would want to buy them.
Because these newcomers would make possible a white
majority within a few years, he stated, the Negroes
could not afford to antagonize them.[25]

Admonishing the freedmen not to be impatient, he
declared that the current generation of blacks lacked
the full capacity to enjoy freedom. By attempting
to make too rapid progress, the freedmen would incur
the danger of falling "by the way-side." To illustrate
his point, Orr cited the Old Testament. Over four
centuries of bondage had disqualified the liberated
Israelites from reaching Canaan immediately. The
biblical lesson was plain, and the freedmen were told
to educate their children. Not until another generation grew up would the blacks find the intelligence
among their race to place them in "the front rank of
civilized life."[26]

The governor's words exuded magnanimity, frankness,
and condescension. He underestimated the political
awareness of the blacks, who, although mostly illiterate,
saw the connection between politics and their vital
interests. He told the blacks that they were not prepared to enjoy the full inheritance of freedom, and
he failed to win their support. The freedmen recognized that the Republican party promised them greater
dignity and hope. They rejected the benevolent conservatism of Orr and Hampton for the equalitarianism
of the Republicans.

133

By the summer of 1867 the races were moving
towards political polarization. The Union Leagues
successfully mobilized the freedmen under the
Republican banner, and simultaneously the number of
eligible white voters was being restricted. Supple-
mental legislation passed in July gave the military
commanders broader authority, including greater discretion in deciding who could vote. (The March
Reconstruction Acts had been vague on the subject of
white disfranchisement.) After Congress passed the
July bill, it became clear that the white conservatives could not manipulate the registration procedures
to their advantage. Disillusionment set in among the
whites. Hopes for a victorious white-black coalition
under conservative auspices faded. Also damaged was
Perry's drive to prevent a convention call.[27]

White opinion moved decisively against the Reconstruction Acts. Hampton, immensely popular among
the whites, abandoned the campaign for compliance and
joined Perry in opposition. Although still favoring
a restricted black suffrage, by the late summer he
denounced the Congressional laws as unconstitutional
and unjust.[28]

Sharing the disenchantment of most whites, Orr
continued to "accept the situation." Disappointed
by the freedman's refusal to align with the conservative whites, he was also repelled by South Carolina
Republicanism. The Union Republican convention which
met in Columbia in July he considered uncouth.
Attending it were dozens of "ignorant plantation
niggers," joined by very few whites "of respectability."
The governor told a reporter:

> From what I have seen of the Radicals
> who have been sent down here to indoctrinate
> the negroes and inflame their minds, and es-
> pecially colored orators who have come among
> them, I have been led to abandon all hope
> of having a Conservative Constitutional Con-
> vention. The obstructive tendency has been
> aided by Governor Perry's letters, which have
> sown dissensions among the people, and have
> tended to unite the colored race against us.
> The blacks have become perfectly conscious of
> their power. This has made them very bold
> and immodest and exacting, and the chances are
> that in the elections for a Convention a large
> majority of colored delegates will be sent.

The man who had addressed black audiences in a friendly manner now spoke of the Negroes disdainfully. He predicted black control of the state and heavy taxation of white property owners. Public revenues would be used to build schools for the blacks, who "will not contribute a dollar for the education of their own children." Because the Republican party was "the organization of the blacks against the whites" and would be dominant, racial conflict was likely. However, the interviewee qualified his grim prophecy. If race warfare could be "kept off for four or five years, intelligence will do here what it does everywhere else--control the votes."[29]

His mind alternated between cynicism and optimism. In late July he spoke of racial strife. "Ultimately, we shall have a war of races, with all the horrors of San Domingo." In a private letter of October 5, he implied that such a catastrophe might not be imminent. Expecting a Republican defeat in the upcoming Northern state elections, Orr was hopeful that Congress would repeal the disfranchisement clause in the Reconstruction Acts. He wrote, "I have a hope, and yet I cannot give you a good reason for it, that suffrage will yet be restricted by Congress to such persons as can read or write or who have a small property qualification, and that the disfranchised will be reinstated in the possession of their former privileges as citizens."[30]

Orr persisted in thinking that the national Republican party might soften the reconstruction policy. On April 29, he told a black audience of a coming division in Republican ranks. "The extreme radical element" would be cast aside, and the "moderate and conservative principles" expounded by such men as William P. Fressenden, John Sherman, Henry Wilson, and Lyman Trumbull would triumph.[31]

The old campaigner continued his effort to dissuade the Negroes from entering the Republican fold. Repeatedly he warned them against oppressing the whites. In Belton on August 29, he asserted that the balance of power could eventually shift against the blacks. He also sought to disabuse them of the notion that they would obtain lands from the government. Besides, he noted, such gifts would not be desirable for them. In the same speech he directed words of caution to the whites. Any white attempt to defeat the convention call was "folly and madness."[32]

135

He was alarmed by the intransigence of whites like
Perry who were unfriendly to the freedmen. At the same
time he feared that a Republican regime, backed by an
ignorant black electorate, would tyrannize the state.
He still held out the hand of friendship to the
Negroes. Although sharing much of the racial prejudice common in this era, he believed that racial
cooperation was the only sensible course. The racial
cooperation that Orr wanted was to be had on the
white man's terms. He desired a government managed
by honest white men, with the collaboration and support
of educated blacks. He neither liked nor trusted
"ignorant plantation niggers." However, he consistently
favored educational opportunities for those blacks who
could, in his judgment, profit from them. He also
wanted fair treatment for all Negroes.

By November the governor was the only white conservative leader who advocated compliance with the
Reconstruction Acts. Most whites, following Perry,
chose to wait for a Northern reaction against the prospect of black rule in the South. (There were grounds
for this expectation. Elections in Connecticut in
April and elsewhere in the North in October showed
Democratic gains.) Shortly before the South Carolina
referendum a "conservative convention" assembled in
Columbia, aiming to solidify white opinion against
the Congressional policy. It was hoped that the
whites refusing to vote and the freedmen who might
fail to participate would comprise a majority and
defeat the Republican program.[33]

On November 19 and 20, the Republicans won a
substantial majority of delegate seats in the constitutional convention. (76 of the 124 members would
be blacks.) Only 4,628 or 46,882 registered whites
voted, 2,350 of them casting affirmative ballots and
2,278 negative. 66,418 of 80,550 eligible blacks went
to the polls. The state's chief executive had
accurately predicted that the convention call would be
approved.[34]

***** ***** ***** ***** *****

The Protestant Ethic and racism, two powerful
currents in American life, affected Orr's attitude
towards the Negro. On April 29, 1867, he lectured a
black audience in Columbia on the need for thrift
and hard work.

136

Save your money; put it into a small house,
or, if you desire a farm, buy five or ten
acres and commence its cultivation. You
will feel that you have a stake in the welfare of the community. There will be something for you to live and labor for; and my
life upon it, when you have thus become the
possessor of property honestly earned and
paid for, you will enjoy more respect for
yourselves, and feel that you are entitled
to the respect of others. I repeat it again
--husband your resources; save the odd
pennies; indulge in no unnecessary extravagance in dress, living or otherwise.

The speaker's values were those of an acquisitive
and capitalistic culture. An exponent of economic
progress and industrial growth, he had criticized
the practices of the great planters in antebellum
days. However, he had defended slavery and regretted
its demise. In 1865 he desired a "white man's
government," although in following years he modified
his position on the Negro's place in politics.[35]

In 1865, before the post-war movement of Negroes
from the state made its impact felt, the governor
privately endorsed colonization. In February 1867,
after the black migration had reached its highest
level, he voiced concern that an unfavorable season
had induced many freedmen to leave. The sight of
many departing blacks caused him regret, he told a
Negro audience in Charleston. "For I desire you to
remain here. I desire you to continue with the people
of South Carolina. I think your interest our interest."
He advised his listeners to exercise sound judgment,
to relocate if the rewards would be better elsewhere,
but to guard against "wild, delusive hopes." Orr
repeated this plea two months later at a black rally
in Columbia, declaring that the state needed every
available person. At this time the promise of rich
lands and high wages was luring many freedmen to the
Southwest. In 1867 an estimated one thousand blacks
passed through Atlanta from South Carolina each week
on the way west.[36]

Orr's sentiment towards the Negro was ambivalent, at times revealing compassion or contempt. In February 1867 he stated that most freedmen had conducted themselves with great propriety since emancipation. In a speech two months later he declared that he had tried to deal impartially with the races.

I have sought to hold the scales of justice equally between you and the white race. I have thrown the protecting arm of the State around you in every instance where acts of oppression have come to my knowledge, and where wrong has been done your people by inconsiderate and vicious white men, I have endeavored to bring all such to justice and to condign punishment. I have had equal occasion to reprobate the conduct of persons of your own color. So long as I continue to discharge the duties of this position--and its sands are running rapidly out--I shall act in this impartial and disinterested manner; but if there be any leaning required, it shall always be to that side which is least able to protect itself.

He also lauded the "intelligent and respectable" blacks who had been moved by the Christian teachings; they were offering moral guidance to the less endowed.[37]

Coexisting with a fatherly good will towards the race "least able to protect itself" was a vehemently angry response to any Negro aggressiveness. In a state where blacks outnumbered whites in many areas, any gathering of Negroes made the governor uneasy. Fear of racial violence instigated by vicious blacks had deep roots in South Carolina's past. Orr requested stern measures against any freedman whose conduct might be presumed as insolent or criminal. In late 1866 he told Brigadier-General Robert K. Scott, head of the Freedmen's Bureau in the state, that blacks in the Kingstree neighborhood were forming military organizations, and he asked that their meetings be stopped. Scott answered that the Negroes had met merely to discuss emigration to Florida in lieu of remaining in a locale where the landowners paid low wages. In October 1867 the governor told General Edwin Canby, who had recently replaced Sickles, that about three hundred freedmen in Abeeville District were meeting on alternate weeks in violation of military orders.

They were drilling, firing, and supposedly "preparing to fight for land." Canby replied that these assemblages were held solely for the purpose of self-protection against threatened white assaults.[38]

As the 1867 Christmas season approached, Orr became distressed by the possibility of Negro disorders. He urged Canby not to concentrate all the troops in three towns--Charleston, Columbia, and Aiken--as was reported. Fearful of racial collision, he thought that federal troops offered the only safeguard against any black attack upon the whites. He was convinced that economic hardship would compel the Negroes to plunder, and "they will operate in organized bands." Alluding to a large number of murders committed by blacks against whites in recent months, he stated, "there is scarcely a District where their incendiary torch has not been applied, and is not being applied to the property of the white man." He was sure that the whites had retaliated with very few acts of violence. Canby replied that a small number of troops in each district would be helpless in the face of serious trouble. The general added that during the first nine months of 1867 the number of blacks involved in murders and attempted murders was not disproportionate to their population ratio.[39]

The governor became indignant when he learned that freedmen in Beaufort District had ignored a summons for road duty. He wanted Canby to dispatch troops to the area to enforce the summons. On another occasion he complained to a military official in Charleston about depredations on some nearby plantations. He requested the stationing of soldiers to protect the planters' property and to drive off the freedmen who had squatted.[40]

He spoke sympathetically of the Negro that he regarded as competent and respectable. For a post-mastership he recommended a black whose sponsor was a Columbia gentleman of "high character and great intelligence." At another time he refused to commute the sentence given a white man for raping a black woman, stating emphatically that it was "high time" that the whites understood the "great enormity" of the crime. The chief executive also denied mercy to a condemned black murderer, pointing out that he had generally been lenient towards the freedmen. "When the record is published, you will be surprised to see how often the executive clemency has been interposed

in their behalf, and mainly on account of their ignorance and inexperience." General Scott commented
that the governor had interposed his official shield
to protect the blacks when the law was not justly
administered.[41]

Orr and Canby disagreed as to whether the freedmen were being mistreated by civil judges. In early
1867 the governor declared that in some localities
violence had been committed against the blacks, but
even in those areas he saw a growing disposition to
give the blacks full legal protection. Later in the
year Canby contended that the civil tribunals had
not been disposed to deal fairly with the freedmen,
and Orr disputed the charge. The governor cited the
testimony of prosecuting officers in the courts that
the Negro had been treated more generously than the
white man.[42]

In September he wrote to President Johnson to
protest Canby's General Order Number Eighty-Nine.
Under this decree all persons assessed for taxes
who had paid them for the current year, and were
registered to vote, could serve as jurors. Among
the excluded were persons disfranchised by the Reconstruction Acts. In December 1866, Orr noted, the
legislature had imposed a one dollar tax upon all
males between the ages of twenty-one and fifty except
those incapable of earning a living; the number of
Negroes who had failed to pay the tax exceeded that
of the whites. He also estimated that only a small
number of blacks in the rural districts were literate.
If juries were formed on the basis of this order,
"ignorance and incompetence" would prevail. He would
have preferred a literary or property requirement,
or a condition, in cases which involved Negroes,
that "a certain proportion of the jury should consist
of their own color."[43]

Canby replied that an 1859 state law excluded
non-voters from juries; the federal policy followed
state precedent. The number of black voters rendered
ineligible exceeded the whites, he asserted, because
the ratio of Negroes failing to pay taxes was greater.
After conferring with the governors of the two Carolinas, Canby altered the ruling. Juries already drawn
would continue to serve during the fall terms. Names
of persons who had paid taxes but were not registered
to vote could be placed in the jury box, but in 1868
a person drawn as a juror could be challenged because
of non-registration.[44]

140

It was in the civil courts that Orr wanted
justice to be administered, and he used his influence
to limit the extension of military authority. In
early 1866 Judge A. P. Aldrich sentenced a man to be
whipped, and Sickles prevented the punishment from
being inflicted. The governor was disturbed when
Aldrich, in reaction to this interference, declined
to hold the remaining sessions on his circuit. Orr
believed that the holding of courts would be "the
best advertisement" that lawlessness would be curbed.
He asked Trescott, who was in Washington, to seek a
modification of Sickles' policy so that punishments
ordered by the civil courts could be administered.[45]

Orr viewed the provost court system as promoting
confusion and conflict between civil and military
authorities. In October 1867 he asked Canby to curtail
or define more clearly the powers of the provost court
at Sumter, maintaining that it had allowed some mis-
carriages of justice. The governor also approved a
suggestion of Chief Justice Benjamin F. Dunkin that
the court of appeals create additional civil court
sessions in order to avoid the establishment of provost
courts in the state's southern circuit. He was
pleased that Dunkin had obtained Canby's consent.[46]

***** ***** ***** ***** *****

With Sickles, the military commander until August
31, 1867, Orr's relations were cordial. In the spring
of 1867 he used his influence with Sickles to circum-
vent the action of the state court of appeals against
the "stay law." In Decmeber 1865 the legislature
had responded to the economic hardship of the day by
continuing in modified form the 1861 "stay law."
Provided that the debtor paid one-tenth of the amount
owed, an execution for indebtedness could be suspended
until the next regular session of the legislature.
Strongly opposed by commercial interests, this measure
was declared unconstitutional by the court of appeals
in the spring of 1866. In September the legislature
moved to suspend the terms of the common pleas courts
until the next spring, but in March 1867 the court
of appeals overruled this action. Understanding the
plight of many debtors, Orr persuaded Sickles to resolve the problem in their favor by military fiat. On
April 11, 1867, the commander issued his General Order
Number Ten, which suspended judgments for actions

occurring between 1860 and 1865, suspended all procedures for the recovery of money in which the purchase of slaves had been involved, stopped foreclos-
ures for twelve months, ended imprisonment for debt,
and granted to the debtor in the sale of property
under execution a house, twenty acres of land, and
five hundred dollars in personal property. On
February 19, before Sickles announced his decree, the
governor instructed the sheriffs not to arrest and
jail any delinquent in a tax execution unless the
person was fraudulently concealing property or
withholding money. On April 12, Sickles endorsed
this instruction.[47]

Orr was concerned that tax collections should pro-
ceed diligently. In the fall of 1867 he asked Canby
to clarify his Order Number Ninety-Two, which suspended collections under the December 1866 tax act.
He described much unwillingness to pay taxes among
people who hoped that through military interference
or the action of the forthcoming convention they
might evade payment entirely. The cause of his concern
was the grim financial status of an impoverished post-
war state. He wanted to reduce as much as possible
the expenses of South Carolina's government. He protested that the state had to support prisoners in its
penitentiary who were sentenced by military tribunals,
and he told Canby that the federal government should
bear this expense.[48]

In dealing with the conqueror Orr was a model of
discretion, urging the military commander to modify
a rule if he thought the request might be successful.
He would never make a challenge on constitutional
grounds. When the secretary of state, Ellison Capers,
questioned Canby's rule that local officers file a
bond with the state treasurer, the governor responded
that his inquiry involved the constitutionality of
the Reconstruction Acts. He regarded controversies
with the military in this sphere as likely to be
injurious.[49]

The test oath, mandated by Congress in July 1862,
posed some problems. On October 20, 1867, Orr asked
Canby to authorize the incumbent commissioners of the
poor to retain their positions until their successors
were appointed, stating that such a policy would obviate
the problem of the test oath. In early December the
general adopted this approach for all local officials.

On December 16, the governor suggested to Canby that
he outrightly dispense with the test oath. Referring
to a vacant sheriff's office in one district, he said
it was most difficult to find a capable man who could
meet the requirement. Canby did not act upon this
request.[50]

After Sickles was removed from his position by
Johnson in August 1867, Orr publicly praised the
"moderation" of his policies. In particular he cited
the general's action in sustaining the "stay law."
In his words, the decree had alleviated much suffering.
This statement drew sharp criticism from several
newspapers, which pictured Sickles as an arrogant
despot.[51]

***** ***** ***** ***** *****

The Bank of the State of South Carolina, chartered
in 1812, was a government-operated fiscal agency. Often
a storm center in antebellum politics, it was a victim
of the Civil War. Its bankruptcy after the war caused
much financial loss and litigation. In November 1866
Orr requested that the bank's existence be terminated.
Ignoring his recommendation, the legislature passed
a bill renewing the bank's life and allowing it the
right of deposit but not of issue. (In the past the
bank had exercised both rights.) The governor vetoed
this bill, contending that the institution, with its
restricted functions, would not be needed. In his
opinion, the treasurer and comptroller-general could
conduct the state's financial business without the
bank. An attempt to override the veto was unsuccessful.[52]

***** ***** ***** ***** *****

Any white support for black education was usually
qualified by the insistence that it be self-supporting.
In a Charleston speech in February 1867 Orr advocated
a system of common schools for both races, with each
providing the revenues for its education. While
favoring education for qualified Negroes, the governor
opposed racial mixing in the schools. Alluding to
"the prejudices of race," he declared in 1868 that
neither whites nor blacks demanded mixing. The
Caucasian race would never recognize "social equality"
with the blacks. He specifically opposed integration
at the University of South Carolina, warning that it
would hinder both whites and blacks in their efforts

143

to obtain an education. The Citadel in Charleston he suggested as a possible Negro institution of higher learning.[53]

***** ***** ***** ***** *****

The South Carolina College in Columbia escaped the ravages of war. In 1865 Governor Perry restored the incumbent trustees to their positions. Perry, a persistent critic of the aristocratic orientation of the school's curriculum, wanted public education to be more utilitarian. The college's traditional emphasis upon classical studies had long been recognized as reflecting a social and political con-servatism.[54]

Perry encountered little serious opposition when he proposed that South Carolina College be converted into a university. With the state impoverished and the old planter class no longer dominant, the classi-cal curriculum was less attractive than in the days of King Cotton. On November 29, 1865, the board of trustees approved Perry's request for a change to university status. On December 6, Orr endorsed the trustees' resolution, asking the legislature to add law, medicine, and modern languages to the list of proposed chairs.[55]

The economic dislocation caused by war, as much as conversion to the university system, induced most post-war students to choose a utilitarian rather than a classical course. The state's dire economic plight also limited the university's capacity to expand the old curriculum. The legislature in 1865 failed to authorize professorships in law, medicine, and modern languages, as Orr had recommended, and in his message of November 1866 he urged once again that these positions be created. The legislators estab-lished the legal and medical chairs.[56]

***** ***** ***** ***** *****

When Orr addressed the Charleston Chamber of Commerce on February 13, 1867, an incident occurred which was generally not reported in the South Caro-lina press. He compared Richmond and Charleston in the rebuilding of their burnt districts, to the dis-advantage of the latter. He also discussed Charleston's longstanding economic loss caused by the relocation of many merchants to other communities. This he

attributed to the exclusiveness in the first circles
of seaboard society, and he maintained that the city
could never become prosperous while the self-made
businessmen were shunned socially. The speaker's
father, "a humble country merchant" from Anderson,
had made purchases in Charleston and felt "the effects
of this evil." In rebuttal, Mayor P. J. Gaillard
stated that the Charlestonians had been very energetic
and deserved no blame for the delay in their city's
rebuilding. He then upheld the right of each citizen to decide who should enjoy social intercourse
with his family. Such a right, the mayor added,
would not be relinquished. The audience reacted to
Gaillard's rejoinder with a long applause. Before
the cheering subsided Orr rose from his seat and
left the banquet room.[57]

In spite of his frustrations the Piedmont politician would not retreat into bitterness. He never
relented in his attempts to make the best of a bad
situation, and he brushed aside the criticisms which
public life brought him. He once remarked that "my
epidermis is very thoroughly case-hardened in consequence of the continual pricking received from
numerous admirers in this and other States." Early
in 1867 the Pickens Keowee Courier called the Andersonian the hardest worked and best abused man in South
Carolina.[58]

He served as the state's chief executive at an
exceptionally difficult time. His task was almost a
thankless one, and his key recommendations to the
legislature were disregarded. In 1866 he asked for
homestead and debtor's relief laws and the abolition
of imprisonment for debt. None of these measures were
passed during his administration.[59]

As the end of his term approached Orr found himself an anomalous figure with no political constituency. His position on Congressional Reconstruction
was spurned by most whites, and his plea for a non-
partisan coalition between blacks and whites was ignored by both races. For urging compliance with the
Reconstruction Acts he was accused of opportunism.

In January 1868 the outgoing governor addressed
the Republican-controlled constitutional convention.
(76 of the 124 delegates were blacks.) He was the
only native white conservative invited to address
the body. The proposal to invite him provoked a

145

heated debate. W. Beverly Nash, one of the state's
most controversial black politicians, denounced the
resolution. Affiliating with Hampton in the spring
of 1867, Nash later joined the Republican party.
(After becoming a Republican, he continued to favor
the removal of disabilities from the disfranchised
whites.) In November 1867 Nash made a speech in
Fairfield District which Orr described as incendiary
and reported to the military authorities. Because the
governor had tried to deny him "the right of free
speech," Nash opposed granting him "the freedom of
this convention." After noting that a military
board had exonerated him of the charge of making an
inflammatory speech, Nash described his antagonist
as the spokesman for a minority opinion. W. J.
Whipper, a black delegate, defended the governor as
one whose chief aim was to "draw parties over to
him." On one occasion Orr had almost succeeded in
winning him over. The convention voted almost unanimously to extend the invitation, with only Nash and
one other delegate dissenting.[60]

On January 17, the governor delivered his
address. He annoyed the black delegates by asserting
that the convention did not represent the state's
wealth, intelligence, or refinement. He then predicted that the convention's work would be in force
until at least 1871. Not until then could the Democrats control the presidency and both houses of Congress simultaneously. Whatever the outcome of the
1868 national election, repeal of the Reconstruction
Acts was unlikely before 1871. Moreover, while he
personally believed these laws unconstitutional, until
they should be voided by the Supreme Court he would
advise compliance with them.[61]

Because he wanted to exercise some influence in
shaping the new state constitution, Orr was present
at the convention, and he appealed for measures which
he had advocated in the past. He recommended a provision for a liberal homestead law, allowing fifty
or one hundred acres of land in the country and a house
and lot in town, none of these liable to attachment
for old debts. He asked his listeners to provide
relief for pre-war debtors and to wipe out all debts
based upon the purchase of slaves. He urged them to
abolish imprisonment for debt, which was "senseless
and cruel."[62]

The prospect of universal black suffrage frightened the speaker, who repeated his argument that many Negroes could not vote judiciously. "You may think that to perpetuate your power, and to preserve your organization, it is necessary to continue the franchise to this class of persons, but eventually you will find that you have been sadly mistaken." Orr further suggested that education be made available to both races, financed by a poll tax rather than a property tax. In addition, he proposed the absence of disabilities imposed upon many whites by the Fourteenth Amendment. The speech closed with a call for racial concord.[63]

> I desire you to adopt a liberal and wise constitution, under which the white and the black man can live together; a constitution which will protect the great interests of the state, and restore to it a degree of prosperity not heretofore enjoyed--a constitution that will dispel that distrust which unfortunately now prevails. You have a great problem to solve, such a one as has rarely been given to man; you are to undertake an experiment which has not thus far in the experience of mankind been successful. That experience shows that, when placed upon terms of equality, the races have not harmonized. It is for you to demonstrate to the contrary.

The 1868 constitution provided for some measures which Orr had advocated in the past--abolition of imprisonment for debt, homestead legislation, and an insolvent law which would remove all indebtedness on the debtor's surrender of his property. The most notable features were universal male suffrage, representation in the lower legislative house on a population basis, the absence of property requirements for officeholding, and the absence of a ceiling on state indebtedness. The Fourteenth Amendment disabilities were incorporated until Congress removed them. Land confiscation, which Perry had forecast, was not included. In April the new organic law was ratified by popular vote, and in July Orr was succeeded by the state's first Republican governor, Brigadier-General Robert K. Scott.

147

Before leaving office, the outgoing chief
executive aired his opinions in a message to the incoming legislature and in "An Address by Governor Orr"
to the people. He was gratified that the new constitution absorbed some of his past suggestions, but
he regretted the lack of a provision for the scaling
of debts, contracted before and during the war, down
to the basis of existing wealth and resources. The
provision securing a homestead to each head of family
he termed "a wise and humane measure."[64]

He had words for those whites who would yield
nothing to the blacks, telling them that some Negro
suffrage was unavoidable. Since the blacks comprised
a majority and numbered some intelligent and educated
persons, any attempt to govern without their consent
would invite discontent. "Would they have patiently
and tamely submitted to a system of laws which they
had no agency in making; or to taxation without
representation?"[65]

The governor was sure that the Republican party
would continue to support universal suffrage, and he
doubted that the Reconstruction Acts would be repealed soon. Should a future Democratic Congress and
president, or the Supreme Court, undo those laws, the
South would be plunged into anarchy. If the governments established under the Reconstruction Acts
were declared to be simply provisional, what authority
would then determine the suffrage question? Should
the Supreme Court void the Reconstruction Acts and
the Southern governments, what governments would
be in existence? In his mind, any tampering with
those laws would imply an acknowledgment of Congressional power to regulate the suffrage in the states. On
constitutional grounds here was a moot question. Democratic victory in the next few national elections could
not, in Orr's judgment, overturn the status quo. (Like
most Southern whites, he denied Congressional authority
to regulate the suffrage. He noted that the Republican
party had been defeated in recent elections in the
North and West, because it had contested the states'
exclusive control over voting.)[66]

Raising these questions revealed the practical bent of his mind. Whatever the theoretical implications, he believed that the white Southerners could help themselves only by participating in politics under the terms of the Reconstruction Acts. The evil inflicted by Congress could be ameliorated only by the whites themselves, aided by the more competent freedmen. In his view, intelligence and wealth had always controlled the votes of the ignorant and dependent throughout the Union. In time such an arrangement would prevail in South Carolina. In his words, responsible Negroes would eventually realize that the native whites were their best friends, and the intelligent people of both races would eventually obtain a dominant voice.[67]

VIII. RADICAL RULE IN SOUTH CAROLINA

The upcountry politician resided on a prosperous
Anderson estate that comprised 225 acres of improved
land, 240 acres of woodland, and 160 acres of other
unimproved land. Wheat, oats, corn, and cotton were
grown, and the livestock numbered about fifty. Trains
on the short branch of the Greenville and Columbia
Railroad passed by the spacious grands of the property,
which was distinguished by a large mansion. The owner
could be seen feeding his animals, or he might be in
the house, lighting his corn-cob pipe and singing with
his children. In 1870 a visitor, who had not seen
him for several years, described his host's "same
rotund physique, errect pose, elastic step, and ruddy
complexion as of old; the same merry twinkle of the
eye; the same social bonhommie that carried its charm
into every circle." He entertained guests frequently
in his home, but he might also be found at a political
meeting, a railroad business meeting, or a fraternal
lodge. Active in the Masonic order, he was South
Carolina's grand master during the 1866-1867 term.[1]

*****   *****   *****   *****   *****

In 1868 the Democratic party was drawing back
most native whites. Perry, urging close ties with
the Northern Democrats, was listened to attentively.
In the meantime Orr weighed the advantages of Republican party membership. In the previous year he had
received overtures to join from J. P. M. Epping,
carpetbagger and federal marshal in Charleston. Epping
stated that dishonest elements were seizing control
of the Republican organization, and he hoped that
reputable men would enter. The Andersonian was also
persuaded by Benjamin Odell Duncan of Newberry, who
later became United States Consul in Naples. Duncan
wanted the party to acquire "sensible men of moderation like yourself."[2]

After the spring of 1867 Orr had no political
affiliation or constituency. Accepting the Reconstruction Acts, he was censured by conservative whites.
Asking the blacks to stand aloof from national parties,
he was a target of Republican organizers.[3] His record
of changing sides left him vulnerable to charges of
opportunism. The Sumter Watchman classified him with
those who had abandoned "their own race, the constitution, the country, and all that is honorable and sacred."[4]

151

In July 1868 the Republican legislature offered him a circuit court judgeship. During the election he was in the Northwest to examine his land holdings. Without having sought the position, he was assigned to the eighth circuit, which comprised some western counties. The former Confederate senator had had his political disabilities removed by Congress. In early October he returned from the West and assumed his new duties.[5]

The Andersonian concluded that opposition to the Republicans was fruitless, and he joined that party. Observing its success in luring the great mass of blacks, he would eventually advise the whites to follow suit. In an 1870 interview he assessed the party's control of the federal government as fortunate. Democratic presidential victory in 1868 would have triggered efforts to overturn existing Southern governments and "undo the entire work of reconstruction." Grant's election, he thought, had prevented violence and bloodshed.[6]

The spiritual wounds of the Civil War did not heal easily. This man saw that time was needed to make the native whites accept the reality of defeat. Had the South obtained Congressional representation without conditions, he added, the section would have remained hostile to the conqueror's policy.

They would not have given universal suffrage to the negro; they would not have permitted the South to be overrun by irresponsible, and in many instances, corrupt men--mere adventurers, having in view solely their own elevation. In fact, such was the temper of the people, that they would not have recognized the right of qualified suffrage to the colored man at the time it was preferred. Of course, at the present time, they would be glad enough to make such a compromise. It is the knowledge of this fact which accounts for the persistency of Republicanism at the North, and for the adoption of a plan of reconstruction which would remove the fangs of the serpent by which that section had been stung. Still, I do not wish to be understood as endorsing all the peculiar manifestations of that political creed which have been exhibited in the South, because Republicanism has gone to extremes here which would never be accepted at the North. A reaction must

necessarily take place, and is already in
progress.

In time, he believed, a "true Republicanism" would
appeal to native white Southerners. Every day "men
of shrewdness and foresight" were realizing that the
Republican party would dominate South Carolina for
another ten years. "Large numbers of the best men"
were willing to espouse Republican principles, but
they were offended by the corrupt persons who ran the
party and manipulated the most ignorant blacks.[7]

The regime of Republican Governor Robert K. Scott,
elected in 1868, displeased many whites. By 1870 they
wanted to challenge the new ruling party, which had increased government expenditures and pressed for racial
equality. The governor's term was two years, and when
Scott ran again in 1870, the conservatives tried to
unseat him. They organized the Union Reform party,
which pledged to uphold the Fifteenth Amendment and
respect the changes stemming from the war. For governor
it chose a Republican, Judge Richard B. Carpenter.
After two blacks declined the nomination for lieutenant-
governor, it selected a Democrat, Matthew C. Butler.
The conservative press backed the new party, although
many whites deplored its acknowledgment of racial
equality.[8]

The Republicans renominated Scott and picked Negro
legislator Alonzo J. Ransier for lieutenant-governor.
Denying the charges of corruption and extravagance,
they pictured the Union Reformers as Democrats in dis-
guise, insincere in their gestures towards the freedmen.
But the Union Reformers made a spirited attempt to cut
into the black majority and unite the white vote.[9]

Orr supported the Republican ticket and belittled
the Union Reform drive as futile. Admitting that incompetence existed in the state government, he maintained that reforms could be accomplished only through
the majority party. Opposition to the dominant party
would only cause the more honest Republicans to unite
with their less scrupulous fellows. He was confident
that the blacks would remain Republican, because it was
only natural that they should affiliate with the party
which had been their benefactor. Reform could be
achieved only if many decent whites would join the Republican organization. Many whites were hesitant to
enter, he believed, because of their dislike of

endorsing Republican principles. In reality the Union Reform platform was essential Republican, and its governorship candidate was a Republican. "How, then, can a voter sustain the Reform party--its nominees and platform--and say his devotion to principles precludes him from joining the Republican party?"[10]

Only in the majority party, the judge argued, could the whites command the Negro's political trust. The whites could not enjoy a political influence over the freedman comparable to that which "we now constantly do in all the other relations and duties of life," until they promised him equal protection in his person, property, and civil rights. Orr understood that the race question was the overriding concern in his state, the real dividing line in politics. In his words, the old issues between parties--banks, tariffs, and internal improvements--had been settled or superseded. Therefore, affiliation with the Republican party "on existing issues" would, for a former Democrat, entail "no sacrifice of principles." At this time many political leaders and analysts in the country thought that present divisions were outdated and a realignment of parties due.[11]

Union Reformers doubted that native whites could gain a strong voice in Republican party councils and thereby effect reforms. Duncan, presently the United States Consul in Naples, asserted that the bad elements in the party were so deeply entrenched that attempts at reform were bound to fail. The few honest men in its councils, such as Daniel H. Chamberlain and Reuben Tomlinson, were "ornamental statues." Duncan derided the prediction that the blacks would remain as a unit in the Republican party, stating that its great corruption would drive out the good and intelligent ones.[12]

The conservative press generally disputed Orr's stand and frequently mentioned his record of changing sides.[13] The Charleston Daily Courier questioned his claim that the Negroes would remain overwhelmingly Republican. In North Carolina, this paper reported, a reform party had framed a platform similar to that of South Carolina's Union Reformers, attracted white and black votes, and ousted a corrupt regime.[14] To the Walhalla Keowee Courier the judge was trying to deceive the freedmen into backing an admittedly corrupt party. This paper accused him of making "low appeals" to the blacks and poor whites.[15] Moreover, the charge circulated that he was maneuvering for a United States Senate seat. He replied that he had never discussed the senatorship with any Republican leaders, and that he had no aspirations for that office.[16]

Allusions were made to Orr's connections with the "Railroad Ring," a group of politicians who took control of the Greenville and Columbia Railroad, which the state partly owned. In 1870 several state officials, who belonged to the ring, offered for sale the state's interest in the road and also the Blue Ridge Railroad. (The latter line ran from Walhalla to Belton, where it linked with the Greenville and Columbia.) Orr, with his former law partner Jacob P. Reid, played a key role in purchasing shares from private individuals. Each of these men earned about twenty thousand dollars for their labors. In addition, the judge sat on the Greenville and Columbia board of directors, elected in April 1870 with other ring members.[17]

With the hope of solidifying white support and gaining black votes, the Union Reformers organized Union Reform clubs. This new party activated much of the white population politically, but most freedmen remained in the Republican camp. The Republicans drew about 85,000 votes, while Carpenter polled over 51,000, and these figures corresponded roughly to the black and white population.[18]

***** ***** ***** ***** *****

The conservative defeat in 1870 led to a resurgence of Ku Klux Klan activity, a factor in the state's political life since 1868. Ku Klux militancy occurred mainly in the central and northwestern counties, and the Klan was often indistinguishable from local Democratic clubs and rifle clubs. In 1870 Klan terrorism was generally sporadic before the election, as the conservatives relied upon a nonviolent strategy, i.e., appealing for black votes. The failure of this effort provoked a new wave of Ku Klux disturbances, which brought countermeasures from President Grant. In October 1871 he suspended the writ of habeas corpus in the counties of York, Laurens, Newberry, Fairfield, Lancaster, Chester, Chesterfield, Spartanburg, and Union. So vigorous was federal action that after 1872 the disorders virtually ceased.[19]

Orr claimed that the counties in his judicial circuit were mainly free of Ku Klux lawlessness, and he commented on the turmoil elsewhere before a Congressional committee in June 1871. In his words, "hatred of the Yankees" motivated the disguised criminals, who were mostly "reckless young men, without a great deal of standing in the community." The judge chided the "better portion" of people who did nothing to stop the violence. Embittered by the political situation, the more respectable whites contributed to a toleration of lawlessness. If these citizens earnestly desired to stop the disorders, "I think the law there is abundantly sufficient to put them down." Blaming the white leaders for their bad example, he cited Wade Hampton as irresponsible. If men of Hampton's stature had spoken out against the Klan, the jurist asserted, peace might have been restored immediately. Since they were disfranchised, they would "let the niggers, carpetbaggers, scalawags, and Ku-Klux send the State to the devil their own way." Had Hampton and the other leading generals chosen to acquiesce in Congressional reconstruction, no more outrages would occur. "But why should they do it? It is nothing to them. They don't suffer."[20]

Also encouraging disrespect for law, in his view, was the corrupt Radical regime. Because the people were misgoverned and robbed by a "swarm of Northern locusts," the incitement to violence was great. With a heavy black majority, the Republicans were able to plunder, because the whites were "stupid enough to insist on being recognized as Democrats." Orr believed that the Democratic party was so obnoxious to the freedmen that the native whites had to disavow it in order to deliver the state from corruption. In 1871 he was declaring that the political course taken by most white South Carolinians was self-defeating. He understood that most whites were bent upon keeping a rigid line between the races. This intransigence aggravated the conditions that produced discord and tension.[21]

The judge exuded an air of cool detachment. On one occasion he remarked that "a public man in South Carolina, who thinks for himself, must have a hide like a rhinoceros, and forty years of antagonism have made mine so tough that all the porcupines in Christendom couldn't draw blood; that is, when I know I'm right."[22]

***** ***** ***** ***** *****

The Union Reform party ceased to exist, and in 1872 the conservatives did not oppose the Republicans. When two Republican slates, the regular and an insurgent, offered themselves to the public, the conservatives endorsed neither. The dominant party had so large a majority that it could afford the luxury of a split. Its preponderance was assured by the freedman's unswerving loyalty.[23]

In addition, a small number of native whites entered the party, mostly from areas where unionism had been strongest before and during the war -- in Charleston, Lexington County, and the mountain districts. The historian Joel Williamson suggests that the Republican program of expanding educational, economic, and political opportunities was primarily appealing to them. The scalawags represented a cross section of South Carolina society, including some persons of much wealth and prominence.[24]

On the whole, few whites would accept the Negro as their political equal, and joining the Republican party implied this. The conservative white who backed a "fusion" movement, i.e., an insurgent Republican ticket, was doing virtually the same, and the freedman recognized his insincerity. The Winnsboro Fairfield Herald openly stated that the whites, to preserve their self-respect, should cease their efforts to conciliate the blacks and "let the ruling party work out the political problems."[25]

In 1872 many Republicans saw the need for reform, and public opinion generally was swayed by the persistent newspaper attacks upon graft in government. In May 1871 a taxpayers convention assembled in Columbia, recommended measures to curb extravagance, and helped to mould public sentiment. Criticisms of the Scott administration came frequently from Republican sources. Among the more outspoken were the Columbia Union and Richard Harvey Cain, black preacher-politician from Charleston. The Republican schism was also fueled by rivalries between machines in the dominant party. In the age of Republican supremacy personal machines proliferated, and the most powerful was led by Scott, who commanded the allegiance of many lesser complexes. This gave the regular Republican ticket a decided advantage over the bolters in 1872. The bolters had their machines, one of them headed by C. C. Bowen of Charleston. The conservatives charged that the Republican wings presented a choice between two sets of thieves.[26]

Appalled by the corruption in the Scott administration, Orr in 1872 was ready to support reform. He
reiterated his view that change could be accomplished
only by the Republican party, because most blacks
would not abandon that organization. While favoring
honesty, they would elect a dishonest Republican over
an honest Democrat. The judge also repeated his contention that the native whites could regain their
natural leadership only by joining the majority party.
They had already shown themselves amenable to the
"fundamental principles of Republicanism." By voting
for either Grant or Greeley they would renounce their
Democratic party allegiance, but only support of Grant
would be regarded by blacks as bona fide Republican.
(The Liberal Republican candidate against President
Grant was Horace Greeley, who was also nominated by
the Democrats.) On July 3, this argument was advanced.

> They cannot gain the control of the minds of
> the colored people unless they absolutely and
> in good faith accept regular Republicanism.
> It is not their votes that our cause needs so
> much as their influence in leading the colored
> people to vote. We ask the white men of this
> State to take up Grant for the sake of State
> reform, in which they have a direct and per-
> sonal interest, and give up Greeley and his
> promises of National reform, in which (if
> such a thing be necessary at all) they can
> have only a remote or secondary interest.
> There is no middle course, and they have got
> to swallow Grant if they want to secure reform
> at home.

In his words, Grant was anxious for the cleaning up of
South Carolina, and leading Republicans in the North
feared that the scandals in the state would hurt the
party nationally.[27]

During the weeks preceding the Republican state
convention Orr continued to berate the Scott regime.
He accused Franklin J. Moses, Jr., the administration's
candidate for governor, of squandering public funds
while presiding over the state house of representatives.
At the same time the judge was determined that the
public should not dissociate him from the national
Republican party. In Belton he praised Grant's
efficiency in suppressing Ku-Kluxism but also denounced
fraud and corruption in the state government.[28]

158

He was a delegate to the Republican convention in Philadelphia which renominated Grant. In a convention speech he lauded the president's enforcement of the Ku Klux Law as merciful and fair. After returning to the state he declared that the Republican rule in South Carolina had caused much anxiety in the party nationally. The anti-Scott wing in the state claimed Grant's support.[29]

Orr was occasionally mentioned for the governorship, and in this regard some conservative newspapers spoke well of him. In February the Columbia Daily Phoenix described him as perhaps the only white Radical with whom the whites could feel secure. Although regarded by many as "time-serving and unreliable" in his partisan affiliations, he would as governor "not be distasteful to us." On the contrary, he was "the best able of any man we know to restore peace and quiet to our disturbed community."[30] In April the Spartanburg Carolina New Era noted that public opinion was fastening upon the upcountry leader "as the man for the crisis."[31] In early July the Charleston Daily News called him "the ablest man" in the Radical ranks.[32]

The Republican state convention gathered in Columbia on August 21. Leading figures in the anti-Moses group were Orr, Daniel T. Corbin, federal district attorney, Benjamin F. Whittemore, carpetbag legislator, F. A. Sawyer, carpetbag educator, and W. Beverly Nash. Mentioned as the reformers' choice for the governorship was Daniel H. Chamberlain, highly cultivated carpetbag attorney, but he stood on the sidelines. The insurgents turned to Reuben Tomlinson, carpetbag educator and legislator. Moses won, and on August 22, after the convention made its decision, Orr announced from the floor that he could not conscientiously support the nominee. He then withdrew, followed by most of the delegates from Anderson, Greenville, and Pickens Counties. As he left, the presiding officer, Thomas J. Mackey, remarked that the Andersonian had been "engaged all his life in jumping from side to side."[33]

Possibly one third of the delegates withdrew, and Orr issued a call for the bolters to hold their own conclave on the following day, August 23. About twenty-five to thirty delegates answered the summons, and they selected the judge as their presiding officer. Upon taking the chair he made a lengthy speech, followed by Bowen, Tomlinson, Corbin, Sawyer, and

others. The organization would be exclusively Republican, he emphasized; it would not conciliate or "buy"
the Democratic party. The 1870 Union Reform movement
had provided no "evidence of good faith" entitling
it to support from "real Republicans." Two years
ago he had felt that reform was needed, but to be
achieved only by Republicans. "I am astonished
that the Democrats should ask the Republicans, with
30,000 or 35,000 majority in the State, to come over
to their views. If they want reform, they must come
over to the Republican party, and there effect it."
The speaker believed that the masses of Republicans
were ready to overthrow the corruptionists. The
success of the reform campaign depended upon the
blacks, and if they were willing to be swindled, "be
it so." He was sure that they would pronounce their
voice of condemnation. He added, "If the white
element choose to vote with us, well, if not, and
they choose to put out their own ticket, let them
take the responsibility."[34]

The bolters selected Tomlinson for governor, and
they named Negroes for three of the six other statewide offices. Tomlinson declared that no alliance
with the Democrats would be considered. At a meeting
in Anderson on August 27, Orr and another bolter,
J. S. Murray, stressed this point. Both asserted
that a Democratic slate would reunite the Republicans
and prevent the defeat of Moses.[35]

Declining to nominate a statewide ticket, the
conservatives concentrated their energies upon local
contests. In counties where they were strong they
offered legislative candidates, and in the predominantly
Republican counties they backed the Republicans most
palatable to them.[36] Early in the campaign the
attitude of the conservative press was reflected by
the Laurensville Herald, which asked every white man
to stand aloof and "await future developments. This
paper called Orr a "Benedict Arnold to his former
party and the Judas of the hour."[37] Most papers endorsed neither Republican ticket, and they frequently
characterized both as odious. One leading insurgent,
Whittemore, had been expelled from Congress for taking
a bribe for a West Point cadetship. This scandal lent
plausibility to the charge that both Republican wings
were despicable. The bolters' warning that they would
reunite with the regulars if the Democrats fielded a
ticket was cited as proof of their insincerity. Moreover, Negro preference for scalawags over carpetbaggers
placed Tomlinson at a disadvantage.[38]

160

Most white ballots went to the bolters, while the blacks stood heavily with the regulars. Moses was decisively elected, and Grant won the state's presidential votes. Greeley's candidacy was not seriously promoted in South Carolina. Although sympathetic, the conservatives realized that an active effort for Greeley would be unavailing.[39]

In late August, while the campaign was in progress, Grant offered to appoint Orr minister to the Argentine Republic. Secretary of State Hamilton Fish wrote that the mission required a highly competent man, particularly in view of Argentina's liberal tendencies, its commerce with the United States, and that country's currently delicate relations with Brazil. The Andersonian, who had been reelected to the circuit court earlier in the year, replied that his private affairs precluded acceptance. However, in December, after the election, he agreed to serve as minister to Russia.[40]

*****   *****   *****   *****   *****

Modernization of the South's economy was the Piedmont leader's great dream. He envisioned a system of small farms and diversified industry, operated mainly by competent white laborers. Throughout his career he desired white immigration into the South. In 1870 he called a liberal immigration policy "an absolute Southern necessity."[41]

Partly affecting his outlook was an unfavorable estimate of black workers. In 1870 he remarked that the South's labor force was "insufficient and to some extent untrustworthy." At the same time Orr was skeptical about the Negro's ability to survive, in competition with the whites, in a free society. The black race was dying out, he believed, and in time there would be an inadequate number of Negroes left to till the crops. Reports of health officers in various Southern cities indicated this trend to him. Within twenty-five years all of the South's colder regions, from Virginia to Georgia, would be populated mainly by "sturdy white immigrants, before whose competing toil the negro will be obliged to give way." The black man would ultimately be confined to the lowlands. The "law of nature" had settled the red man's fate, and it "has applied to the negro" whenever he has tried to work side by side with the white.[42]

161

In spite of the great wartime losses, Orr saw
the South blessed by an immense land area, productive
soil, and a good climate. Capital and labor were
needed. He wanted to tap the world's population
reservoirs, and he maintained that an immigrant
would find larger rewards in South Carolina than in
the West.

> Our products are nearer the great markets
> of the world, our soil is far more fertile,
> and the emigrant will come to a State al-
> ready settled and possessing the advantages
> of age if not of progress. The same causes
> which have developed Wisconsin, Minnesota
> and Iowa may be applied with equal if not
> greater success in South Carolina. We
> only require a multitude of farmers to
> raise the produce for which we have hereto-
> fore paid the North and West, and in my
> judgment the owners of large tracts of
> valuable plantation lands will be glad to
> dispose of their surplus possessions rather
> than attempt the cultivation of crops on
> the gigantic scale which belonged to our
> former system of labor. Experiment has
> demonstrated, both here and abroad, the
> value of small farms and diversified indus-
> try.

If South Carolina could imitate New Jersey in exploiting water power and manufacturing resources,
"a truly golden dream of prosperity" would come.
Although the presently unstable political situation
frightened people from investing, he predicted that
the return of stability would bring a generous flow
of money.[43]

The stability that he desired was predicated upon
racial concord. In 1870 he declared that the majority
of blacks would eventually want to work in harmony
with the whites. He still spoke of an identity of
interests between the races, and he forecast that the
South would use the Fifteenth Amendment, a "two-edged
sword," to its advantage and obtain greater influence
in national politics.[44]

Although Orr stated that the Negro race would
ultimately die out, for the present he acknowledged
the black majority, with its political consequences.
Pessimistic about the Negro's ability to contribute to

the region's growth, he tolerated his presence grace-fully. The Negro himself made his presence bearable.[45]

> I think the negro race is a very controllable
> and manageable race. While they have not a
> very high sense of right of property, (and
> that could not be expected of them,) yet I
> do not think they are wanting in gratitude
> upon all proper occasions. But when you
> consider the sudden change wrought in the
> condition of the slave from 1865 to the
> present time, the matter of surprise is
> that the negro has not become much more
> insulting, exacting, and domineering than
> he has. . .

> I think the moral power of the white race
> over the colored race, which was acquired
> during two hundred years of slavery,
> exists to a very great extent yet. I
> think you may take colored men and train
> them and make good soldiers of them, if
> you have officers who will lead them.
> But if you trust to their individuality in
> resisting aggression and outrage upon them,
> it would be an exceptional case where the
> white race would be resisted.

He did not think that the whites had to pay a
price for stability and racial concord. Entry into
the Republican party, with the acknowledgment of
the Negro's political equality, was the price, a
price which most whites refused to pay. In 1871 Orr
contended that if the Southern whites had turned
Republican, they would have acquired absolute control,
even though there existed a corrupt element within that
party.

> The very moment that the colored man could
> have been satisfied that it was not the pur-
> pose of his old master to put him back into
> slavery, the old master would have obtained
> influence over him. And as conclusive proof
> of the correctness of my statement, I think
> if you will deem it worth while to put the
> question to every gentleman of the South who
> may come before you, you will be told that
> in everything outside of politics the white
> population, the democratic population, the
> old slaveholders, the men of most intelligence

in the community, have just as much influence over the negro and his conduct,
and the management of him, as they ever
had. He goes to them for advice, and
takes their advice on everything except
on the subject of voting.

Racial amity was attainable, so he asserted. Unfortunately, he saw an increasing tendency among blacks
and whites to polarize in politics.[46]

IX. JUDGE AND DIPLOMAT

The 1868 constitution divided South Carolina into eight judicial circuits, each having a judge elected for four years by the legislature. The circuit judge presided over the common pleas court, which dealt with civil and equity cases, and the general sessions court, which heard criminal cases. The constitution also provided for probate courts headed by popularly elected judges. In addition, local justices of the peace were to be chosen by popular vote; this provision was not carried out. In September 1868 the legislature empowered the governor to name "magistrates," and in February 1870 a new law established the courts of the trial justice, who would be appointed by the governor.[1]

Orr presided over the eighth judicial circuit, which comprised the counties of Anderson, Greenville, Oconee, and Pickens. (In 1870 Abbeville was transferred into this jurisdiction.) In this circuit the whites outnumberd the blacks. In Anderson and Greenville the ratio was about two-to-one, in Pickens four-to-one, and in Oconee five-to-one. In Abbeville there were about two black citizens to each white.[2]

General sessions cases involved numerous offenses, among them larceny, assault and battery, riot, malicious trespass, retailing liquor without a license, and keeping a bawdy house. The judge believed that the people in his circuit were generally law abiding. In January 1872 he told the Anderson County grand jury that the area had been entirely free of the disorders occurring elsewhere in the state. This overall peacefulness he attributed to the high caliber of the black leaders, whom he considered "the best and most intelligent of the former slaves and the issue of the old free negroes."[3]

He also described race relations as amicable, and the experiment with "mixed juries" he deemed successful. White jurors, the judge noted, were usually less severe towards Negroes than whites committing the same offense, on the ground that the white man "ought to have more intelligence than to do such a thing." Moreover, in his words, juries composed mostly of Negroes had not hesitated to convict black defendants.[4]

As governor, Orr had advocated a generous policy
towards debtors, and on the bench he worked for
leniency. His commons pleas courts usually awarded
the plaintiffs in debt cases much less than what they
demanded. In 1869 the Greenville jury established
the practice of "scaling" debts, usually to one-half
the sum of the principal and interest. Thereafter
many pleas were withdrawn by consent, and the
docket was rapidly cleared. On one occasion the
judge stated that the crowded dockets had hindered
all of the business enterprise of the community. In
his view, the ante-bellum and war debts had survived
the loss of property and nearly all means for debt
liquidation. Under a liberal debtor policy "all the
material interests of society in your midst will be
stimulated and developed. The losses of the past
will be swallowed up in the efforts, hopes and
achievements of the future."[5]

In Detheridge vs. Earle (1871) the state supreme
court voided "scaling." At issue was a promissory
note dated April 5, 1861; the Greenville court had
awarded the plaintiff one-half of the original sum.
Observing that the debt had not involved Confederate
notes or their equivalent, the higher tribunal insisted that no court could negate or partially negate
the obligation of contracts. "To permit persons to
get rid of paying one-half of their just, honest and
equitable debts, because there has been a rebellion
in the State, is no more nor less than offering a
premium for such rebellion."[6]

At issue in Blease and Baxter vs. Pratt (1869)
was an 1863 slave purchase, negotiated after the
Emancipation Proclamation took effect. Orr, as
visiting judge, instructed the Newberry jury that
Lincoln's decree, "emancipating all the slaves in
this State," nullified the sale and the promissory
note. The state supreme court overturned this decision, ruling that Lincoln's edict had not freed the
slaves in South Carolina. Even though the slaves
had been "afterwards liberated," the higher court
declared, there was no justification for a "breach of
the warranty of title contained in a bill of sale
of slaves."[7]

During his governorship the Andersonian had desired homestead legislation, and in 1868 the Republican regime enacted such a law. Under this measure,
whenever the real estate of a head of a family was
levied upon by court process, a homestead valued at
one thousand dollars should be measured off and
awarded to the debtor. The law applied to liens
existing at the time of its passage as well as to
those contracted thereafter. In Joseph R. Shelor vs.
John Mason, Sr., and John Mason, Jr., in Oconee
County, Orr upheld the new law. He cited judicial
decisions from other states which sustained the right
of legislatures to exempt a debtor's property from
levy or sale even for antecedent debts. He also
named the United States Supreme Court verdict in
Planter's Bank vs. Sharp, which admitted that states
could pass laws exempting tools or household goods
from levy or sale under existing contracts. The judge
ruled that since property of small value could be
exempted from levy for contracts existing before the
law's passage, then such an enactment must be constitutional when the property's value was enlarged.
In his words, the justification for the Homestead Act
had been accepted by the United States Supreme Court
in cases where state legislatures had changed the
statute of limitations, discharged insolvent debts,
and abolished imprisonment for debt. In Sturgis vs.
Crowninshield, John Marshall had distinguished between
the obligation of a contract and the remedy given
by a legislature to enforce it. The late chief justice was quoted, "Without impairing the obligation of
contract, the remedy may certainly be modified, as
the wisdom of the nation shall direct."[8]

The state supreme court reversed the circuit
court's decision in Shelor vs. Mason and Mason and
restricted the scope of the Homestead Law. The
plaintiff contested the legislature's power to allow
a homestead exemption as against the claim under a
mortgage executed prior to the adoption of the 1868
constitution. The higher tribunal maintained that the
mortgagee was entitled to the whole mortgaged premises,
or whatever portion was necessary to satisfy the mortgage. "This right constitutes, in part, the obligation
of the contract expressed by the mortgage." Otherwise,
the court ruled, the obligation of contracts would be
impaired.[9]

167

*****   *****   *****   *****   *****

The Palmetto state was the last in the Union to
allow divorces. Its people were, according to a Kentucky newspaper, "remarkable for an exalted conception
of the sacredness of the marriage tie." During the
Reconstruction era there was a brief interruption in
South Carolina's rigid anti-divorce tradition. The
1868 constitution gave to the common pleas courts
"exclusive jurisdiction in all cases of divorce,"
while specifying also that divorces could be allowed
only "by the judgment of a court as shall be prescribed by law."[10]

Although the legislature had not authorized the
courts to issue divorces, Orr in 1869 approved two
requests and dismissed a third. One of these decisions,
rendered at Greenville, contained a lengthy defense of
the judicial power to grant divorces. "There is,
perhaps, no other civilized country, either protestant
or catholic, that has not made some provision, either
legislatively or judicially, for dissolving marriage
for adequate cause, except this State." He contended
that if the equity courts could assume jurisdiction
from "necessity" and without legislative authorization
in alimony cases, they could act similarly in divorce
litigation. Before the 1868 constitution took effect
the state supreme court ruled that the equity courts
could decide alimony questions but not divorce cases.
Chief Justice Benjamin F. Dunkin had stated that the
equity courts possessed "no inherent power," aside
from any legislative mandate, to issue divorces. The
Anderson jurist cited a contradictory opinion, that
of New York's Chancellor Kent.[11]

The circuit judge was confident that the 1868
constitution obviated all doubts. He quoted those
sections which gave to the common pleas courts jurisdiction in all divorce and equity matters. Article
XIV, Section 5, allowed divorces "by the judgment of
a court, as shall be prescribed by law." Orr
asserted that this clause did not imply the requirement
of a legislative statute.[12]

In 1872 the legislature provided authorization for
the courts to dissolve marriages; six years later this
law was repealed. The 1895 constitution prohibited
divorces, and over fifty years elapsed before this ban
was lifted. In 1948 the voters approved a constitutional amendment permitting divorces; in the following
year enabling legislation was enacted.[13]

***** ***** ***** ***** *****

The upcountry judge was on the losing side in
the South Carolina election of 1872. Benjamin Perry
believed that the election result moved him to accept
the United States ministership to Russia, offered in
December. The legislature had re-elected him to the
bench earlier in the year, but the overseas mission
promised to be more remunerative. At this time the
Andersonian was a man of considerable wealth, with
a personal estate valued in the twenty thousand
dollar range.[14]

In Perry's opinion, the diplomatic appointment
manifested Grant's intention to reward the judge for
his speech at the Republican national convention in
June. The desire to name a prominent Southerner may
also have been a factor. Fifteen years earlier, in
1857, James Buchanan made a good will gesture to the
Palmetto state by naming Francis W. Pickens to the
Russian mission. In 1872 another leading South Carolina moderate entered the same position. At an
Anderson banquet Orr attributed the appointment to
Grant's purpose "to fully recognize the South as an
integral part of our common country." According to
this interpretation, the appointment was part of
the president's effort to bind up the nation's wounds.[15]

Undoubtedly the jurists' reputation as a competent public figure was weighed in Grant's mind. American-Russian relations were currently strained. Con-
stantine de Catacazy's presence as the Russian envoy
in Washington had caused some unpleasantness, and the
Russian foreign minister, Prince Gorchakov, regarded
him as meddlesome. Catacazy, whose recall was requested
by the United States, had spoken harshly of Grant and
had tried to prevent the execution of the Anglo-American
Treaty of Washington.[16]

In February 1873 Orr sailed from New York, and in
March he was in St. Petersburg to undertake his last
public service. Accompanying him were his son James
Lawrence, Jr., who served as his secretary, and his
daughter Mary, who enrolled at a girls school in
Weimar, Germany. Before embarking the new diplomat
contracted a cold, which prevented his full enjoyment
of the trip. Five or six days were spent in London,
followed by stays in Paris, Weimar, and Berlin. Many
traditional tourist sights were on their agenda--
Westminster Abbey, the Tower of London, the Tuileries,

169

the Louvre, and others. Orr recorded his impressions
of Europe in a letter to his brother Jehu.[17]

Throughout his life he was deeply interested in
economic development, and the letter contained his
appraisal of the European economy.

> The soil of France appears to me to be
> better than that of England or Germany and I
> thought in a higher state of cultivation.
> The farms are very small, many not exceeding
> an acre, and a furrow not a fence, marks the
> dividing line between the holders. I did not
> see a field in England or Germany or France,
> enclosed by a fence. All people are required
> to keep up their stock, and if they graze them,
> they must have herdsmen to protect their stock.
> If the farmers in these three empires were re-
> quired to fence their land it would absolutely
> bankrupt them. In western Germany the land,
> where it was level, was rich, and I was sur-
> prised, in travelling from Cologne to Cassel
> to see such a large number of furnaces, forges
> and foundries, with inexhaustable supplies of
> coal.

His social conservatism also showed itself. The conduct
of the 1871 Paris Commune he called "vandalic beyond
description or imagination." After describing the
damage caused by the insurrectionaries, he noted that
the elder Napoleon's Arch of Triumph "was spared by
the mob."[18]

When the minister met Tsar Alexander II on March
18, they discussed the Catacazy problem and the re-
ception given Grand Duke Alexis during his United
States tour in 1871 and 1872. In the American's words,
the tsar regarded the warm greeting accorded Alexis
as "a manifestation of friendship and respect" to
Russia as the "old and most steadfast friend" of the
United States in Europe. Orr informed Secretary of
State Hamilton Fish that all ill feelings arising
from the Catacazy affair had vanished. Evidently
the tsar was eager to improve relations between the
two countries.[19]

Two other matters of state were pressing. The letter to Jehu alluded to imminent hostilities between Russia and the Khivans, "who seem as great outlaws as our Comanches." The envoy called Khiva a "very contemptible" state and predicted an easy Russian conquest. Also, on May 2, he notified Fish of Russian designs on Japanese-held Sakhalin.[20]

Previous American ministers to St. Petersburg had disliked the damp and depressing weather.[21] The incumbent, who had already contracted a cold before sailing from New York, found the Russian weather uncongenial. He did not recover from his illness. On April 10, James Lawrence, Jr., wrote that his father's health was "improving slowly, though the climate is a great drawback to him, being very changeable just at this season of the year." On May 6, as he was approaching his fifty-first year, death came.[22]

*****   *****   *****   *****   *****

Orr's public career spanned a period in which a slaveholding society was in crisis. Like most other white South Carolinians, he defended slavery and supported secession when Lincoln won the presidency. Slavery was destroyed in the Civil War, and the South was challenged to create a new system of race relations. Although slavery died, many of the old racial prejudices lingered, and resistance to change remained strong. With the passage of the Reconstruction Acts, Orr urged his fellow whites to recognize the political rights of the freedmen. For proposing this course, and for entering the Negro's political party, he was severely censured. Racial polarization in politics, which he sought to avert, developed in the state. By the end of the century the blacks were largely disfranchised and removed as a factor in South Carolina's political life.

Orr's vision of manufacturing growth and economic diversification became a reality in the decades after his death. Particularly in the cotton mill industry did the Palmetto state make notable strides. In this endeavor growth was moderate in the immediate post-Civil War years. However, between 1880 and 1920 the textile industry expansion was considerable. By the latter date South Carolina was producing about one-fourth of the country's cotton yarn and cotton cloth.[23]

171

Only one of his descendants became active in state politics. James Lawrence, Jr. (1852-1905), textile mill executive in Anderson, was a Wade Hampton Democrat in the years after his father's death. Opposed to Benjamin F. Tillman's movement of downtrodden whites, which became a powerful force in the 1880's, he was the defeated candidate of the anti-Tillman conservatives for lieutenant-governor in 1892.

During his career the Piedmont politician was accused of opportunism. In 1932 Francis B. Simkins and Robert H. Woody, in their study of Reconstruction, took essentially this view. They saw elements of wisdom in his pragmatism, but they described as "devious" his efforts to promote white acquiescence in the Reconstruction Acts. William Arthur Sheppard's Red Shirts Remembered (1940), a rabidly anti-Radical work, was unfriendly to the Andersonian. "Corruption dragged a trail of slime through the State, and men whom the white people had delighted to honor were pleased with the feel of the ooze." Such a man, in Sheppard's mind, was Orr, who "denounced reform movements, was elected Judge by the Negroes, and rewarded by Grant with the portfolio of Minister to Russia." Other conservative historians of the twentieth century have written more respectfully. Commenting on his entry into the Republican party, John S. Reynolds in 1905 called him "a gentleman whose ability was everywhere recognized and of whose personal honesty there has never been a question." In 1926 Henry T. Thompson pictured the post-Civil War governor as "an able executive" whose task was complicated by the tension between civil and military jurisdictions. Thompson did not discuss his later affiliation with the Republicans.[24]

In early 1867 one newspaper remarked that the governor "has met the fate that so many renegrades have met before him--he is spurned by both parties." At about the same time, according to another journal, he was arousing much anger by proposing the suffrage for all literate blacks. Several years later Martin W. Gary, leading conservative Democrat, asserted that Orr had "betrayed his State by going over to the enemy and dividing the whites."[25]

172

The historian Joel Williamson has shown that anti-scalawag sentiment was more a post-Reconstruction myth than a Reconstruction reality. Many scalawags of good reputation enjoyed much deference in their society. Although Orr's political stands were often sharply attacked, he was widely esteemed in his community.[26]

When the news of death reached Anderson his fellow townsmen were stunned. The bells of the city chimed, while businesses closed. Upon reaching New York, the body was met by a delegation of Masons and other citizens, who conducted memorial services. When the body arrived in Columbia, some Anderson residents were there to accompany it to the diplomat's home town. The large attendance at the funeral, held on June 19, 1873, revealed the great admiration for this well known public figure. The Anderson Intelligencer, reporting his death, stated that Orr "had won his way easily to the hearts of all, whether high or low, rich or poor."[27]

NOTE ON SOURCES

This bibliographical note is not inclusive. Rather, it is limited to those materials that have been most heavily used in the preparation of this book.

Indispensible manuscript sources were the Orr-Patterson Papers at the University of North Carolina Library, the governorship papers at the South Carolina Archives, the James H. Hammond Papers at the Library of Congress, and the Benjamin F. Perry Papers at the Alabama Archives. Also useful were the Orr Papers at the South Caroliniana Library and the James J. Pettigrew Papers at the North Carolina Archives.

The Orr Pamphlets in the South Caroliniana Library contain significant materials, including the 1855 speech on political economy before the South Carolina Institute, the 1855 address on education at Furman University, and some campaign letters. Many of his speeches and statements will be found in the South Carolina press. Worth mentioning are the Anderson Gazette, the Anderson Intelligencer, the Charleston Daily Courier, the Charleston Daily News, the Charleston Mercury, the Columbia Daily Phoenix, the Pendleton Messenger, the Pickens (and later Walhalla) Keowee Courier, and the Spartanburg Carolina Spartan. These and other newspapers recorded much political activity and exude the flavor of public controversy and opinion.

Legislative documents have been vital. In the Congressional Globe and in the "Proceedings of the Confederate Congress," Southern Historical Society, Papers, volumes XLIV-L, one can grasp the quality of Orr's mind, his parliamentary acumen, and his political philosophy. The journal of the South Carolina legislature and The Journal of the Congress of the Confederate States of America, 1861-1865 were essential. Of similar value were the records of the state conventions which he attended, such as the secession convention and the 1865 constitutional convention.

Key sources for the judgeship were the local court judgment rolls in the South Carolina Archives, and the South Carolina Reports: Reports of Cases Heard and Determined in the Supreme Court of South Carolina.

Many secondary works have been relied upon for understanding the nation, section, and state in which Orr lived. The most important were the following:

Cauthen, Charles. South Carolina Goes to War, 1860-1865 (Chapel Hill, 1950).

Channing, Steven. Crisis of Fear: Secession in South Carolina (New York, 1970).

Craven, Avery O. The Growth of Southern Nationalism, 1848-1861 (Baton Rouge, 1953).

Hamer, Philip. The Secession Movement in South Carolina, 1847-1852 (Allentown, Pa., 1918).

Kibler, Lillian. Benjamin F. Perry: South Carolina Unionist (Durham, 1946).

Nevins, Allan. Ordeal of the Union (2 vols., New York, 1947).

Nevins, Allan. The Emergence of Lincoln (2 vols., New York, 1950).

Nichols, Roy F. The Disruption of American Democracy (New York, 1948).

Olsberg, R. Nicholas. "A Government of Class and Race: William Henry Trescot and the South Carolina Chivalry, 1860-1865" (Ph.D. dissertation, University of South Carolina, 1972).

Perman, Michael. Reunion Without Compromise: The South and Reconstruction, 1865-1868 (Cambridge, England, 1973).

Schultz, Harold S. Nationalism and Sectionalism in South Carolina, 1852-1860 (Durham, 1950).

Simkins, Francis B., and Woody, Robert H. South Carolina During Reconstruction (Chapel Hill, 1932).

Williamson, Joel. After Slavery: The Negro in South Carolina During Reconstruction, 1861-1877 (Chapel Hill, 1965).

Wiltse, Charles M. John C. Calhoun: Sectionalist
    (Indianapolis, 1951).

Yearns, Wilfred B. The Confederate Congress
    (Athens, Ga., 1960).

ABBREVIATIONS USED IN NOTES

A. H. R.   American Historical Review

Ala. Arch.   Alabama Department of Archives and History

C. U. Lib.   Clemson University Library

Cong. Globe   Congressional Globe

D. U. Lib.   Duke University Library

J. S. H.   Journal of Southern History

L. C.   Library of Congress

M. V. H. R.   Mississippi Valley Historical Review

N. C. Arch.   North Carolina Department of Archives and History

S. C. Arch.   South Carolina Department of Archives and History

S. C. H. M.   South Carolina Historical Magazine

S. H. C.   Southern Historical Collection, University of North Carolina Library

U. S. C.   South Caroliniana Library, University of South Carolina

U. Va. Lib.   University of Virginia Library

NOTES

CHAPTER I

1. On the sectional conflict and symbols, see
Avery O. Craven, The Growth of Southern Nationalism,
1848-1861 (Baton Rouge, 1953), 392-97. On cultural
federalism, Roy F. Nichols, The Disruption of American
Democracy (New York, 1948), 514.

2. 1800 Census of Pendleton District, South Carolina, ed. William C. Stewart (Washington, 1963), 5-6,
12; Anderson Intelligencer, May 8, 1873; Louise A.
Vandiver, Traditions and History of Anderson County
(Atlanta, 1928), 15.

3. Lillian Kibler, Benjamin F. Perry: South
Carolina Unionist (Durham, 1946), 10-11.

4. William W. Freehling, Prelude to Civil War:
The Nullification Controversy in South Carolina, 1816-
1836 (New York, 1965), 18; Alfred G. Smith, Jr.,
Economic Readjustment of an Old Cotton State (Columbia,
1958), 1-12, 9-32.

5. Ibid., 23-24; R. Nicholas Olsberg, "A Government of Class and Race: William Henry Trescot and the
South Carolina Chivalry, 1860-1865" (Ph.D. diss.,
Univ. of South Carolina, 1972), 36-43; Kibler, Perry,
17.

6. David D. Wallace, South Carolina: A Short
History (Columbia, 1961), 710.

7. Vandiver, Anderson County, 10, 15; Mss. returns
of the U.S. Census, 1840 (on microfilm at S. C. Arch.).

8. John Livingston, Biographical Sketches of
Distinguished Americans, Now Living (New York, 1853),
393.

9. Ibid., 393-94; Univ. of Virginia Faculty
Minutes, 1840, U. Va. Lib.; W. H. Topping, "Hon. James
L. Orr," National Democratic Review, I (1856), 328.

10. Gerald S. Henig, Henry Winter Davis (New York,
1973), 30-31; Univ. of Virginia Matriculation Books,
1834-1842, U. Va. Lib.

11. _Ibid._, Orr to John Reuben Thompson, Dec. 9, 1849, Thompson Papers, U. Va. Lib.; Henig, _Davis_, 28-31; Livingston, _Biographical Sketches_, 394; Topping, "Orr," 328.

12. _Ibid._, 328; _Charleston Daily Courier_, May 9, 1856.

13. Benjamin F. Perry, _Reminiscences of Public Men_ (Philadelphia, 1883), 185-86; Topping, "Orr," 341.

14. _Ibid._, 328; Anderson _Highland Sentinel_, Oct. 13, 1843.

15. Albert S. Thomas, _A Historical Account of the Protestant Episcopal Church in South Carolina_ (Columbia, 1957), 496-97.

16. Anderson _Highland Sentinel_, Oct. 13, 1843; Anderson _Gazette_, Feb. 27, July 17, July 24, Sept. 11, Nov. 27, 1846, Dec. 9, 1847; Vandiver, _Anderson County_, 20-21.

17. _Pendleton Messenger_, Aug. 11, Oct. 6, Oct. 13, 1843. Orr led in the four infantry regiments from Pendleton election district. Bonham won the other cavalry and infantry units in the division.

18. Vandiver, _Anderson County_, 109; Livingston, _Biographical Sketches_, 396.

19. Anderson _Highland Sentinel_, Oct. 13, 1843; Joel H. Silbey, "John C. Calhoun and the Limits of Southern Congressional Unity, 1841-1850," _The Historian_, XXX (1967), 62.

20. Anderson _Gazette_, Dec. 9, 1843. Opposition to the state-sponsored bank faded in the 1840's, as the Mexican War and the sectional quarrel absorbed public attention. Wallace, _South Carolina_, 427-28.

21. Charles M. Wiltse, _John C. Calhoun: Sectionalist, 1840-1850_ (Indianapolis, 1951), 181-83.

22. Rhett, low-country politician, editor, and planter, was the state's foremost disunionist of the pre-Civil War years.

23. Wiltse, Calhoun: Sectionalist, 185-97; Laura A. White, Robert Barnwell Rhett: Father of Secession (New York, 1931), 68-79.

24. Ibid., 79-81. Cheves, prominent in politics since the 1830's, was a former speaker of the national House of Representatives.

25. Pendleton Messenger, June 7, June 14, July 19, 1844; Anderson Gazette, July 5, July 12, 1844. Orr's newspaper denounced the protective tariff "by which the South is ground to the dust by iniquitous Taxation, for the benefit of Northern manufacturers."

26. Pendleton Messenger, Oct. 25, 1844.

27. Orr to Calhoun, Nov. 9, 1844, Calhoun Papers, C. U. Lib.

28. Greenville Mountaineer, Dec. 13, 1844; Journal of the House of Representatives of the States of South Carolina, 1844, pp. 236-37, S. C. Arch. (hereafter cited as S. C. House Journal).

29. Ibid., 1844, pp. 91-92.

30. The Wilmot Proviso, a rider to a Congressional bill, sought to ban slavery in all lands taken from Mexico. The Proviso was passed in the House but defeated in the Senate.

31. James W. Gettys, "To Conquer a Peace: South Carolina and the Mexican War" (Ph.D. diss., Univ. of South Carolina, 1974), 375; Ernest M. Lander, Jr., "The Reluctant Imperialist: South Carolina, the Rio Grande, and the Mexican War," Southwestern Historical Quarterly, LXXVIII (1975), 257-67.

32. Ibid., 256-57; Charleston Daily Courier, May 16, 1846; Charleston Mercury, Nov. 30, 1846.

33. Lander, "Reluctant Imperialist," 258-60; Lander, "The Palmetto Regiment Goes to Mexico," South Carolina Historical Association, Proceedings, 1973, pp. 83-84.

34. Gettys, "To Conquer a Peace," 375-80.

35. Orr to Calhoun, Aug. 9, 1847, Calhoun Papers, C. U. Lib.

36. Wiltse, Calhoun: Sectionalist, 289-90. Under the "Compromise of 1808" each election district received one senator, except for Charleston's two. Representatives were apportioned by white population and taxable wealth.

37. Freehling, Prelude to Civil War, 90-91, 330-33. While universal white male suffrage was in effect since the early nineteenth century, the only state and federal officials elected directly were members of the state legislature and the lower house of Congress.

38. S. C. House Journal, 1844, pp. 134-35, 137-38; 1845, pp. 199-200; 1846, pp. 138-40; 1847, pp. 59, 127-28; Charleston Daily Courier, Dec. 2, 1847; Anderson Gazette, Sept. 20, 1844, Dec. 12, 1845.

39. Ibid., Dec. 9, 1843.

40. Simms to Hammond, Jan. 7, 1847, The Letters of William Gilmore Simms, eds. M. C. Oliphant, A. T. Odell, and T. C. D. Eaves (5 vols., Columbia, 1954), II, 255-56. Simms wrote that Orr backed Hammond in the U. S. Senate election in 1846, when A. P. Butler beat Hammond.

41. Charleston Daily Courier, Oct. 20, 1846. David S. Taylor won 2,327 votes, Orr, 2,274, and John T. Broyles, 1,976. A legislator's stipend was between 200 and 250 dollars. S. C. Treasury Journal, 1845-1849, pp. 38, 69, 109, S. C. Arch.

42. Orr to Calhoun, Aug. 9, 1847, Calhoun Papers, C. U. Lib.; Anderson Gazette, May 27, June 10, June 24, 1847; J.N. Whitner to Benjamin F. Perry, Aug. 9, 1847, Perry Papers, Ala. Arch.

43. Anderson Gazette, May 27, June 10, June 24, 1847.

44. John G. Van Deusen, Economic Bases of Disunion in South Carolina (New York, 1928), 238-39.

45. Ibid., 240-43.

46. Kibler, _Perry_, 214-15.

47. _Ibid._, 214-15; Van Deusen, _Economic Bases_, 241-44; _Anderson Gazette_, Feb. 27, Sept. 11, Nov. 27, 1846; _Pendleton Messenger_, Sept. 11, Oct. 16, 1846, Aug. 6, 1847, Jan. 14, 1848; _Greenville Mountaineer_, Nov. 26, 1847.

48. _S. C. House Journal_, 1845, pp. 146-47.

49. Journal of Proceedings of the Town Council of Anderson, 1845-1866, pp. 1, 6-7, W. P. A. Transcripts of County Records, U. S. C.

50. _Ibid._, 9, 14-15.

51. _Anderson Gazette_, Sept. 5, Dec. 19, 1845.

CHAPTER II

1. Wiltse, _Calhoun: Sectionalist_, 241-42; Craven, _Southern Nationalism_, 21-35.

2. _Ibid._, 21-35.

3. Silbey, "Calhoun and..Congressional Unity," 60-63. Aspects of the 1848 campaign in South Carolina are described in Jon L. Wakelyn, "Party Issues and Political Strategy of the Charleston Taylor Democrats of 1848," _S. C. H. M._, LXXIII (1972), 72-86.

4. Joseph G. Rayback, _Free Soil: The Election of 1848_ (Lexington, 1970), 268-70, 275-76; Kibler, _Perry_, 223-24.

5. _Greenville Mountaineer_, Oct. 23, 1840, Oct. 14, 1842; _Pendleton Messenger_, Oct. 25, 1844; Charleston _Daily Courier_, Oct. 20, 1846. Simpson's Whig predecessors in Congress were Waddy Thompson and William Butler. See Gettys, "To Conquer a Peace," 65-70.

6 Kibler, _Perry_, 222-25; Orr to Calhoun, Aug. 9, 1847, Calhoun Papers, C. U. Lib.; Philip Hamer, _The Secession Movement in South Carolina, 1847-1852_ (Allentown, Pa., 1918), 17-18, 26.

7. Kibler, Perry, 222-23; Perry Diary, Oct. 1, 1848, Perry Papers, S. H. C.; Greenville Mountaineer, July 28, 1848.

8. Perry Diary, May 18, Dec. 24, 1848, Perry Papers, S. H. C.; Kibler, Perry, 224-25.

9. Ibid., 224-25; Greenville Mountaineer, Oct. 27, 1848; Pendleton Messenger, Nov. 3, 1848.

10. Ibid., May 4, May 18, 1849; Hamer, Secession Movement, 29-35.

11. Ibid., 35, 42-44.

12. Ibid., 45-48.

13. Congressional Globe, 31 Cong., 1 Sess. (May 8, 1850), Appendix, part I, 543-44.

14. Ibid., 544.

15. Ibid., 545-46.

16. Ibid., 546.

17. Ibid., 546.

18. Other parts of the Compromise of 1850 were abolition of the slave trade in the District of Columbia, adjustment of the Texas-New Mexico boundary, and compensation to Texas for yielding on the bounary question.

19. Hamer, Secession Movement, 58-59. Even the proposed fugitive slave law was eyed with suspicion in South Carolina, because it allowed the slave a jury trial. There was also doubt that the law could be enforced.

20. Ibid., 59-61; Allan Nevins, Ordeal of the Union (2 vols., New York, 1947), I, 315-17. Hammond and Pickens, both from Edgefield, were major South Carolina politicians. Hammond was a former governor, Pickens a former Congressman.

21. Cong. Globe, 31 Cong., 1 Sess. (June 12, 1850), 1189.

22. Pendleton Messenger, Sept. 20, 1850.

23. Nevins, Ordeal of the Union, I, 361-65.

24. Ibid., 358-61; Kibler, Perry, 243-48.

25. Nevins, Ordeal of the Union, I, 361-65.

26. Ibid., 365-66; Silbey, "Calhoun and..Congressional Unity," 66; Craven, Southern Nationalism, 108-11.

27. Ibid., 111-14; Pendleton Messenger, Oct. 31, Nov. 7, 1850, April 10, 1851; Orr to William Choice, Jan. 17, 1851, clipping from unidentified newspaper, Orr-Patterson Papers, S. H. C.

28. Kibler, Perry, 244-48. Butler and Barnwell, both U. S. Senators, were the leading cooperationist advocates. See John G. Barnwell, Jr., "Robert W. Barnwell and South Carolina Politics, 1850-1852" (M. A. thesis, Univ. of North Carolina, 1972).

29. Kibler, Perry, 252-53; Hamer, Secession Movement, 80-81.

30. Pendleton Messenger, April 10, 1851; Charleston Daily Courier, May 30, 1851.

31. Ibid., May 30, 1851. In the event of a blockade, Orr stated, Great Britain probably would not intervene, because British commerce with South Carolina was not great enough to induce intervention. Pendleton Messenger, July 31, 1851.

32. Ibid., July 31, 1851.

33. Ibid., July 31, 1851.

34. Proceedings of the Meeting of Delegates from the Southern Rights Associations of South Carolina Held at Charleston, May 1851 (Columbia, 1851), 6; Charleston Mercury, May 7, 1851; Hamer, Secession Movement, 93-98.

35. Ibid., 99-101; Charleston Mercury, July 30, 1851; Pendleton Messenger, July 31, 1851.

Some radical newspapers chided Orr for inconsistency. In the spring of 1851 he asked that delegates chosen for the state convention be uninstructed, and he wanted the state to abide by their policy. By the late summer he believed that the decision on secession should not be left to the delegates' discretion. He wanted the people, through public meetings, to instruct the delegates against separate secession. Ibid., August 14, 1851.

36. Charleston Mercury, Oct. 28, 1851; Kibler, Perry, 271-72.

37. Ibid., 272-78; White, Rhett, 114-15, 132-33. In December 1850 Rhett was elected to the U. S. Senate seat vacated by Calhoun's death in the previous March. Between Calhoun's death and Rhett's election Robert W. Barnwell held the seat by appointment.

CHAPTER III

1. Charles Cauthen, South Carolina Goes to War, 1861-1865 (Chapel Hill, 1950), 6; Manning to Orr, Jan. 11, 1853, Orr-Patterson Papers, S. H. C.

2. Pickens Keowee Courier, August 28, 1858; Cong. Globe, 32 Cong., 1 Sess. (June 9, 1852), Appendix, 658-59.

3. Ibid., 658-59.

4. Ibid., 658-59.

5. Harold S. Schultz, Nationalism and Sectionalism in South Carolina, 1852-1860 (Durham, 1950), 19-25, 79-83, 148-49; Kibler, Perry, 278-79.

6. Charleston Mercury, June 11, June 18, June 26, 1852.

7. Kibler, Perry, 278-301; Steven A. Channing, Crisis of Fear: Secession in South Carolina (New York, 1970), 168-70; Schultz, Nationalism and Sectionalism, 19-25.

8. Ibid., 97-101.

9. Charleston Mercury, June 22, 1852, quoting the Darlington Flag; John B. Edmunds, Jr., "Francis W. Pickens: A Political Biography" (Ph.D. diss., Univ. of South Carolina, 1967), 164.

10. U. S. Census Mss. returns, 1850; Pickens County Sessions Journal, 1843-1857 and 1857-1885 (W. P. A.

Historical Records Survey, 1938-39), U. S. C.; Anderson County, Minutes of the Court of Equity, S. C. Arch. During the 1850's a Congressman's salary was about three thousand dollars. Receipts and Expenditures of the U. S. Government, 1851-52, National Archives and Records Service.

11. Orr to J. D. B. DeBow, Nov. 7, 1855, DeBow Papers, D. U. Lib.; Orr to James J. Pettigrew, April 20, 1857, Pettigrew Papers, N. C. Arch.; South Carolina: The Grand Tour, ed. Thomas D. Clark (Columbia, 1973), 300; Paul W. Gates, "Southern Investments in Northern Lands Before the Civil War," J. S. H., V (1939), 156, 176-78.

12. U. S. Census Mss. returns, 1860; Virginia Clay-Clopton, A Belle of the Fifties (New York, 1905), 52.

13. Ibid., 52.

14. Loose Legislative Papers, S. C. Arch.

15. Cong. Globe, 32 Cong., 1 Sess. (Apr. 12, 1852), 1050; 33 Cong., 2 Sess. (Jan. 10, 1855), 230-31, 235; 34 Cong., 2 Sess. (March 2, 1857), 962-63.

16. Ibid., 32 Cong., 1 Sess. (Dec. 10, 1851), 60; Nevins, Ordeal of the Union, II, 24-25.

17. Cong. Globe, 32 Cong., 1 Sess. (Feb. 24, May 31, June 10, 1852), 1412-15, 1551-52, Appendix, 272-73; Schultz, Nationalism and Sectionalism, 43, 66.

18. Cong. Globe, 33 Cong., 2 Sess. (Jan. 10, 1855), 231.

19. John Forney, Anecdotes of Public Men (2 vols., New York, 1873), I, 57; Spartanburg Carolina Spartan, March 26, 1857, quoting the Newberry Rising Sun.

20. New York Times, Nov. 28, Dec. 5, Dec. 6, 1853; Orr to Perry, Dec. 9, 1853, Perry Papers, Ala. Arch.

21. Charleston Mercury, Dec. 7, 1853; Simms to Orr, August 30, 1856, Letters of..Simms, III, 440-41; Pickens to Milledge Bonham, Dec. 11, 1857, Bonham Papers, U. S. C.

22. Laura White, "The National Democrats in South Carolina, 1852 to 1860," South Atlantic Quarterly, XXVIII (1929), 370-71; Channing, Crisis of Fear, 168-69.

23. Pickens to Bonham, Dec. 11, 1857, Bonham Papers, U.S.C.; Olsberg, "A Government of Class and Race," 67-78, 86-100; Kibler, Perry, 226-30.

24. Ibid., 303-09; Chauncey Boucher, "Sectionalism, Representation, and the Electoral Question in Ante-Bellum South Carolina," Washington University Studies, IV (1916), 60.

25. Orr to Hammond, Sept. 17, 1859, Hammond Papers, L. C.; Schultz, Nationalism and Sectionalism, 24-25, 148-49, 176-77.

26. Daniel W. Hollis, University of South Carolina (2 vols., Columbia, 1956), II, 7-14; Kibler, Perry, 308-09; White, "National Democrats," 376.

27. Orr, Address Delivered before the Philosophian and Adelphian Societies of the Furman University, at their Annual Meeting, July 18, 1855 (Greenville, 1855), pamphlet.

28. Smith, Economic Readjustment of an Old Cotton State, 115-18; White, "National Democrats," 376-77; Kibler, Perry, 209.

29. Orr, Address Delivered before the South Carolina Institute (Charleston, 1855), pamphlet. This speech was also printed in DeBow's Review, XIX (1855), 1-22.

30. Ibid.

31. Ibid.

32. Ibid.

33. Ibid.; White, "National Democrats," 376-77.

34. Ronald Takaki, "The Movement to Reopen the African Slave Trade in South Carolina," S. C. H. M., LXVI (1965), 38-39, 47-52; Schultz, Nationalism and Sectionalism, 183.

35. Charleston Mercury, Oct. 31, Nov. 4, 1854.

36. Pickens Keowee Courier, Aug. 28, 1858; Cong. Globe, 34 Cong., 3 Sess. (Dec. 15, 1856), 123-26.

37. Craven, Southern Nationalism, 177-78.

38. Orr to Perry, March 6, 1854, Perry Papers, Ala. Arch.; Spartanburg Carolina Spartan, Aug. 10, Sept. 7, 1854.

39. Charleston Daily Courier, May 9, 1856.

40. Craven, Southern Nationalism, 238-43; White, "National Democrats," 372.

41. Spartanburg Carolina Spartan, Aug. 10, 1854; Aug. 30, 1855; Charleston Mercury, Aug. 4, 1855.

42. Robert E. May, The Southern Dream of a Caribbean Empire, 1854-1861 (Baton Rouge, 1973), 30-37.

43. Spartanburg Carolina Spartan, Sept. 7, 1854; Pickens Keowee Courier, Aug. 28, 1858; Schultz, Nationalism and Sectionalism, 53, 121, 178-79.

44. Cong. Globe, 32 Cong., 1 Sess. (Aug. 26, 1852), 2368-69; 32 Cong., 2 Sess. (Feb. 24, March 1, 1853), 825-26, 1001-02.

45. Ibid., 33 Cong., 1 Sess. (March 22, 1854), 718.

46. Ibid., 33 Cong., 1 Sess. (May 1, 1854), 1032-36; Spartanburg Carolina Spartan, May 18, 1854; John Savage, Our Living Representative Men (Philadelphia, 1860), 388-89.

47. Frederick Douglass Paper, Sept. 1, 1854; Hanson Pardon Records, National Archives Record Group Nos. 59, 204, National Archives and Records Service.

48. Charleston Mercury, Aug. 4, 1855.

49. Ibid., Aug. 4, 1855.

50. Ibid., Aug. 4, 1855.

51. Ibid., Aug. 7, 1855.

52. Ibid., Aug. 31, 1855; Spartanburg Carolina Spartan, Aug. 30, 1855; Schultz, Nationalism and Sectionalism, 84-85; Kibler, Perry, 281.

53. Letter from James L. Orr, of South Carolina, to Hon. C. W. Dudley (Washington, 1855), pamphlet.

54. Ibid., Charleston Daily Courier, May 9, 1856.

55. Spartanburg Carolina Spartan, Aug. 30, 1855; Schultz, Nationalism and Sectionalism, 96-102; Kibler, Perry, 283-85; Olsberg, "A Government of Class and Race," 12-17.

56. Fred H. Harrington, "The First Northern Victory," J. S. H., V (1939), 186-205; "A Congressman's Letters on the Speaker Election in the Thirty-Fourth Congress," ed. T. R. Hollcroft, M. V. H. R., XLIII (1956), 444-45.

57. Cong. Globe, 34 Cong., 1 Sess. (Jan. 9, 1856), 175; Charleston Mercury, Jan. 29, 1856.

58. New York Times, Feb. 23, 1856; Topping, "Orr," 339; Roy F. Nichols, Franklin Pierce: Young Hickory of the Granite Hills (Philadelphia, 1931), 451.

59. White, "National Democrats," 377-78; Charleston Daily Courier, May 7, May 8, 1856.

60. Ibid., May 9, 1856.

61. Ibid., May 9, 1856.

62. Schultz, Nationalism and Sectionalism, 121. Nichols, Disruption of American Democracy, 519-20, contains the text of the Cincinnati plank on slavery.

63. Charleston Daily Courier, June 5, June 6, June 27, 1856; Schultz, Nationalism and Sectionalism, 121-23.

64. Ibid., 113-20.

65. Charleston Mercury, July 12, 1856; Cong. Globe, 34 Cong., 1 Sess. (July 9, 1856), Appendix, 805-06.

66. Robert W. Johannsen, Stephen A. Douglas (New York, 1973), 535; Charleston Mercury, Oct. 14, 1856.

67. Nevins, Ordeal of the Union, II, 511; Schultz, Nationalism and Sectionalism, 124-28.

68. Buchanan to Orr, Jan. 1, 1857, Orr-Patterson Papers, S. H. C.; Orr to Pickens, Jan. 6, 1857, Pickens Papers, D. U. Lib.

69. Cong. Globe, 34 Cong., 3 Sess. (Jan. 9-22, Feb. 19-28, 1857), 274-76, 403-13, 426-33, 760-73, 924-53; Henig, Davis, 93-94.

70. Orr to James J. Pettigrew, April 20, 1857, Pettigrew Papers, N. C. Arch.; Spartanburg Carolina Spartan, May 14, 1857. Senator Douglas, who saw Orr in Minnesota during the summer, described him as "familiar with speculations in Government lands." Douglas to the Chicago Times editor, Aug. 29, 1857, The Letters of Stephen A. Douglas, ed. Robert W. Johannsen (Urbana, 1961), 394.

71. Schultz, Nationalism and Sectionalism, 139-41; Charleston Daily Courier, June 10, 1857.

72. Charleston Mercury, June 6, Aug. 6, 1857 (quoting the Newberry Mirror on Aug. 6).

73. Charleston Mercury, Aug. 15, 1857, quoting the Anderson Gazette and Advocate; Cobb to Alexander H. Stephens, July 21, 1857, The Correspondence of Robert Toombs, Alexander H. Stephens, and Howell Cobb, in Amer. Historical Assn., Annual Report, 1911, II (Washington, 1913), 406-07; Thomas Bocock to Hunter, July 23, 1857, The Correspondence of Robert M. T. Hunter, ed. C. H. Ambler (New York, 1971), 211; Nichols, Disruption of American Democracy, 150-51.

74. Orr to Pettigrew, April 20, 1857, Pettigrew Papers, N. C. Arch.; Orr to Breckinridge, Aug. 13, 1857, Breckinridge Papers, L. C.

75. William F. Russell to Orr, Aug. 31, 1857, Orr-Patterson Papers, S. H. C.; Orr to A. D. Banks, Aug. 17, 1857, Ibid.; James C. Allen to Stephen A. Douglas, Nov. 30, 1857, Douglas Papers, Univ. of Chicago Library; James McCook to Douglas, Nov. 30, 1857, Ibid.,; Ben Perley Poore, Perley's Reminiscences of Sixty Years in

the National Metropolis (2 vols., Philadelphia, 1886),
I, 530-31; Nichols, Disruption of American Democracy,
150-51.

76. Clay-Clopton, A Belle of the Fifties, 42-44,
51-52; Perley's Reminiscences, II, 21-22; Allan Nevins,
The Emergence of Lincoln (2 vols., New York, 1950),
I, 124; W. A. Swanberg, Sickles the Incredible (New
York, 1956), 15. The Speaker's salary was over twelve
thousand dollars. Receipts and Expenditures of the
U. S. Government, 1858-59, National Archives and
Records Service.

77. Orr to James J. Pettigrew, Jan. 18, 1858,
Pettigrew Papers, N. C. Arch.

78. Cong. Globe, 35 Cong., 1 Sess. (Feb. 2, Feb. 8,
1858), 535-41, 621-23.

79. Ibid., 35 Cong., 1 Sess. (April 14, May 4,
1858), 1589-90, 1905-06.

80. Schultz, Nationalism and Sectionalism, 147-49,
175-77.

81. Ibid., 156-69; Kibler, Perry, 292-95.

82. Schultz, Nationalism and Sectionalism, 157,
164, 181-85; James H. Adams to Hammond, Sept. 22,
1858, Hammond Papers, L. C.

83. Pickens Keowee Courier, Aug. 7, 1858; Orr to
Hammond, July 25, 1858, Hammond Papers, L. C.

84. Pickens Keowee Courier, Aug. 14, 1858.

85. Ibid., Aug. 28, 1858.

86. Ibid., Aug. 28, 1858.

87. Ibid., Aug. 28, 1858.

88. Spartanburg Carolina Spartan, March 11, 1858;
Ashmore to Perry, Jan. 7, July 14, 1858, Perry Papers,
Ala. Arch.

89. Pickens Keowee Courier, Dec. 4, 1858, Jan. 8,
1859; Spartanburg Carolina Spartan, April 21, 1859;
White, "National Democrats," 381.

Adding to Orr's disillusionment was his opinion that the Buchanan presidency was a failure. In late 1859 he spoke harshly of Buchanan, chiefly because of the tariff and "general inefficiency." Ashmore to Perry, Nov. 22, Nov. 23, 1859, Perry Papers, Ala. Arch.

90. Cong. Globe, 34 Cong., 3 Sess. (Dec. 11, 1856), 103-04.

91. Robert W. Johannsen, "Stephen A. Douglas, 'Harper's Magazine,' and Popular Sovereignty," M. V. H. R., XLV (1959), 608, 617; Orr to Hammond, Sept. 17, 1859, Hammond Papers, L. C.

92. Orr to Hammond, Sept. 17, 1859, Ibid.

93. Orr to Hammond, Sept. 17, 1859, Ibid.; Pickens Keowee Courier, April 9, 1859.

94. Hammond to William Porcher Miles, Nov. 23, 1858, Miles Papers, S. H. C.

95. Channing, Crisis of Fear, 87, 92-93.

96. Ollinger Crenshaw, The Slave States in the Presidential Election of 1860 (Baltimore, 1945), 199-200; Schultz, Nationalism and Sectionalism, 194.

97. Ibid., 189-91; Channing, Crisis of Fear, 127-30.

98. Ibid., 157-60.

99. Ibid., 172-77.

100. Ibid., 199-200; Orr to Perry, March 5, 1860, Perry Papers, Ala. Arch.; Orr to Pettigrew, Feb. 8, 1860, Pettigrew Papers, N. C. Arch.

101. Charleston Mercury, April 18, 1860.

102. Ibid., April 18, 1860.

103. Ibid., April 20, 1860.

104. Maxcy Gregg to A. P. Aldrich et al, Oct. 23, 1858, Hammond Papers, L. C.; Edward Spann to Hammond, April 21, 1860, Hammond Papers, U. S. C.; Hammond to William Porcher Miles, July 16, 1860, Miles Papers, S. H. C.

CHAPTER IV

1. Three Against Lincoln: Murat Halstead Reports the Caucuses of 1860, ed. William B. Hesseltine (Baton Rouge, 1960), 14-15.

2. Schultz, Nationalism and Sectionalism, 215-16. After the South Carolinians exited, the delegations from Florida, Texas, Arkansas, and Georgia followed them.

3. Ibid., 216-19.

4. Ashmore to Orr, May 25, 1860, Orr-Patterson Papers, S. H. C.; Edgefield Advertiser, Aug. 8, 1860, printing Orr letter of July 23.

5. Ibid., Aug. 8, 1860. Breckinridge was over-whelmingly favored in South Carolina.

6. Ashmore to Hammond, July 10, 1860, Hammond Papers, L. C.

7. Edgefield Advertiser, Aug. 8, 1860.

8. Ibid., Oct. 3, 1860.

9. Channing, Crisis of Fear, 239n; Cauthen, South Carolina Goes to War, 27. The Anderson Intelligencer, Oct. 4, 1860, predicted that Orr's pronouncement would induce the "ultra Unionists" to reconsider their views.

10. Schultz, Nationalism and Sectionalism, 223-24; Channing, Crisis of Fear, 242-43; Olsberg, "A Government of Class and Race," 238-41.

11. Yorkville Enquirer, Nov. 1, 1860; Channing, Crisis of Fear, 240.

12. Spartanburg Carolina Spartan, Nov. 8, 1860.

13. James J. Pettigrew to W. S. Pettigrew, Oct. 24, 1860, Pettigrew Papers, S. H. C.; Ashmore to Perry, Nov. 14, 1860, Perry Papers, Ala. Arch.; Channing, Crisis of Fear, 261-64; Olsberg, "A Government of Class and Race," 213-15, 219-22, 246-68.

14. _Ibid._, 242-44; Nichols, <u>Disruption of American Democracy</u>, 366-67.

15. Cauthen, <u>South Carolina Goes to War</u>, 51-60; Olsberg, "A Government of Class and Race," 269-72.

16. Pickens <u>Keowee Courier</u>, Nov. 24, Dec. 1, 1860; Ashmore to Perry, Nov. 19, 1860, Perry Papers, Ala. Arch. In Anderson Orr again upheld cooperative action. If the other Southern states "submitted tamely" to Lincoln's rule, he reserved the right to oppose South Carolina's lone departure.

17. <u>Anderson Intelligencer</u>, Dec. 13, 1860; <u>Charleston Mercury</u>, Dec. 18, 1860; <u>Journal of the Convention of the People of South Carolina, held in 1860, 1861, and 1862, together with the Ordinances, Reports, Resolutions, etc.</u> (Columbia, 1862), 23. Hereafter cited as <u>Journal of the Convention..1860, 1861, 1862</u>. The other Anderson delegates were Joseph N. Whitner, J. P. Reed, R. F. Simpson, and B. F. Mauldin.

18. _Ibid._, 59; <u>Charleston Mercury</u>, Dec. 22, 1860.

19. "Narrative and Letter of William Henry Trescot, concerning the Negotiations between South Carolina and President Buchanan in December, 1860," <u>A. H. R.</u>, XIII (1908), 543.

20. _Ibid._, 543; <u>The War of the Rebellion: A Compilation of the Official Records of the Union and Confederate Armies</u> (Washington, 1880-1901), Series I, I, 115.

21. Samuel W. Crawford, <u>The Genesis of the Civil War: The Story of Fort Sumter</u> (New York, 1887), 148-49. Crawford quoted a letter written to him by Orr, dated September 21, 1871.

22. <u>War of the Rebellion</u>, Series I, I, 109-110, 115-18.

23. _Ibid._, Series, I, I, 120-25.

24. Journal of the Convention..1860, 1861, 1862, 156, 172; Trescot to Cobb, Jan. 14, 1861, "Three Letters of William Henry Trescot to Howell Cobb, 1861," ed. M. Foster Farley, S. C. H. M., LXVIII (1967), 26.

25. Journal of the Convention of the People of Georgia, held in Milledgeville and Savannah, in 1861, Together with the Ordinances Adopted (Milledgeville, 1861), 305-06.

26. Journals of the South Carolina Executive Councils of 1861 and 1862, ed. Charles Cauthen (Columbia, 1956), 21-22.

27. Anderson Intelligencer, Jan. 24, 1861.

28. Ibid., March 7, March 21, 1861; Thomas, Protestant Episcopal Church in South Carolina, 496-97.

29. Pickens Keowee Courier, May 25, June 8, June 22, 1861; Spartanburg Carolina Spartan, June 20, 1861; Charleston Daily Courier, Aug. 23, 1861.

30. War of the Rebellion, Series I, LIII, 180, Series IV, I, 404-05; J. W. Mattison, "Orr's South Carolina Rifles," Southern Historical Society, Papers, XXVII (1899), 157-59; Pickens Keowee Courier, July 13, 1861.

31. Charleston Mercury, Feb. 3, 1862.

32. Ralph A. Wooster, The Secession Conventions of the South (Princeton, 1962), 22-23; Journal of the Convention..1860, 1861, 1862, 216-21, 236-37, 243-48, 255-62. Orr himself proposed a change, which the convention endorsed: "That Congress shall not contract any debt, except for war purposes, and all expenditures in excess of revenues from imports, which shall not exceed fifteen per cent ad valorem, and other services, shall be met by direct taxation, to be provided for by Congress authorizing the expenditure." Ibid., 260.

33. Cauthen, South Carolina Goes to War, 139-40.

34. Olsberg, "A Government of Class and Race," 391-92.

35. Journal of the Convention..1860, 1861, 1862, 333.

36. Cauthen, South Carolina Goes to War, 142-44; Olsberg, "A Government of Class and Race," 392-93.

37. Ibid., 392-93; Laura White, "The Fate of Calhoun's Sovereign Convention in South Carolina," A. H. R., XXXIIII (1929), 759-60; Lowry P. Ware, "Attorney General Isaac W. Hayne and the South Carolina Executive Council of 1862," South Carolina Historical Association, Proceedings, 1952, pp. 8-11; Cauthen, South Carolina Goes to War, 144.

38. Ibid., 152-56; Journal of the Convention..1860, 1861, 1862, 399.

39. Charleston Daily Courier, Dec. 4, 1862; William Gilmore Simms to Hammond, Dec. 4, 1862, Hammond Papers, L. C.; White, "Calhoun's Sovereign Convention," 770; Cauthen, South Carolina Goes to War, 161-62.

CHAPTER V

1. Journal of the Congress of the Confederate States of America, 1861-1865 (7 vols., Washington, 1904-05), I, 844, 849. Hereafter cited as Jour. Cong.

2. Trescot to Miles, Dec. 6, 1861, Miles Papers, S. H. C.; Edward S. Hammond to James H. Hammond, June 10, 1861, Hammond Papers, U. S. C.; A. P. Aldrich to Milledge Bonham, Jan. 5, 1862, Bonham Papers, U. S. C.; Mary Chesnut, A Diary from Dixie (Boston, 1949), 157, 168; Olsberg, "A Government of Class and Race," 391.

3. On Feb. 21, 1862, when the Senate classified its members, South Carolina was designated "four years --six years." Barnwell drew the short term and Orr the long one. Jour. Cong., II, 12-14.

4. "Proceedings of the Confederate Congress," Southern Historical Society, Papers, LI, 26-29, hereafter cited as "Proc. Cong."

5. David Donald, Why the North Won the Civil War (New York, 1962), 80-84.

6. "Proc. Cong.," XLVI, 247-49.

7. Jour. Cong., II, 153-54.

8. "Proc. Cong.," XLV, 250-53.

9. Ibid., XLVIII, 187-90; Jour. Cong., III, 97-98.

10. Ibid., III, 497-99; "Proc. Cong.," L, 127-34, 150-58. Orr proposed the drafting of all principals liable to service who had, since May 19, 1862, furnished substitutes who were liable. Men who had since September 8, 1862, offered substitutes under age eighteen or in a partisan corps would also be subject to the draft. Those who had since July 20, 1863, provided substitutes who had been lost (not as casualties) would be similarly affected. He contended that this plan would procure "all who did not have good substitutes." It lost by a 5-15 vote.

11. Ibid., XLVI, 74-79.

12. Ibid., XLVI, 189-92.

13. Ibid., XLVIII, 105-07; Jour. Cong., II, 295-96, 310-13.

14. Ibid., II, 261-62, III, 546-47, 559, 567-68, 572-73, 582, 765-68; IV, 575; "Proc. Cong.," L, 45-46, LII, 326-28, 359-62, 370-71.

15. Ibid., XLIX, 17, 174-77; Jour. Cong., III, 354-55; Wilfred B. Yearns, The Confederate Congress (Athens, Ga., 1960), 129-30.

16. Jour. Cong., IV, 268; "Proc. Cong.," LI, 406-07.

17. Ibid., LII, 2-6; Jour. Cong., III, 712, IV, 387, 723.

18. "Proc. Cong.," XLVII, 206-10, XLVIII, 2-5, 13-16, 25-27, 39-40, 53-54, 60-61, 75-76, 318-25; Yearns, Confederate Congress, 38.

19. Ibid., 228; "Proc. Cong.," XLVIII, 287-90.

20. Ibid., LI, 192-93, 198-99.

21. Ibid., LII, 270.

22. Michael Musick, "The South Carolina Delegation in the Confederate Congress" (M. A. thesis, Emory Univ., 1968), 52-55, War of the Rebellion, Series I, XIV,

897-900; "Proc. Cong.," XLVIII, 73, XLIX, 75-77.

23. Orr to Beauregard, April 4, 1863, Orr File, Civilian Records, War Dept. Collection of Confederate Records, National Archives and Records Service.

24. "Proc. Cong.," XLVI, 61, 113-19, 127-31.

25. Ibid., LII, 290-91; Jour. Cong., IV, 266, 326; Sens. Wigfall, Orr, et al, to Gen. Robert E. Lee, Feb. 4, 1865, Wigfall Papers,L. C.

26. Yearns, Confederate Congress, 122, 233; Jour. Cong., III, 453; "Proc. Cong.," L, 14, 43-44. On Dec. 14, 1863, Orr stated that the impressment law had become "an instrument of oppression."

27. Ibid., XLVIII, 154-58; Jour. Cong., II, 73-74, 243, III, 216-17.

28. Ibid., IV, 552-53. Benjamin was prominent in the drive to enlist black soldiers, and the opposition to black troops became entangled with the movement to demand his resignation. N. W. Stephenson, "The Question of Arming the Slaves," A. H. R., XVIII (1913), 295-96.

29. "Proc. Cong.," XLV, 222-24; Jour. Cong., III, 371. In Sept. 1862 and May 1863 Congress passed legislation regulating hospital conditions and procedures for granting furloughs and discharges.

30. Ibid., IV, 267.

31. Bell I. Wiley, Southern Negroes, 1861-1865 (New Haven, 1938), 148-51.

32. Jour. Cong., III, 194, 584, 740-41; "Proc. Cong.," L, 334.

33. Wiley, Southern Negroes, 148-59; Bill G. Reid, "Confederate Opponents of Arming the Slaves," Journal of Mississippi History, XXII (1960), 249-70.

34. "Proc. Cong.," LII, 289-93.

35. Ibid., LII, 289-93, 296-98, 300-06.

36. Jour. Cong., IV, 585, 670-71.

37. Orr to Perry, Feb. 17, 1865, Perry Papers, Ala. Arch.

38. Jour. Cong., IV, 298; "Proc. Cong.," LI, 322, 435. The United States apologized to Brazil and agreed to return the Florida. The steamer sank mysteriously in Hampton Roads before it could return.

39. Yearns, Confederate Congress, 169-70.

40. Orr to Benjamin, May 27, 1862, Orr File, Civilian Records, War Dept. Collection of Confederate Records, National Archives and Records Service.

41. Yearns, Confederate Congress, 162.

42. Jour. Cong., III, 140; "Proc. Cong.," XLIX, 230-35.

43. Orr to Perry, May 12, 1863, Perry Papers, Ala. Arch.

44. "Proc. Cong.," L, 22-39; Yearns, Confederate Congress, 175.

45. Orr to Hammond, Jan. 3, 1864, Hammond Papers, L. C.

46. Jour. Cong., III, 515-16.

47. Orr to "McCalla," Feb. 7, 1864, Bell I. Wiley Collection on the Confederate Congress, Emory Univ.

48. Reminiscences of Jehu A. Orr, typescript in Mississippi Dept. of Archives and History, 4-5.

49. Ibid., 4-5; Jour. Cong., IV, 143-212.

50. Robert M. T. Hunter, "The Peace Commission of 1865," Southern Historican Society, Papers, III, 168-69; Yearns, Confederate Congress, 178-80.

51. Reminiscences of Jehu A. Orr, 11-13; Yearns, Confederate Congress, 181.

52. Orr to Perry, Feb. 17, 1865, Perry Papers, Ala. Arch.; Memoirs of Williamson Oldham, Confederate Senator, typescript, Univ. of Texas Lib., 301-02.

53. Jefferson Davis, "Reply of Jefferson Davis to Robert M. T. Hunter," Southern Historical Society, Papers, V, 223; Jour. Cong., IV, 633; Reminiscences of Jehu A. Orr, 13.

54. Anderson Intelligencer, April 7, 1870; Orr to Pickens, April 29, 1865, Pickens-Dugas Papers, S. H. C.

55. Orr to Pickens, April 29, 1865, Ibid.

CHAPTER VI

1. Edgefield Advertiser, May 24, 1865.

2. Michael Perman, Reunion Without Compromise: The South and Reconstruction, 1865-1868 (Cambridge, England, 1973), 27-30, 57-60; John R. Kirkland, "Federal Troops in the South Atlantic States, 1865-1877" (Ph.D. diss., Univ. of North Carolina, 1968), 33-35.

3. Kibler, Perry, 375-76.

4. Kirkland, "Federal Troops," 68-69.

5. Kibler, Perry, 377-86; Perman, Reunion Without Compromise, 74; Columbia Daily Phoenix, July 31, 1865; Perry, Reminiscences of Public Men, with Speeches and Addresses (Greenville, 1889), 247-49, 275.

6. Ibid., 184; John L. Bell, Jr., "Constitutions and Politics: Constitutional Revision in the South Atlantic States, 1864-1902" (Ph.D. diss., Univ. of North Carolina, 1970), 62-63; The Diary of Gideon Welles, ed. H. K. Beale (3 vols., New York, 1960), II, 358-59.

7. Journal of the Convention of the People of South Carolina, held in Columbia, South Carolina, September 1865 (Columbia, 1865), 5-25.

8. Ibid., 59-65; Charleston Daily Courier, Sept. 22, 1865; Perry, Reminiscences (1889 ed.), 277; Sidney Andrews, The South Since the War (Boston, 1866), 62-63.

9. Kibler, Perry, 406-09.

10. Joel Williamson, After Slavery: The Negro in South Carolina During Reconstruction (Chapel Hill, 1965), 350; Eric McKitrick, Andrew Johnson and Reconstruction (Chicago, 1960), 210-11; Perman, Reunion Without Compromise, 106-07.

11. Journal of the Convention..1865, 21, 33-36, 79-82, 86-87, 93; Charleston Daily Courier, Sept. 19, 25, 28, 1865; Andrews, South Since the War, 48, 68-73. Charleston was given two senators, and each of the other districts received one.

12. Donald H. Breese, "Politics in the Lower South During Presidential Reconstruction, April to November 1865" (Ph.D. diss., Univ. of California at Los Angeles, 1964), 306.

13. Charleston Daily Courier, Sept. 25, 28, 1865; Andrews, South Since the War, 40.

14. Ibid., 49; Journal of the Convention..1865, 147-48; Charleston Daily Courier, Sept. 28, 1865.

15. Bell, "Constitutions and Politics," 69-70, 134; Breese, "Politics in the Lower South," 239-42; Andrews, South Since the War, 96.

16. Ibid., 40, 49-50; Columbia Daily Phoenix, Sept. 27, 1865; Perry, Reminiscences (1889 ed.), 280; Charleston Daily Courier, Sept. 28, 1865.

17. Ibid., Nov. 3, 1865; Report of the Joint Committee on Reconstruction, at the First Session, Thirty-Ninth Congress (Washington, 1866), Part II, 216-17; Perry, Reminiscences (1889 ed.), 278. There were reports that many Hampton ballots were voided on grounds of faulty marking.

18. Ibid., 278-79; Francis B. Simkins and Robert H. Woody, South Carolina During Reconstruction (Chapel Hill, 1932), 43; The Ku-Klux Conspiracy: Testimony Taken by the Joint Select Committee to inquire into the condition of affairs in the late insurrectionary States (Washington, 1872), III, 18; J. Rutherford Worcester to Orr, Dec. 11, 1865, Orr Papers, S. C. Arch.; New York Times, Feb. 17, 1867; Harper's Weekly, IX (1865), 721.

19. Sumter Watchman, Dec. 13, 1865.

20. Ibid., Dec. 13, 1865; Orr to William D. Kelley, Dec. 21, 1865, Orr Papers, S. C. Arch.

21. Thomas Wagstaff, "Call Your Old Master 'Master': Southern Political Leaders and Negro Labor During Presidential Reconstruction," Labor History, X (1969), 336-37; Sumter Watchman, Dec. 13, 1865.

22. Theodore B. Wilson, The Black Codes of the South (University, Ala., 1965) discusses the codes in South Carolina and elsewhere.

23. Williamson, After Slavery, 75-77; Charleston Daily Courier, Feb. 16, 1866; William H. Trescot to Orr, Jan. 1, 1866, Orr Papers, S. C. Arch.; Sickles to Orr, Jan. 4, 1866 (telegram), and Orr to Sickles, Jan. 4, 1866 (telegram), Sickles Papers, D. U. Lib.; Kirkland, "Federal Troops," 118-19.

24. New York Times, Jan. 4, 1866.

25. Orr to Sickles, Dec. 13, 1865, Orr Papers, S. C. Arch. Fears of Christmas uprisings were widespread in the South. Dan T. Carter, "The Anatomy of Fear: The Christmas Day Insurrection Scare of 1865," J. S. H., XLII (1976), 345-64.

26. Orr to Sickles, Dec. 13, 1865, Orr Papers, S. C. Arch.

27. Orr to Johnson, Jan. 19, 1866, in Charleston Daily Courier, Feb. 3, 1866; Pickens to Orr, Feb. 16, 1866, Orr Papers, S. C. Arch.; Williamson, After Slavery, 62.

28. Columbia Daily Phoenix, Sept. 27, 1865; Andrews, South Since the War, 96; Sumter Watchman, Dec. 13, 1865. In his inaugural speech Orr credited the high tariff, which he expected to be retained for many years, with making the present time "auspicious' for new manufacturing projects.

29. Rowland T. Berthoff, "Southern Attitudes Towards Immigration," J. S. H., XVII (1951), 328-31; Williamson, After Slavery, 118; Orr to secretary of the German Society of New York, March 2, 1866, in Charleston Daily Courier, March 6, 1866.

30. Sumter Watchman, Dec. 13, 1865; McKitrick, Johnson and Reconstruction, 191, 210-11; William Gillette, The Right to Vote: Politics and the Passage of the Fifteenth Amendment (Baltimore, 1965), 25-26.

31. Orr to Kelley, Dec. 21, 1865, Orr Papers, S. C. Archives.

32. Orr to Kelley, Dec. 21, 1865, Ibid.

33. V. Jacque Voegeli, Free But Not Equal: The Midwest and the Negro During the Civil War (Chicago, 1967), discusses Northern dislike of Negroes and fear of black migrations from the South.

34. Trescot to Orr, Feb. 28, March 4, March 6, March 31, April 15, April 20, May 6, May 13, May 20, 1866, Orr Papers, S. C. Arch.

35. Ronald E. Bloom, "The National Union Convention of 1866," (M.A. thesis, Univ. of Pittsburgh, 1963), 71-72, 93-95, 103-04, 122.

36. Ibid., 88-89, 100, 109; Joseph B. James, "Southern Reaction to the Proposal of the Fourteenth Amendment," J. S. H., XXII (1956), 487; Perman, Reunion Without Compromise, 211.

37. Ibid., 209; Charleston Daily Courier, Aug. 3, 1866; Sumter News, Aug. 9, 1866; Edgefield Advertiser, Aug. 1, 1866; Yorkville Enquirer, July 12, 1866; Anderson Intelligencer, July 12, 1866; Winnsboro Tri-Weekly News, June 30, Aug. 16, 1866; Winnsboro Fairfield Herald, Aug. 1, 1866; Columbia Daily Phoenix, July 7, 1866.

38. Ibid., July 7, 1866; James, "Southern Reaction..Fourteenth Amendment," 478.

39. Orr to Stephens, Oct. 30, 1866, Stephens Papers, Emory Univ. Lib.

40. Sumter Watchman, Aug. 8, 1866.

41. New York Times, Aug. 14, 1866.

42. Perry, Reminiscences (1889 ed.), 302-03.

43. Ibid., 299-302; Bloom, "National Union Convention," 110, 122-27.

44. Perry, Reminiscences (1889 ed.), 299-302.

45. Thomas Wagstaff, "The Arm-in-Arm Convention," Civil War History, XIV (1968), 108, 116-17; Perman, Reunion Without Compromise, 225.

46. Charleston Daily Courier, Sept. 6, 1866.

47. New York Times, Sept. 23, 1866; Sickles to Orr, Oct. 4, 1866, Orr Papers, S. C. Arch.; Orr to Stephens, Oct. 30, 1866, Stephens Papers, Emory Univ. Lib.

48. Perman, Reunion Without Compromise, 231; Orr to Jenkins, Oct. 22, 1866, Orr Papers, U. S. C.

49. Orr to Jenkins, Oct. 22, 1866, Ibid.; Orr to Johnson, Nov. 11, 1866, Johnson Papers, D. U. Lib.

50. Charleston Daily Courier, Nov. 14, 1866; Avery O. Craven, Reconstruction: The Ending of the Civil War (New York, 1969), 196-97.

51. Charleston Daily Courier, Nov. 28, 1866; E. Merton Coulter, The South During Reconstruction, 1865-1877 (Baton Rouge, 1947), 99-100.

52. Charleston Daily Courier, Nov. 28, 1866.

53. James, "Southern Reaction..Fourteenth Amendment," 478, 496-97; Williamson, After Slavery, 350-51.

CHAPTER VII

1. Michael Les Benedict, A Compromise of Principle: Congressional Republicans and Reconstruction (New York, 1974), 210-12; Martin E. Mantell, Johnson, Grant, and the Politics of Reconstruction (New York, 1973), 22.

2. Edgefield Advertiser, Jan. 9, 1867; McKitrick, Johnson and Reconstruction, 470-72; James, "Southern Reaction..Fourteenth Amendment," 493-94.

3. Larry G. Kincaid, "The Legislative Origins of the Military Reconstruction Act, 1865-1867," (Ph.D. diss., Johns Hopkins Univ., 1968), 161-62; Perman, Reunion Without Compromise, 262; Benedict, Compromise of Principle, 216-24.

4. J. G. deR. Hamilton, Reconstruction in North Carolina (New York, 1914), 190; John S. Reynolds, Reconstruction in South Carolina, 1865-1877 (Columbia, 1905), 52; Pickens Keowee Courier, Feb. 2, 1867; Sumter News, Feb. 14, 1867; "Notes of Colonel W. G. Moore, Private Secretary to President Johnson, 1866-1868," ed. St. George L. Sioussat, A. H. R., XIX (1913), 105.

5. Ibid., 105; New York Times, Feb. 5, 6, 7, 1868; Charleston Daily News, Feb. 5, 1867; Kincaid, "Military Reconstruction Act," 165.

6. New York Times, Feb. 8, 1867; Perman, Reunion Without Compromise, 264; Mantell, Johnson, Grant, and.. Reconstruction, 23.

7. Pickens Keowee Courier, Feb. 23, 1867.

8. Ibid., Feb. 23, 1867.

9. Charleston Daily Courier, Feb. 15, 1867.

10. Hamilton, Reconstruction in North Carolina, 190; Worth to Orr, Feb. 22, 1867, Orr Papers, S. C. Arch.; New York Times, Feb. 22, 1867.

11. Orr to Stephens, Feb. 21, 1867, Stephens Papers, L. C.

12. W. R. Brock, An American Crisis: Congress and Reconstruction, 1865-1867 (New York, 1963), 182-85; Perman, Reunion Without Compromise, 263.

13. Orr to Stephens, Feb. 21, 1867, Stephens Papers, L. C.

14. Kirkland, "Federal Troops," 140-44.

15. Mantell, Johnson, Grant, and..Reconstruction, 38-40; Perman, Reunion Without Compromise, 278; Kibler, Perry, 449.

16. Charleston Daily News, April 3, 1867.

17. Ibid., April 3, 1867.

18. Ibid., April 3, 1867; Mantell, Johnson, Grant, and..Reconstruction, 40-41; Columbia Daily Phoenix, May 2, 1867.

19. Ibid., June 7, 1867.

20. Mantell, Johnson, Grant and..Reconstruction, 41; Charleston Daily Courier, March 23, 1867.

21. Williamson, After Slavery, 372-73; Simkins and Woody, South Carolina During Reconstruction, 74-77.

22. Ibid., 83-85; Kibler, Perry, 450-55.

23. Columbia Daily Phoenix, May 2, 1867.

24. Ibid., May 2, 1867.

25. Ibid., May 2, 1867.

26. Ibid., May 2, 1867.

27. William A. Russ, Jr., "Political Disfranchisement in South Carolina, 1867-1868," Susquehanna Univ. Studies, I (1939), 149-52; Kibler, Perry, 453-54.

28. Simkins and Woody, South Carolina During Reconstruction, 84-86; New York Times, Sept. 4, Sept. 11, 1867.

29. Ibid., Aug. 9, Aug. 11, 1867.

30. Ibid., Aug. 11, 1867; Orr to John W. Burbridge, Oct. 5, 1867, Orr Papers, S. C. Arch.

31. Columbia Daily Phoenix, May 2, 1867.

32. Charleston Daily Courier, Sept. 7, 1867.

33. Charleston Daily News, Nov. 9, 1867; Simkins and Woody, South Carolina During Reconstruction, 86-88; Kibler, Perry, 460-61. C. Vann Woodward, American Counterpoint: Slavery and Racism in the North-South Dialogue (Boston, 1971), 173-75, discusses the impact of the 1867 Northern state elections upon Southern opinion.

34. Kibler, _Perry_, 460-61; Simkins and Woody, _South Carolina During Reconstruction_, 88-89.

35. Columbia _Daily Phoenix_, May 2, 1867.

36. Ibid., May 2, 1867; Charleston _Daily Courier_, Feb. 15, 1867; Orr to Kelley, Dec. 21, 1865, Orr Papers, S. C. Arch.; Williamson, _After Slavery_, 108-09; Coulter, _South During Reconstruction_, 99-100.

37. Charleston _Daily Courier_, Feb. 15, 1867; Columbia _Daily Phoenix_, May 2, 1867.

38. _The Nation_, IV (1867), 2; Orr to Canby, Oct. 31, 1867, and Canby to Orr, Nov. 25, 1867, Orr Papers, S. C. Arch.

39. Orr to Canby, Nov. 29, 1867, Orr to Gen. John S. Preston, Dec. 11, 1867, Orr to Canby, Dec. 18, 1867, Canby to Orr, Dec. 24, 1867, _Ibid._

40. Orr to Canby, Sept. 13, 1867, and Orr to Gen. H. B. Clitz, July 13, 1868, _Ibid._

41. Orr to A. W. Randall, Dec. 9, 1867, Orr to S. G. Goodlet, Nov. 29, 1865, Orr to A. J. Ransier, Sept. 17, 1867, _Ibid._; _Charleston Daily News_, Feb. 15, 1867.

42. _Ibid._, Feb. 15, 1867; Orr to Canby, Oct. 5, 1867, Orr to Gen. John S. Preston, Dec. 11, 1867, Orr Papers, S. C. Arch.

43. Orr to Johnson, Sept. 30, 1867, _Ibid._

44. Canby to Johnson, Oct. 12, 1867, and Orr to I. W. Dawkins, Oct. 15, 1867, _Ibid._

45. Orr to Trescot, March 27, 1866, Andrew Johnson Papers, L. C.

46. Orr to Canby, Oct. 5, 1867, and Orr to Benjamin F. Dunkin, Oct. 31, 1867, Orr Papers, S. C. Arch.

47. Simkins and Woody, _South Carolina During Reconstruction_, 46-47; _Newberry Herald_, April 24, 1867. In his legislative message of September 1866, Orr noted that the court of errors had voided the "stay law," and he urged creditors to act fairly and

liberally. Charleston Daily Courier, Sept. 6, 1866.

48. Orr to Canby, Sept. 30, Oct. 5, 1867, Feb. 27, 1868, and Orr to commandant at post in Columbia, Feb. 17, 1868, Orr Papers, S. C. Arch.

49. Orr to Ellison Capers, Oct. 19, 1867, Ibid.

50. Orr to Canby, Oct. 20, Dec. 16, 1867, Orr to W. E. Holcombe, Dec. 9, 1867, Orr to J. B. Tollison, Jan. 22, 1868, Orr to James Hemphill, Charles S. Price, and Giles J. Patterson, Feb. 1, 1868, Ibid.

51. Sumter Watchman, Oct. 2, 1867; Yorkville Enquirer, Oct. 3, 1867; Winnsboro Fairfield Herald, Oct. 2, 1867; Charleston Daily Courier, Sept. 25, Sept. 26, 1867.

52. Ibid., Nov. 28, 1866; J. Mauldin Lesesne, The Bank of the State of South Carolina (Columbia, 1970), vii, 171-72.

53. Charleston Daily Courier, Feb. 15, 1867; Charleston Daily News, July 8, 1868; Coulter, South During Reconstruction, 83-85; Rembert Patrick, The Reconstruction of the Nation (New York, 1967), 235-36.

54. Hollis, University of South Carolina, II, 7-14.

55. Ibid., II, 14-16; Charleston Daily Courier, Dec. 9, 1865.

56. Ibid., Nov. 22, 1866; Hollis, University of South Carolina, II, 34-35. The legislature also acted upon Orr's proposal that South Carolina take advantage of the 1862 Morrill Act, which made available to the states land scrip for the building of agricultural and mechanical schools. After the legislature passed a resolution accepting this officer, Orr sent an agent to Washington to obtain the scrip. But a law of March 29, 1867, disqualified the former Confederate states, except Tennessee, from the Morrill Act benefits.

57. New York Herald, Feb. 21, 1867; New York Times, Feb. 28, 1867.

58. Orr to James Conner, Oct. 19, 1867, Orr Papers, S. C. Arch.; Pickens Keowee Courier, May 11, 1867.

His governorship salary was thirty-five hundred dollars. S. C. Treasury Journal, 1866, p. 105, S. C. Arch.

59. Charleston Daily Courier, Nov. 28, 1866; Newberry Herald, Dec. 5, 1866; New York Times, Dec. 27, 1866, Jan. 24, 1867.

60. Ibid., Aug. 11, 1867, Jan. 21, 1868; Orr to Canby, Nov. 2, 1867, Orr to Gen. John S. Preston, Dec. 14, 1867, Orr Papers, S. C. Arch.; Columbia Daily Phoenix, Dec. 11, 1867; Charleston Daily Courier, Jan. 17, 1868.

61. New York Times, Jan. 15, Jan. 23, 1868; Sumter News, Jan. 25, 1868. Orr expected that the next president, elected in 1868, would be someone representing the "Conservative and Democratic element in the North and West."

62. Ibid., Jan. 25, 1868.

63. Ibid., Jan. 25, 1868.

64. Charleston Daily News, July 8, July 11, 1868. Contending that the homestead law was constitutional when applied to debts already existing, Orr cited several court decisions in other states.

65. Ibid., July 11, 1868.

66. Ibid., July 11, 1868.

67. Ibid., July 11, 1868.

CHAPTER VIII

1. U. S. Census Mss. Returns, 1870; Anderson Intelligencer, April 7, 1870. He sat on the Greenville and Columbia Railroad board of directors.

2. New York Times, Feb. 25, 1868; J. P. M. Epping to Orr, May 14, Sept. 23, 1867, and Benjamin Odell Duncan to Orr, May 25, 1868, Orr Papers, S. C. Arch.

3. In Orangeburg a white Republican orator be-littled Orr's habit of "sliding down and edging off from one platform to another, in order to be equal to the situation," with the result that his party affilia-tion was difficult to perceive. Orangeburg Carolina Times, May 22, 1867.

4. Sumter Watchman, July 15, 1868.

5. Charleston Daily News, July 6, 1868; Walhalla Keowee Courier, Sept. 4, 1868; Anderson Intelligencer, Sept. 2, Sept. 23, 1868.

6. Ibid., April 7, 1870.

7. Ibid., April 7, 1870.

8. Robert H. Woody, "The South Carolina Reform Movements of 1870 and 1872" (M.A. thesis, Duke Univ., 1928), 16-17, 20-26; Woody, "The South Carolina Election of 1870," North Carolina Historical Review, VIII (1931), 168.

9. Ibid., 170-76.

10. Anderson Intelligencer, Aug. 25, 1870.

11. Ibid., Aug. 25, 1870; Hans L. Trefousse, The Radical Republicans: Lincoln's Vanguard for Racial Justice (New York, 1969), 449.

12. Newberry Herald, Aug. 24, 1870; Charleston Daily Courier, Oct. 15, 1870.

13. Under the caption, "Keep it before the people," several newspapers reprinted an excerpt from the March interview in which Orr admitted the corruption in the Radical regime. Winnsboro Fairfield Herald, Sept. 21, 1870; Sumter Watchman, Aug. 31, 1870; Anderson Intelligencer, Aug. 25, Sept. 1, 8, 15, 22, 19, Oct. 6, 1870.

14. Quoted in Ibid., Aug. 25, 1870.

15. Quoted in Ibid., Sept. 1, 1870.

16. Ibid., Sept. 15, 1870.

17. Ku-Klux Conspiracy, III, 111-12, 165, 234, 264, 271; Dr. J. W. W. Marshall to "My dear friend," April 12, 1870, Marshall Papers, D. U. Lib.; Simkins and Woody, South Carolina During Reconstruction, 203-06; Williamson, After Slavery, 384-85.

18. Woody, "South Carolina Election of 1870," 176-79, 184-86.

19. Allen W. Trelease, White Terror: The Ku Klux Klan Conspiracy and Southern Reconstruction (New York, 1971), 70-73, 115-17, 349-53; Simkins and Woody, South Carolina During Reconstruction, 457, 462-64.

20. Ku-Klux Conspiracy, III, 21-22; Charleston Daily News, June 2, 1871.

21. Ibid., June 2, 1871.

22. Anderson Intelligencer, April 7, 1870.

23. Simkins and Woody, South Carolina During Reconstruction, 465.

24. Williamson, After Slavery, 349.

25. Ibid., 354-56; Winnsboro Fairfield Herald, June 27, 1872.

26. Woody, "South Carolina Reform Movements of 1870 and 1872," 78, 81-85; Williamson, After Slavery, 396-97.

27. Anderson Intelligencer, July 18, 1872. In the spring of 1871 Orr stated that Grant would be the only Republican who could defeat the Democrats in 1872. He added that he had no faith in the Democrats, who were "a lot of confounded idiots." In his view, the Democratic party had thrown away a good opportunity to win with Salmon P. Chase in 1868, but instead the party chose Horatio Seymour, whose "draft-riot reputation" was offensive. (Seymour had been New York's wartime governor.) Orr confessed that he "went with the crowd" and voted unwillingly for Seymour in 1868. He thought the Democrats might wisely nominate someone with a sound war record, perhaps a general, in 1872. Hancock he mentioned favorably, but Sherman he thought overrated and odious to the South. Charleston Daily News, June 2, 1871.

28. Ibid., July 30, 1872; Anderson Intelligencer, Aug. 8, 1872.

29. New York Times, June 6, 1872; Charleston Daily Courier, June 15, Aug. 21, 1872; Charleston Daily News, July 9, 15, 23, 1872.

30. Quoted in Anderson Ingelligencer, Feb. 15, 1872.

31. Quoted in Ibid., May 2, 1872.

32. Charleston Daily News, July 6, 1872.

33. Charleston Daily Courier, Aug. 22, 23, 24, 1872; Anderson Intelligencer, Aug. 29, 1872.

34. Ibid., Aug. 29, 1872; Charleston Daily Courier, Aug. 24, 1872.

35. Ibid., Aug. 24, Aug. 26, Sept. 3, 1872; Anderson Intelligencer, Aug. 29, 1872.

36. Woody, "South Carolina Reform Movements of 1870 and 1872," 100-01.

37. Quoted in Charleston Daily Courier, Sept. 3, 1872.

38. Ibid., Sept. 26, 1872; Charleston Daily News, Sept. 3, 9, 16, 1872; Orangeburg Times, Sept. 11, 25, 1872; Whittemore to Orr, Sept. 9, 1872, Orr-Patterson Papers, S. H. C.; Williamson, After Slavery, 361.

39. Woody, "South Carolina Reform Movements of 1870 and 1872," 106, 116.

40. Fish to Orr, Aug. 30, 1872, and Orr to Fish, Sept. 8, 1872, Orr-Patterson Papers, S. H. C. The Charleston Daily News, Sept. 24, 1872, reported the tendered appointment with the caption, "Argentine --The Thirty Pieces of Silver."

41. Anderson Intelligencer, April 7, 1870.

42. Ibid., April 7, 1870.

43. _Ibid._, April 7, 1870. He expected that the South would meet Western opposition to any attempt to divert the tide of immigration southward.

44. _Ibid._, April 7, 1870.

45. _Ku-Klux Conspiracy_, III, 14-15.

46. _Ibid._, III, 14.

CHAPTER IX

1. Simkins and Woody, _South Carolina During Reconstruction_, 141-42.

2. _Anderson Intelligencer_, March 10, 1870; U. R. Brooks, _South Carolina Bench and War_ (2 vols., Columbia, 1908), I, 186; _Ku-Klux Conspiracy_, III,1; Walhalla _Keowee Courier_, Sept. 4, 1868.

3. _Ibid._, April 2, 1869; Judgment Rolls, Anderson County, Court of General Sessions, Sessions Journal, Box 78, S. C. Arch.; _Anderson Intelligencer_, Jan. 25, 1872; _Ku-Klux Conspiracy_, III, 1, 15.

4. _Ibid._, III, 1, 5, 14-15.

5. _Anderson Intelligencer_, Nov. 18, 1869.

6. _South Carolina Reports: Reports of Cases Heard and Determined in the Supreme Court of South Carolina_ (St. Paul, 1916), III, 192.

7. _Ibid._, III, 245-46. The supreme court cited other court opinions in support of its verdict.

8. _Anderson Intelligencer_, July 29, 1869.

9. _South Carolina Reports_, II, 233-35.

10. _Anderson Intelligencer_, April 22, 1869, quoting the Louisville _Courier_; J. D. Sumner, Jr., "The South Carolina Divorce Act of 1949," _South Carolina Law Quarterly_, III (1950-51), 257.

11. Walhalla _Keowee Courier_, May 28, 1869; _Anderson Intelligencer_, June 3, Sept. 2, 1869.

12. Ibid., Sept. 2, 1869.

13. Sumner, "The South Carolina Divorce Act," 257-59.

14. Perry, Reminiscences (1883 ed.), 186-87. Circuit court judges were paid $3,500. S. C. Treasury Journal, 1868-1872, pp. 128, 200, 270, S. C. Arch. The salary for the Russian ministership was $17,500. Hamilton Fish to Orr, Dec. 7, 1872, Fish Papers, L. C. For his financial holdings, see Anderson County, Office of the Probate Judge, Estate Papers, S. C. Arch.

15. Fish to Orr, Dec. 7, 1872, Fish Papers, L. C.; Anderson Intelligencer, Jan. 23, 1873.

16. "A Letter of James L. Orr, Minister to Russia, 1873," ed. Joseph C. Baylen, S. C. H. M., LXI (1960), 225. (This letter is in the possession of James A. Carpenter, State University, Mississippi.) Edward H. Zabriskie, American-Russian Rivalry in the Far East (Philadelphia, 1946), 16n.

17. "A Letter of James L. Orr, Minister to Russia," 226-29. Also in the party was Miss Fannie Goodman, one of Mary Orr's friends, who enrolled with her at the Weimar school.

18. Ibid., 228-29.

19. Orr to Fish, March 18, 1873, Papers Relating to the Foreign Relations of the United States, 1872-1873 (Washington, 1873), II, 782; Zabriskie, American-Russian Rivalry, 16n.

20. "A Letter of James L. Orr, Minister to Russia," 230; Orr to Fish, May 2, 1873, Papers Relating to the Foreign Relations..1872-1873, II, 783. The prediction that Russia would conquer Khiva proved accurate.

21. Thomas A. Bailey, America Faces Russia: Russian-American Relations from Early Times to Our Day (Ithaca, 1950), 45-48.

22. James L. Orr, Jr., to "My dear Sister," April 10, 1873, Orr-Patterson Papers, S. H. C.

23. Ernest M. Lander, Jr., A History of South Carolina, 1865-1960 (Chapel Hill), 82-83.

24. Simkins and Woody, South Carolina During Re-construction, 44; William Arthur Sheppard, Red Shirts Remembered (Atlanta, 1940), 5; Reynolds, Reconstruction in South Carolina, 148; Henry T. Thompson, Ousting the Carpetbagger from South Carolina (Columbia, 1926), 23.

25. Edgefield Advertiser, March 6, 1857, quoting the Memphis Bulletin; New York Herald, Feb. 21, 1867; Sheppard, Red Shirts Remembered, 15.

26. Williamson, After Slavery, 374-75.

27. Samuel A. Ashe and Edward McCrady, Jr., Cyclopedia of Eminent and Representative Men of the Carolinas of the Nineteenth Century (2 vols., Madison, Wis., 1892), I, 117; Anderson Intelligencer, May 8, 1873.

ABOUT THE AUTHOR

Roger P. Leemhuis was born and raised in Erie, Pennsylvania, and holds degrees from Villanova University, the University of Massachusetts, and the University of Wisconsin. Since 1967 he has been on the History faculty at Clemson University in South Carolina.

He has had a lifelong interest in the American Civil War period and in the postwar decades of the late nineteenth century. He has written an article on William W. Boyce, a controversial South Carolinian who sat in the Confederate Congress. Currently Leemhuis is doing research on South Carolina in the 1890's.